W9-ATG-306

# Contemporary Poetry and Contemporary Science

# Contemporary Poetry and Contemporary Science

EDITED BY

ROBERT CRAWFORD

OXFORD
UNIVERSITY PRESS

Great Clarendon Street, Oxford OX2 6DP

Oxford University Press is a department of the University of Oxford.
It furthers the University's objective of excellence in research, scholarship,
and education by publishing worldwide in

Oxford New York

Auckland Cape Town Dar es Salaam Hong Kong Karachi
Kuala Lumpur Madrid Melbourne Mexico City Nairobi
New Delhi Shanghai Taipei Toronto

With offices in

Argentina Austria Brazil Chile Czech Republic France Greece
Guatemala Hungary Italy Japan Poland Portugal Singapore
South Korea Switzerland Thailand Turkey Ukraine Vietnam

Oxford is a registered trade mark of Oxford University Press
in the UK and in certain other countries

Published in the United States
by Oxford University Press Inc., New York



First published 2006



British Library Cataloguing in Publication Data
Data available

Library of Congress Cataloging in Publication Data
Data available

Typeset by RefineCatch Limited, Bungay, Suffolk
Printed in Great Britain
on acid-free paper by
Biddles Ltd., King's Lynn

ISBN 0–19–925812–0 978–0–19–925812–3

1 3 5 7 9 10 8 6 4 2

to Ian Wall

*with thanks for his encouragement and patience*

and in memory of

Michael Donaghy
and
Miroslav Holub

*distinctive, carrying voices*

## ACKNOWLEDGEMENTS

Firstly, thanks are due to Ian Wall of the Edinburgh International Science Festival, who knew I had written a number of poems about science, and talked me into running a programme of events from which this book grew. At a later stage the Sciarts scheme run by the Wellcome Trust with support from the Arts Council of England made it possible to bring together poets and scientists for the meetings which resulted in the poems in this book. Birgit Arends was very helpful in supporting this project, and a particular debt is owed to Dr Louisa Gairn who acted as project assistant at the University of St Andrews, and helped to run a series of events there. The Natural History Museum in London, Dundee Contemporary Arts Centre, the Scottish Poetry Library, the Poetry Society in London, the Scottish Science Centres, the University of Newcastle upon Tyne, and other institutions also lent support as matters developed. In St Andrews both StAnza and The Poetry House at the University of St Andrews provided continuing support. Special thanks are due to Dr Lilias Fraser, Jill Gamble, Brian Johnstone, Jane Sommerville, and all my colleagues in the School of English, University of St Andrews, as well as to Professor Wilson Sibbett of the School of Physics at St Andrews, who acted as the project's overall scientific adviser. Nick Wetton helped clear copyright permissions with his customary geniality and efficiency. Great gratitude is due to my family and to all the book's contributors who waited patiently for the better part of a decade as this book matured. Thanks also to all at Oxford University Press.

The following sources and permissions for the use of copyright material should be acknowledged: Diane Ackerman: 'We are Listening', from *Jaguar of Sweet Laughter* (Random House, 1991), © 1991 by Diane Ackerman, reprinted by permission of Random House Inc; Simon Armitage: 'Newton's Third Law', from *Zoom!* (Bloodaxe Books, 1989), reprinted by permission of the publisher; 'The Shout', from *The Universal Home Doctor* (Faber and Faber, 2002); John Berryman: 235 ('The marker slants, flowerless, day's almost done'), from *The Dream Songs* (Farrar, Straus and Giroux, 1969); John Burnside: 'By Kautokeino', from *The Good Neighbour* (Jonathan

Cape, 2005), reprinted by permission of The Random House Group; Robert Crawford: from 'Photonics', and 'Scotland', from *A Scottish Assembly* (Chatto and Windus, 1990); 'The Handshakes', from *Masculinity* (Jonathan Cape, 1996); 'Deincarnation' and 'Alford', from *Spirit Machines* (Jonathan Cape, 1999), all reprinted by permission of The Random House Group; Rebecca Elson: 'Let there always be light (searching for dark matter)', from *A Responsibility to Awe* (Oxford Poets, 2001), reprinted by permission of Carcanet Press; Veronica Forrest-Thomson: 'Cordelia: or, "A Poem Should not Mean, but Be" ' and 'The Dying Gladiator', from *Collected Poems and Translations*, edited by A. Barnett (Allardyce, Barnett, Publishers, 1990), © Jonathan Culler and The Estate of Veronica Forrest-Thomson, 1990, reprinted by permission of the publisher; Jorie Graham: from 'Event Horizon', in *Materialism* (The Ecco Press, 1993); Miroslav Holub: 'In the Microscope' and 'The Corporal who killed Archimedes', from *Poems Before and After: Collected English Translations*, translated by Ian and Jarmila Milner, Ewald Osers, and George Theiner (Bloodaxe Books, 1990), reprinted by permission of the publisher; Miroslav Holub: 'Spacetime' and 'Kuru, or the Smiling Death Syndrome', from *Vanishing Lung Syndrome* (Faber and Faber, 1990); 'The Rampage', from *The Rampage* (Faber and Faber, 1997); A. E. Housman: 'Here are the skies, the planets seven', *Additional Poems V*, in *Collected Poems and Selected Prose*, edited by Christopher Ricks (Penguin Twentieth-Century Classics, 1989), reprinted by permission of The Society of Authors as the Literary Representative of the Estate of A. E. Housman; Aldous Huxley: 'Fifth Philosopher's Song', from *The Collected Poems*, edited by Donald Watt (Chatto and Windus, 1971), reprinted by permission of The Random House Group; Elizabeth Jennings: 'Delay', from *New Collected Poems* (Carcanet Press, 2002), reprinted by permission of David Higham Associates; Velimir Khlebnikov: from *The Longer Poems of Velimir Khlebnikov* (Greenwood Press, 1975); Robert Lowell: 'Home After Three Months Away', from *Robert Lowell: Collected Poems* (Farrar, Straus and Groux, 2003); Hugh MacDiarmid: 'Of John Davidson', from 'To a Friend and Fellow-Poet', and from 'Crystals Like Blood', from *Selected Poems*, edited by Alan Riach and Michael Grieve (Penguin Twentieth-Century Classics, 1994), reprinted by permission of Carcanet Press; Edwin Morgan: 'Poetry's like a gull, protesting, sheering off . . .', 'We saw how he cheated at the Ishihara . . .',

'Golden Apples', 'Submarine Demon', 'March', 'The professor-dissector . . .', 'Early Days', 'Gibson Gibson . . .', 'Why would the lord of life confine his write', and 'Trilobites', from *Collected Poems* (Carcanet Press, 1990), reprinted by permission of the publisher; Adrienne Rich: 'Planetarium', from *Collected Early Poems 1950–1970* (W. W. Norton, 1993), reprinted by permission of the publisher; Leslie Scalapino: from *Way* (North Point Press, 1988); Frederick Seidel: 'The New Cosmology', from *These Days* (Knopf, 1989), © 1980, 81, 82, 83, 84, 86, 87, 88, 89 by Frederick Seidel, reprinted by permission of Alfred A. Knopf, a division of Random House Inc; Wallace Stevens: from 'Of Modern Poetry', in *The Collected Poems of Wallace Stevens* (Knopf, 1954), copyright 1954 by Wallace Stevens and renewed 1982 by Holly Stevens, reprinted by permission of Alfred A. Knopf, a division of Random House Inc; John Wilkinson: 'Laboratory Test Report', from *Flung Clear: Poems in Six Books* (Parataxis Editions, 1994), reprinted by permission of Parataxis Editions and John Wilkinson; 'Sweetness and Light', from *Oort's Cloud: Earlier Poems* (Barque Press, 1999), reprinted by permission of the publisher; William Carlos Williams: 'Some Simple Measures in the American Idiom and the Variable Foot', from *Collected Poems 1939–1962, Volume II* (Carcanet Press, 2000), © 1962 by William Carlos Williams, reprinted by permission of New Directions Publishing Corporation.

Every effort has been made to contact copyright holders of poems published in this book. The editor and publisher apologize for any material included without permission or without appropriate acknowledgement, and would be pleased to rectify any omissions or errors brought to their attention at the earliest opportunity.

R.C.

*St Andrews, 2005*

# CONTENTS

*Notes on Contributors* xiii

INTRODUCTION 1
Robert Crawford

RAMPAGE, OR SCIENCE IN POETRY 11
Miroslav Holub

'AS ABOVE' 25
Don Paterson, introduced by Andrew Riches

POETRY AND VIRTUAL REALITIES 27
Edwin Morgan

'GRIMOIRE' 48
Michael Donaghy, introduced by Kevin Warwick

SPIRIT MACHINES: THE HUMAN AND THE COMPUTATIONAL 52
Robert Crawford

'BIOLOGY' 69
Robert Crawford, introduced by Rona R. Ramsay

TESTAMENT AND CONFESSIONS OF AN INFORMATIONIST 72
W. N. Herbert

'THE WORKING SELF' 88
W. N. Herbert, introduced by Martin Conway

A SCIENCE OF BELONGING: POETRY AS ECOLOGY 91
John Burnside

'STEINAR UNDIR STEINAHLITHUM' 107
John Burnside, introduced by R. M. M. Crawford

MODELLING THE UNIVERSE: POETRY, SCIENCE, AND THE ART OF METAPHOR 110
Simon Armitage

'CIRCADIAN' 123
John Glenday, introduced by Eric Priest

Astronomy and Poetry 125
Jocelyn Bell Burnell

'A Fistful of Foraminifera' 141
Sarah Maguire, introduced by Norman MacLeod

The Act of the Mind: Thought Experiments in the Poetry of Jorie Graham and Leslie Scalapino 146
Adalaide Morris

'Once I Looked into Your Eyes' 167
Paul Muldoon, introduced by Warren S. Warren

The Art of Wit and the Cambridge Science Park 170
Drew Milne

'The Organ Bath' 188
David Kinloch, introduced by Alison Gurney

Contemporary Psychology and Contemporary Poetry: Perspectives on Mood Disorders 191
Kay Redfield Jamison

Afterword 204
Gillian Beer

*Notes* 211

*Index* 227

## NOTES ON CONTRIBUTORS

**Simon Armitage**'s *Selected Poems* was published by Faber and Faber in 2001, and followed by his collection *The Universal Home Doctor* (Faber, 2002). He teaches creative writing at Manchester Metropolitan University.

**Gillian Beer**'s books include *Darwin's Plots* (2nd edn., Routledge, 2000) and *Open Fields: Science in Cultural Encounter* (OUP, 1996). She is an Honorary Fellow of Clare Hall, University of Cambridge.

**Jocelyn Bell Burnell** discovered pulsars (stars that release regular bursts of radio waves) in 1967. She has held senior appointments at the Royal Observatory in Edinburgh, at the Open University, the University of Bath, and the University of Oxford.

**John Burnside**'s *Selected Poems* was published by Cape in 2006; his novels include *Living Nowhere* (Cape, 2003). He is Reader in English at the University of St Andrews.

**Martin Conway**'s books include *The Psychology of Memory* (1993) and *Theories of Memory* (1998). He is Professor of Cognitive Psychology at the University of Leeds.

**Robert Crawford**'s *Selected Poems* was published by Cape in 2005; his critical books include *The Modern Poet* (OUP, 2001). He is Professor of Modern Scottish Literature at the University of St Andrews.

**Robert M. M. Crawford** is Professor Emeritus in the School of Biology, University of St Andrews. He studies climatic change and species adaptations for survival in the arctic as well as the photo-ecology of Scotland since 1840.

**Michael Donaghy** (1954–2004) was born in the Bronx, studied at the University of Chicago, and moved to London in 1985. His collections of poetry include *Shibboleth* (OUP, 1988), *Errata* (OUP, 1993), and *Conjure* (Picador, 2000).

**John Glenday**'s collections of poetry include *The Apple Ghost* (Peterloo, 1989) and *Undark* (Peterloo, 1995). He has worked for a number of years as a drugs counsellor, and lives in north-east Scotland.

**Alison Gurney** is Professor of Pharmacology at the University of Manchester. The main themes of her research are the mechanisms that underlie the control of tone in healthy and diseased blood vessels, and the mechanisms of action of vasodilator drugs.

**W. N. Herbert**'s collections of poetry include *The Big Bumper Book of Troy* (Bloodaxe, 2002); his critical work includes *To Circumjack MacDiarmid* (OUP, 1992). He teaches creative writing at the University of Newcastle upon Tyne.

**Miroslav Holub** (1923–98) worked in the field of immunology in Prague. In English translation his collections of poetry include *Vanishing Lung Syndrome* (Faber and Faber, 1990) and *The Rampage* (Faber and Faber, 1997). His volumes of essays include *The Dimension of the Present Moment* (Faber and Faber, 1990).

**Kay Redfield Jamison**'s books include *Night Falls Fast: Understanding Suicide* (Knopf, 1999) and *Exuberance* (Knopf, 2004). She is Professor of Psychiatry at the Johns Hopkins University School of Medicine and Honorary Professor of English at St Andrews.

**David Kinloch**'s collections of poetry include *Un Tour d'Ecosse* (Carcanet, 2001) and *In My Father's House* (Carcanet, 2005). He is a Senior Lecturer in English at the University of Strathclyde.

**Norman MacLeod** grew up in the United States, then moved to London in 1993. He is Keeper of Palaeontology at the Natural History Museum. His interests range from historical palaeoecology to palaeontological informatics.

**Sarah Maguire**'s collections of poetry include *The Invisible Mender* (Cape, 1997) and *The Florist's at Midnight* (Cape, 2001). She is editor of *Flora Poetica: The Chatto Book of Botanical Verse* (Chatto and Windus, 2001). She lives in London.

**Drew Milne**'s collections include *Modern Critical Thought: An Anthology* (Blackwell, 2003) and *The Damage: New and Selected Poems* (Salt, 2001). He is a Fellow of Trinity Hall, University of Cambridge.

**Edwin Morgan**'s *Collected Poems* was published by Carcanet in 1990; his recent collections include *Cathures* (Carcanet, 2002). He holds the appointment of Scotland's National Poet.

**Adalaide Morris** is John C. Gerber Professor of English at the University of Iowa. Her books include *Wallace Stevens: Imagination and Faith* (Princeton University Press, 1974) and *Sound States: Innovative Poetics and Acoustical Technologies* (University of North Carolina Press, 1997).

**Paul Muldoon**'s *Poems 1968–1998* was published by Faber in 2001; his recent work includes *Moy Sand and Gravel* (Faber, 2002). He is Howard G. B. Clark Professor of the Humanities at Princeton University and Honorary Professor of English at St Andrews.

**Don Paterson**'s collections of poems include *The Eyes* (Faber, 1999) and *Landing Light* (Faber, 2003). His prose works include *The Book of Shadows* (Picador, 2004). He is Lecturer in English at the University of St Andrews.

**Eric Priest** holds the Gregory Chair of Mathematics at the University of St Andrews. His research interests include Solar Magnetohydrodynamics, the study of the subtle, and often nonlinear, interaction between the Sun's magnetic field and its plasma interior or atmosphere, treated as a continuous medium.

**Rona R. Ramsay** is a biochemist whose research focuses on the action and interaction of chemicals in the body at a cellular level: bioenergetics, membranes, and cell communication. She is a Reader in Biochemistry at the University of St Andrews.

**Andrew Riches** is Head of Medical Science and Human Biology at the University of St Andrews. His research centres on the study of cancer in humans and methods of treatment, especially radiation. His main areas of interest include molecular mechanisms of growth control in haematopoieses, breast cancer risk, and radiation carcinogenesis.

**Warren S. Warren** has recently taken up a post as Professor of Chemistry at Duke University. He was previously Director of the New Jersey Center for Ultrafast Laser Applications, and Associate Director of the Princeton Center for Photonics and Optoelectronic Materials. His work focuses on using controlled radiation fields to alter dynamics in ultrafast laser spectroscopy, nuclear magnetic resonance, or magnetic resonance imaging.

**Kevin Warwick**'s books include *I, Cyborg* (Century, 2002). He is Professor of Cybernetics at the University of Reading, where he carries out research in artificial intelligence, control, and robotics. His favourite topic is pushing back the frontiers of machine intelligence and in 1998 he shocked the international scientific community by having a silicon chip transponder surgically implanted in his left arm.

# Introduction

Robert Crawford

At the start of the 1920s Einstein's visit to England excited not only writers but also the general, newspaper-reading public. 'Einstein the Great', T. S. Eliot called him, with an ironic smirk, surveying the press coverage for a 'London Letter' contributed to the American magazine *The Dial* in July 1921. Rose Macaulay, writing 'probably the first significant novel in the English language to make direct use of Einstein's theories', presents in her media story *Potterism* (1920) the newspaper headline 'Light Caught Bending'.[1] In Scotland, later in the same decade, Hugh MacDiarmid ended one of his greatest lyric poems, 'Empty Vessel', by writing of a woman's grief for her dead child, 'The licht that bends ower a' thing | Is less ta'en up wi't.'[2] So it was that Einstein caught the imagination of American, English, and Scottish writers.

A scientist who considered imagination more important than knowledge, Einstein was likely to appeal to poets. Readers now take it for granted that those Modernist impulses which dominated much of early twentieth-century literature from Joyce to Mayakovsky and from Paul Valéry to T. S. Eliot were engaged with the epoch's scientific revolutions. Hugely influential work by Gillian Beer has demonstrated the pervasiveness of scientific thinking in late nineteenth- and early twentieth-century English literature. More narrowly focused studies, such as Ian F. A. Bell's work on Ezra Pound, show just how interested in scientific thought was an individual poet and *animateur*, while research into Einstein and Modernism suggests how ideas such as relativity permeate the writing of the period.[3] With its focus on a poetics of the particle and a poetics of the wave, Daniel Albright's *Quantum Poetics* (1997) relates scientific ideas and metaphors to the poetry of the first half of the twentieth century, and especially to the work of Yeats, Pound, and Eliot. A number of studies, like Albright's, show how science provided metaphors for poetry and its understanding.

Whether it is Portugal's Fernando Pessoa writing pseudonymously his poem 'Newton's Binomial Theory' or England's I. A. Richards speculating as a philosopher and critic of verse in *Science and Poetry* (1926), there is plenty of evidence for engagement with science on the part of earlier twentieth-century European poets. If not all wrote, like MacDiarmid, of ' "hohlraum" oscillators' and 'liquid helium', nevertheless many poets, from London to Moscow and from Lisbon to the Shetlands, were attracted by scientific work.[4] In America too, as Adalaide Morris has shown in studies of H.D., a poet might engage with science to enhance, deepen, and add resonance to an innate lyricism.[5] One of the challenges for poetry was to digest and add metaphorical resonance to scientific terminology—a challenge which persists today. But there was also a sense that even the structure of a poem might be aligned with emerging scientific principles. So *The Waste Land* can be read as a poem of relativity, as can some of Wallace Stevens's poems with their interest in the way objects are changed according to ways of looking.

Einstein quickened an interest in the multiplication of perspectives. The emergence of computing technology further developed the way information gained from such a multiplication may be processed and reprocessed. Elsewhere, I have drawn attention to the shared intellectual interests between two student friends: the young philosopher poet T. S. Eliot and the philosophically trained scientist Norbert Wiener, who went on to develop the study of cybernetics.[6] Modernist poetry often assumes the dynamics of a cybernetic system, all feedback loops and schemata of knowledge-control. Recent poets' interests in computing, in computer-like iterations of language, and in virtual reality, may be part of a genealogy that goes back not only to poets fascinated, like Eliot, by 'unreal' reality, but also to a scientist such as Wiener, attracted to a Bergsonian questioning of apparently objective phenomena.

If earlier twentieth-century poets' interest in science is fairly obvious, then scientists' engagement with poetry, or even with literature or philosophy more generally, can be harder to trace. Nevertheless, facets of earlier twentieth-century science which we now take for granted—the terminology of the atom, for instance—had been sacralized and given cultural currency by older poets. As Edwin Morgan points out in this present book, the narrative of atomic physics was given its classic form by Lucretius, long, long before any atoms were split. It is not just that individual scientists such from Clerk Maxwell to Einstein and Wiener may have enjoyed poetry—its patternings and imaginative investigations—but that science itself is often underwritten by the formulations and imaginative structures developed and articulated by poets. Even today poets may side with Simon Armitage in this book when he argues that poetry with its mythmaking power may *precede*, rather than simply follow, science. This makes poetry exciting but also sometimes culpable. It is the mythmaking imagination of poetry, claims Armitage, that dropped the atomic bomb.

Whatever their excitement or culpability, it is evident with hindsight that early last century poetry and science were intertwined. Many people suppose that nowadays this has ceased to be so. A few exceptional books seek to question this assumption, but these tend to be specialist academic monographs. Professor N. Katherine Hayles, in *The Cosmic Web: Scientific Field Models and Literary Strategies in the Twentieth Century* (1984) and ensuing studies, challenges the idea that literature (including poetry) operates very differently and separately from scientific thinking. A scholar like Hayles, however, is the exception that proves the rule. This annoyingly unhelpful rule is one that was given conventional and, for many, compelling articulation by C. P. Snow in a 1959 lecture on the idea of *Two Cultures*.[7] For Snow poetry and science certainly belonged in very different cultural camps. For half a century now the opposition of the poetic and the scientific has been a given assumption of much thinking, including that of journalists, scientists, and philosophers. When the philosopher Mary Midgley writes her book *Science and Poetry* (2001), she uses the term 'poetry' to denote those elements of life which we assume to be unscientific. Midgley is far from alone in her misty use of the word. Many scientists use 'poetry' or 'poet' similarly; poets are people who haven't a clue. Hence such a book title as Robert H. March's *Physics for Poets* (1970), or the university course title 'Astronomy for Poets', which, as Simon Armitage points out in his essay here, turns out to mean simply astronomy for people who can't count. On occasion, readers of the present book will encounter the assumption that scientific thinking and poetic dreaming are importantly different, or even completely at loggerheads. Not all scientists and poets line up in bland accord. Yet, more provocatively and interestingly perhaps, readers of the following essays, poems, and reflections may be challenged to see poetry and science as potently aligned modes of discovery.

*Contemporary Poetry and Contemporary Science* is in several senses a 'crossover' book. It presents the deliberations of literary critics alongside the musings of poets and scientists; it allows distinguished scientists such as Jocelyn Bell Burnell and Kay Redfield Jamison to express an enthusiasm for poetry, writing not as literary critics but as scientists drawn to particular poets' works which express something of what scientists value when they do science. There are differences, even clashes of tone among this book's contributors. This may annoy academic specialists wedded to the tone and assumptions of one particular discipline. Yet the contributors' aim has been to write in a style comprehensible to an audience beyond their immediate peer group. Some of the essays and poems here are immediately accessible; others, such as that of the Cambridge-based literary critic Drew Milne, may require more effort on the part of readers whose background is very different from that of the writer. Eventually, however, all the contributions to the book should make sense to poets, to scientists, and to readers who are neither one nor the other.

*Contemporary Poetry and Contemporary Science* is a crossover project in another sense too. With some glee, it goes against the present-day decorum of its academic publishing house by mixing specially commissioned verse with its prose. It does so because, with its accent on the contemporary, the volume aims to demonstrate through its form, and through practice as well as through reflection, that poetry and science can meet with productive results. While the essays for this volume were being written, some of the poets and scientists involved read and listened to each other's work. This process began, with the encouragement of Ian Wall, at the Edinburgh International Science Festival in 1998, when Simon Armitage, W. N. Herbert, Miroslav Holub, Edwin Morgan, and the present writer met. Miroslav Holub sent in his essay almost immediately; sadly, it was one of the last things he wrote. The project then developed over several years, and in several countries, with some of the contributors visiting each other's work places. Between the essays of the book appear the results of a considerable number of meetings between pairs of poets and scientists which took place, largely in 2002–3, thanks to the generous sponsorship of the SciArts project (funded by the Wellcome Trust and the Arts Council of England). These poet–scientist encounters happened over lunches, where the poet and scientist talked about their work, and the scientist more often than not brought to the lunch table an object or a concept to which the poet reacted by producing a poem. The relationship between poem and object is often tangential, and all the better for that. After reading the poems produced, the scientists then responded with a short piece of prose that considered the encounter and reacted specifically to the poem. In this book, these reactions function as introductions to the poems themselves. On occasion, most notably when Paul Muldoon and Warren S. Warren met, the making of the poem then gave rise to further scientific work.

The project of this book may sound contrived, or at least eccentric. Yet, as *Contemporary Poetry and Contemporary Science* progresses, the realization may strengthen that today, whether or not all poets and scientists expect it, there is the real possibility of meaningful interchange between poetry and science. Crossing between these disciplines, and between prose and verse, this book is not intended as a comprehensive or definitive account of how these two modes of discovery—the poetic and the scientific—interact. Instead, it is content to hint that there are today areas where they do so. Through bringing together writers of verse, scientists, and literary critics, it shows simply that some poets and some scientists may be sympathetically interested in what each other gets up to.

Even to suggest this is to move productively beyond the stereotyping of 'two cultures' promulgated by C. P. Snow in mid-twentieth century England. A glance at literary and scientific history suggests that Snow's view was itself particularly and unhelpfully eccentric. Poetry (from the Greek word for making) and science (from the Latin word for knowledge) had been bound together from pre-Socratic times until eighteenth- and early nineteenth-century Romanticism; in Western culture, this meant from Hesiod and Lucretius to Goethe and Shelley. For a comparatively short time, in the later nineteenth and earlier twentieth centuries, it seemed that the professional specialization of knowledge was separating poetry and science, the cave of making from the white-coated lab. Yet, looking back, as more recent critics have done, we may detect correspondences between Darwinian thought and the poetry of Tennyson, or between Einstein and *The Waste Land*. The poetic prose of James Joyce helped conceptualize the poetics of quantum physics.

Even as C. P. Snow's 1959 notion of two cultures established itself as a journalistic orthodoxy, a poet such as Edwin Morgan in Scotland was experimenting imaginatively with the evolving technology of the computer, and the Czech scientist Miroslav Holub was establishing his poetic reputation. Though it was not the fashion to say so, modes of scientific knowledge and modes of poetic making continued to be intertwined.

Today we know that there were other twentieth-century ways of viewing the cultural–scientific spectrum, ways which may have been eclipsed by Snow's catchy notion of 'two cultures'. In Scotland George Davie's historical theorizing about 'the democratic intellect' saw knowledge in terms of an educational system considerably different from that of Snow's Oxbridge, and set philosophy at the heart of a 'generalist' model of education which might lead towards scientific or humanistic knowledge, and which mediated between both. The Scottish philosopher John Macmurray, in works such as *Religion, Art and Science* (1961) argued that 'The subject matter of a poem can be scientific', though the poem must move beyond that to an essential 'phase of contemplation'; again, Macmurray wrote that 'there is an aesthetic moment in scientific discovery—a flash of insight that fuses a mass of data and reveals the law of their unity—which is indispensable', even if this has to be 'subordinated immediately and strictly to the scientific demand for generality and experiment'.[8] Although Macmurray saw poetry and science as growing apart, he could detect elements of each within the other. It is surely this impulse which has always attracted some poets towards science and some scientists towards poetry: a perception of something shared as well as of many differences, and an insight that poetry and science might at times provide material, images, metaphors, and procedures that might be mutually enriching, illuminating, or pleasurable. If we adopt a Wittgensteinian framework of family resemblances, rather than Snow's binary model, we can see that in recent decades poetry and science, each obsessed with hidden, often uncertain structures, have continued to operate in sometimes related ways. Both have been part of the ever-shifting weather of postmodern culture; each has sought at times a clarity seldom associated with postmodernism.

Were this book attempting a global survey of how contemporary poetry and contemporary science interact, it might include the Australian poet Les Murray's reading of James Gleick's *Chaos*, and the way in which chaos theory more generally may appeal to poets for its bringing together the structured and the aleatory. The complex, aleatory nature of rhyme provides a semantic randomness within a sonnet, for instance, even as that sonnet imposes a remarkable fixity of acoustic pattern upon its contents. On the one hand, rhyme drives in a clearly controlled acoustic direction; on the other hand, if rhyme is in control of the imagination, it constantly moves the intellectual content of a poem in surprising and surprisingly unpredictable or barely predictable directions governed principally by sound-patterning—'*From C. S. Lewis to C. S. Gas*', as Paul Muldoon puts it in a characteristic phrase.[9] For an Irish poet like Muldoon, attuned to Irish and Gaelic poetry, where a complex system of internal rhymes operates alongside and sometimes predominates over end-rhyme, the sound system of a poem may encourage a density of word-gaming that leads both to an intensification of aleatory shifts of idea and to a simultaneous reinforcing of rule-driven acoustics—so that, in the elaborate double-sestina form which Muldoon so relishes, the poem becomes both more and less predictable. Such paradoxes have their analogues in contemporary scientific principles of uncertainty and of complexly intersecting multiple systems of 'chaos'.

Though Muldoon is one of this book's contributors, it is beyond the scope of the volume to provide a full explanation or analysis of his or other poets' work as part of some grand narrative that links up all contemporary poetry and contemporary science. Some literary critics such as Daniel Tiffany (whose work is discussed here by Adalaide Morris) have begun to move towards presenting attempts at an overarching theoretical context for the understanding of recent poetry alongside recent science, but it is on the whole too soon to do so convincingly in a way that takes proper account of poets as different as Edwin Morgan, Paul Muldoon, and Jorie Graham, let alone sciences as different as the immunology investigated by Miroslav Holub in Prague and the psychiatry researched by Kay Redfield Jamison at the Johns Hopkins University. This book does include work by or about all of these poets and scientists, and readers may notice filiations—as when Holub mentions Jamison's particular preoccupation (bipolar disorder), or when poets from such different and even opposing perspectives as Morgan and Armitage regard virtual reality as a challenge for poetry to engage with—but

*Contemporary Poetry and Contemporary Science* presents samplings, juxtapositions, and provocations, rather than aiming to suggest that all poets and scientists are in covert, let alone overt, agreement about some master narrative to which they all conform in suspect unison.

The essays in this book are offered simply as instances where contemporary poets are attracted towards science and where contemporary scientists are attracted towards poetry. The reasons for the attraction are not always the same. For the astrophysicist Jocelyn Bell Burnell there is a sheer pleasure in collecting poems which articulate something of the wonder and procedural quirkiness of her subject; for the psychiatrist Kay Redfield Jamison, it may be that the accuracy of poetic expression yields something of scientific value; for the poet Simon Armitage, science, however obliquely regarded, offers fascinating poem-fuel. The essays in this book are not intended to cohere as part of one all-governing, neat argument, a unified theory. Instead they are gathered to function as a mosaic, a tessellation, suggesting straightforwardly that comings together between contemporary poetry and contemporary science are relatively common, indeed to be expected. Whether a critic such as Adalaide Morris sees the development of scientific theories of uncertainty as operating both within and alongside recent poetry, or a poet like W. N. Herbert is drawn to the ear-worthy vocabulary of science, the challenge of its sonorous lexis, attractions between contemporary poetry and contemporary science exist and flourish. Sometimes, when they met as this book took shape, poets and scientists were rather wary of each other; often each was rather excitedly in awe of his or her counterpart. Yet there were also moments of recognition, as when the solar physicist Eric Priest, working with the poet John Glenday, realized that poet and scientist might share rather a lot when it comes to working methods:

Stimulated by observations of the Sun, lots of ideas are continually floating around in my conscious and subconscious mind, and occasionally, when I wake up in the morning or am walking in the hills or working in the garden, one of them will take on a life of its own and crystallise. I then know in general terms the way I want to go, but have to spend many weeks discovering the detailed steps, using all the skills and mathematical techniques at my disposal—and often I will be led in unexpected directions on my journey to a fuller understanding. Indeed, the creative process of making poetry for

John seemed very similar, including the initial spark of inspiration, the hard work (often taking a couple of months!) and the sense of the poem taking on its own life.

Working with sound and the contours of words, the materiality, roots, and adriftness of language, many poets will recognize in Eric Priest's account something of how a poem can take off in unexpected directions on its trajectory towards completion. There are moments when doing science and making poems can seem very close. Repeatedly each discipline seeks a honed elegance dependent on careful pruning, leaving out, editing until only what is most needed remains. Yet this is not to deny that poetry and science are in many ways different activities. In science (often to the frustration of the scientist) there seems an obligation to suppress emotion, including the emotion of exuberant discovery, while poetry, however modulated and oblique, is often reliant on a fusion of musical and emotional pitch. Certainly tensions between poetic and scientific approaches will be apparent in the essays that follow. So will instances of consonance and attunement. Topics from a need to confront the implications of computing technology to the interplay between poetry, science, and religious belief recur in several essays. Too often over the past few decades the relationship between poetry and science has been assumed to be antagonistic; or simply, and to the annoyance of at least some poets and scientists, it has been taken for granted that scientists and poets have no interest in each other's work. At times, as when the pharmacologist Alison Gurney concludes that 'scientists and poets both make use of lateral thinking in formulating ideas, but otherwise they work in quite different ways', there are indications that, despite a momentary engagement with 'crossover' between poetry and science, the truth lies on the side of disengagement. At other moments, though, there is a sense of engagement working out, as the palaeontologist Norman MacLeod puts it, 'much better than I'd dare hope.'

Such positive engagement produced stunning results when the scientist Warren Warren at Princeton, after working with Paul Muldoon on their joint project for this book, was spurred to conduct a new experiment. Warren scanned the brain of a person concentrating on Muldoon's poem and then concentrating on passages from the regulations of Princeton University. When Warren and Muldoon presented their work to an audience of poets and scientists at The Poetry House at the University of St Andrews in 2003, the poets in the audience were clearly delighted to hear that there was a different, more intense pattern of brain activity that went with the reading of the poem, as compared with that which attended the bureaucratic prose. Writing in this book about the same experiment, Kay Redfield Jamison seems excited too. This shared enthusiasm hints that both poets and scientists may be attracted to the idea that poetry is a powerful medium and that its practitioners may have more in common with—and more to share with—practitioners of science than is supposed by most contemporary commentators who still regard as valid the malingering assumptions of the misguided C. P. Snow.

The essays in this book are individual counter-examples that prove such assumptions wrong. There are too many of them for any one to be the exception that proves a rule. Though they do not add up to a general theory, or sing together in perfect, rhyming accord, they do, along with several recent anthologies and collaborations, suggest that contemporary poetry and contemporary science are often interested in one another. Whether he knows it or not, John Burnside follows Aldous Huxley, who stressed the importance of ecology in his 1963 response to C. P. Snow, *Literature and Science*. Some scientists might argue with Burnside's poetico-eco-philosophical perception of what science is; some poets might argue with some of the immunologist Miroslav Holub's strictures about the use of rational scientific material in the dreamworld and soundscape of poems. Yet this book should furnish plenty of evidence that, however debatable the ground, there is certainly a wide variety of terrains where contemporary poetry and contemporary science parley, entertain each other, and even, in sometimes surprising ways, combine.

# Rampage, or Science in Poetry

Miroslav Holub

When asked what is the difference between a poet and a scientist-poet, I usually reply that for the scientist-poet ten minutes is exactly ten minutes. This definition comes, of course, from long experience with poetry readings by thoroughbred poets, and from scientific workshops where the chairperson would turn off the microphone after the allotted ten minutes even if you were just presenting a new Theory of Everything. But my ten minutes definition also has a broader meaning. In science one very soon makes an important personal developmental step: self-restraint. One learns that the individual is unique more because of his molecular structures, like the major histocompatibility complex, than because of his psyche, so deeply affected and shaped by social atmosphere, culture, market-place, friends, foes, and editors. One learns too that revelations are the function of hard everyday work and discipline; that tuition comes in most cases before intuition and that intuition is a very plastic word.

When an active scientific worker feels entitled to write poetry, he would rather accept his writing as tiny discoveries than as large revelations. For him poetry is a way of human communication, not the way of spiritual personal expansion. Human communication should be economical, as condensed as possible, allowing the other party enough time and space to reach his or her own answers and conclusions. It was Ezra Pound who underscored the fact that poetry means condensation (German *dichten* means condensare).[1] In science one learns very soon that one is at best one tiny knot in the planetary network of knowledge, intelligence, and emotionality, not the greatest event in the Universe since the Big Bang.

My argument is that there may be something like a scientific approach incorporated into something which may still be poetry, but not vice versa. Science in poetry may be represented by the hard-centred scientific thinking, by the elegance or incisiveness of scientific questions and temporary solutions, but not by interpretations or versifications of scientific data of the sort seen in many learned magazines where biochemists may publish verses on the action of prostaglandins and physicists on quarks.

There used to be an American Association of Physicians-Poets. I was the only foreign member. They published a magazine and an anthology, full of diabetes, kidney failures, psychoneuroses, and arthritis. Only an anthology of German-speaking physicians writing poetry (1971) contained worse poetry, also on roses, night shadows, and morning walks in the fields. Both anthologies were almost as bad as the *International Who's Who in Poetry Anthology* (1972). Even with a professional background, people who just want to be poets are very different from poets. More than that, the notion of 'poetry in science' is an unfortunate misunderstanding. The best one can get from poetry in a scientific career is some kind of vivid imagination which must stay at all times under the strict control of available knowledge. Science is art of the soluble, said Peter Medawar: poetry is the art of the insoluble.

Poets love to speak a lot, mainly about poetry. Scientists tend to avoid the terrifying word science. Nobody can discuss 'immunology' or 'palaeontology'. The only thing to speak about in 'science' are fullerones, CD 45* cells, or trilobites. Poetry has gone on being discussed in about the same manner for the last 2000 years; over the same time-span science has changed in a fundamental way at least three times, from speculative to classificatory and experimental, from comprehensible to almost incomprehensible in terms of human everyday logic, struggling with the 'fluent nature of things'. A poet may find this fact important, proving the immortality of poetry and the temporary nature of science. For me, the necessity of science is immanent to mankind, and so is the necessity of poetry. However, it is a lot easier to chat about something so indefinable and personal as poetry. I utterly dislike this sort of intellectual chatter, as is evident from the first stanzas of my poem 'Literary Bash':

> Like eggs of hail
> from the blue sky,
> the buzz of greasy bluebottles,
> the twitter of eggheads.

Interior sounds
of matter fatigue.

Never stopping.[2]

Had I not started both careers in about the same time, with science as the profession and poetry as a 'supporting pastime', I would be gravitating nowadays towards science anyway, because of its viability and vigour. Traditional intellectuals rooted in the traditional humanistic disciplines are losing credibility, not only because of the rising importance of pragmatic global enterprises, solutions, and ways of thinking, but always because of the fact that they are involved basically only in defence of the *status quo ante*; with the possible exception of sociologists and experimental psychologists, they are growing more and more alienated from real life and vocabulary. They neglect, in favour of 'eternal values', the fact that with science and technology we are creating our own new environment, our new nature. According to the physicist, Alan Lightman, every twenty years mankind is learning more than it did in all previous history.

Scientific activity becomes more and more something like a dynamic planetary process, an offensive, a result of concentrated human energy, 'the only one which is obviously and undoubtedly cumulative and progressive' (George Sarton), in spite of the fact that 'unlike art, science destroys its past' (Thomas S. Kuhn). This process is analogous to the manner in which a modern city destroys its nineteenth-century predecessor by building on and from its stones. I will refer later to my poem 'The Rampage', which renders the cellular offensive at the very onset of life. I feel that such a scientific hidden rampage is now occurring at the onset of a new quality of our life.

Because of the effective increase of public education, traditional intellectuals have lost their monopoly of knowledge. They are losing ground, because they can't be popularized, in contrast with science which is becoming popular by its mere practical and applicable results. As Michael Ignatieff has written in *Prospect*, the community has never been more educated and the intellectuals have never had less prestige. The only exceptions, escaping the crisis of authority, are the exact scientists. Not because of what they know, but because they have the methodology and openly visible results.

In my book of essays *Shedding Life* I quoted George Steiner: 'I remain unrepentant in my hunch that intellectual energies, imaginative boldness and sheer fun are currently more abundant in the sciences than they are in the humanities. Courteous inquiries by colleagues in the sciences render more embarrassing the casuistic jargon, the pretentious triviality which now dominate so much of literary theory and humanistic studies.'[3]

So I am proud to have a rather scientific mentality, not so much dependent on casuistic jargon and pretentious triviality. As a medical student, I was attracted only by psychiatry and as an aspiring poet by existentialism, all kinds of poetism, and the ethical pathos of the Czech philosophy as represented by Jan Patocka. I loved philosophy before I learned what science is about, how instructive it is to do something with your own hands, and how important it is to join a more or less collective project in a lab and to share the group's thoughts.

Science is labelled by philosophers as morally neutral, but the practice of experimental and/or theoretical scientific disciplines is a moral lesson in a kind of modesty, scrupulosity, perseverance, and silence. One must have the guts to do the same thing again and again and to accept or respect any qualified criticism. Of course, there are one-track scientists that may show some hubris and arrogance, but the scientist-poet mutation is by definition not one-tracked.

On the other hand, a scientist-poet does not, as a rule, experience the personal abyss which gapes before the poet who is existentially dependent on his Words, words, words, and who fumbles among his emotions and depressions. The poetry-writing scientist has his safeguards in his everyday laboratory routine, in the work which may bring positive or negative results, but is almost never a total failure, a solitary tragedy: he has other people around and they may help with technology and with the formulation of basic questions. There is harsh scientific competition, but even the person who never 'makes it' by publishing a paper in *Nature* or in *Science* magazine can be useful. A failed poet has no options, except to survive on a microscopic level of small magazines which have more contributors than readers. A scientific worker's career is mostly short of and far from a tragedy.

This has nothing to do with so-called rationality. I hate that cliché. Laboratory work is driven by as many emotions as any artistic performance. A 'rationalist' in any profession and in practical life is more likely to suffer from emotional stress, he is less likely to handle the situations (i.e., most situations) which escape human logic. A 'rationalist' is a rare phenomenon anywhere, and is in fact a deviation with a sort of obsessive neurosis.

What is generally labelled as rationality is in fact just education and concrete knowledge, as opposed to that lack of learning supposedly needed for primary or natural insight, sensitivity, and geniality. Intentional lack of knowledge is supposed to restore the 'natural' sensibility, letting it be open to the 'natural world' as if science were unnatural or inhuman. Rationality has little to do with the field of study or research. Any Lévi-Strauss studying the myths of Inuits is as rational as any immunologist studying natural killer cells. Only for understanding myths you need the imagination cultivated by all our fairy tales, for natural killer cells you need to remember the biology lessons in any US or European high school.

A frenzied poet, then, may be the individual who prefers to forget his school years, the more or less quiet scientist-poet is an individual who prefers to remember, because he does not believe in his privileged poetic instincts. I am astonished by the frequent incidence of failure at high school (or failure at university) that features in the biographies of poets, writers, and publicists in general. Sometimes, the literary career seems to be some kind of revenge or compensation.

Of course, it may well be that poetry is 'in the genes'. I am not sure. In some cases, poetry and art in general might well be a magnificent personal attempt to cope with the imminent disorder, labelled by psychiatrists as a bipolar (manic-depressive) reaction, illness, or psychosis. In some cases, maybe, but not in all cases. The 'poetic and artistic' attitude is, in my experience, mostly some sort of group infection, not a genetic affection. It is true, however, that the incidence of bipolar psychosis is above the average of the given population among 'artists' (and below the average among scientific workers).

In poetry we also tend to forget what poems we have read years ago; otherwise we would be hardly able to believe that the new poem is really new and not just some re-emergence of the *déja vu*, of the half-forgotten. Half-forgetting is the basis of intuition.

Now it is time to move from personality problems to the writing process, to poetry itself. In the first place, a person who lives with scientific images of the world, who has an intimate knowledge of his concrete field of research, who has a personal relation to a thymus or to adhesion molecules, and who reads with interest and astonishment about the tremendous achievements in most dynamic scientific disciplines, from astrophysics to molecular genetics—such a person has a broader concept of the natural world. He has really challenging themes other than his own biography, his own impressions from a landscape or from a bedroom. He finds new discoveries much more intriguing than the old myths. He lives with another concept of reality, in which his own inner life and emotional movements are not the safest ground, but the most precarious area.

Consequently he doesn't like too much of his personal presence in his poems. He finds that his approach and eventual (very rare) ideas are personal enough. So, typically, he chooses themes which do not involve too much description, but require rather a dramatic rendering, themes that develop as if by themselves. Sometimes he has utterly unpoetic topics, in my case, for example, anencephaly, intensive care units, heart transplants, and a mouse universe. Even in a love poem he prefers a metaphoric use of stick insects and molecules fitting molecules to the pink and velvet skin and bleeding heart.

I remember that at a very early stage of my writing I very much wanted to escape from the narrow limits of a spectrum of metaphors that used menagerie, roses, cabbage, and, at best, garlic. Eventually such a spectrum might extend to planets, called stars, and love, instead of testosterone. Why not refer to the subtotal extent of so-called reality, from pulsars to leptons, from prokaryotic organisms to our lymphocytes and interferons, provided they can be used in a comprehensible way? From the beginning, I had simply more *comparata* in mind and would use a lot more of the fantastically poetic stuff like RNA and DNA, provided they could make some sense for the reader or listener, not because these odd terms would be *that* well known, but because they could be made comprehensible from the context, or because they could be accepted as dark images or sounds in an otherwise clear development of the poem.

The title poem of my last book, *The Rampage*, may be an example:

> The last time
> there was a genuine rampage,
> herds stampeding

with the zest of hurricanes,
with the pulsations of a storm,
and the force of destiny,

when the roar went up
against the villous ceiling,
when the stronger ones
pushed forward to the cruel
thunder of whips while the zombies
fell back into permanent darkness,

the last time
the cavalry charged
across the whole width of the enemy line
into the gap between life and death,
and not even one single droplet of misery
dripped,

the last time
something really won
and the rest turned into compost

that was when the sperm
made the journey
up the oviduct.

That was 'to be or not to be'.

Since that time we've been tottering round
with the embarrassment of softening skeletons,
with the wistful caution
of mountain gorillas in the rain;
we keep hoping for the time-lapse soul,
secreting
marital problems and
a stationary home metaphysics

against which
the adenosine triphosphate of every fucked-up cell
is like the explosion of a star
in a chicken coop.[4]

The poem starts as a report from a battle so that the reader could be present at the scene which is, however, a microscopic 'scientific' landscape. The poem makes use of the fact that spermatozoa are very popular cells and the fact that the process of fertilization may be familiar to most practitioners. Of course, I can't expect that everybody would be ready to see the herds of cells as real in the way that somebody who has spent some forty years looking on live cells in the microscope might, but the cellular stampede is not beyond imagination and at any rate readers may know the fibre-optic recording of the sperm travelling up the oviduct. At least in its first four stanzas the poem might be thought of as offering some sort of subtitles for a Lennard Nilsson film and I have assumed—perhaps incorrectly—that it is sufficiently visual. So I dared to include the term 'villous ceiling' (meaning surface of a mucous membrane covered with minute elongated projections or folds, as in the oviduct). In case the reader would not accept the villi, he still has the sound of the word, not far from villainous, which may add to the setting of the cellular drama.

The main leap of the poem brings us to a situation completely familiar in adult life. It presents hesitations, time-lapse souls, metaphysics, and marital problems, that appear so far from the real 'rampage' deep inside. Typically, I used the professional term adenosine triphosphate, not in the hope a poetry reader would be aware of the cellular energy metabolism, but just as an impressive, hard, reliable, chemical term in an intelligible metaphoric situation. There is nothing scientific about adenosine triphosphates and villous membranes in 'The Rampage', but there may be something of the scientific hard-centred approach in the essential idea or theme of the poem, the lingering counterpoint of the cellular drive and the human. In my mind, this is not an apocalyptic poem, it's a realistic biological one, opposing optical illusions present in any human biography.

It may be meaningful that an analogous poem has been written by Aldous Huxley, a man of letters with an eager and family-conditioned interest in science:

Fifth Philosopher's Song

A million million spermatozoa,
  All of them alive:
Out of their cataclysm but one poor Noah
  Dare hope to survive.

And among that billion minus one
Might have chanced to be
Shakespeare, another Newton, a new Donne—
But the One was Me.

Shame to have ousted your betters thus,
Taking ark while the others remained outside!
Better for all of us, froward Homunculus,
If you'd quietly died![5]

The microscopic scene here is identical to that of my poem. In addition, the sceptical image of the one who 'took the ark' is not far from my 'mountain gorillas in the rain' and 'softening skeletons'. Huxley, however, is much more personal and lyrical, whereas I stay with the cellular counterpoint to our psychological setting and tend to escape any trace of sentiment (and consequently any exclamation mark). Huxley clearly felt apologetic about the theme, using the excuse of a 'philosopher's song'; I don't have any excuse. Of course, there is also a fifty years' gap between the two poems.

A crystalline example of the use of a scientific statement or sentence in a poem occurs in the quotations from theoretical physics in my poem, 'Spacetime'.

When I grow up and you get small,
then—

(In Kaluza's theory the fifth dimension
is represented as a circle
associated with every point
in spacetime)

—then when I die, I'll never be alive again?
Never.
Never never?
Never never.
Yes, but never never never?
No, not never never never,
just never never.

So we made
a small family contribution
to the quantum problem of eleven-dimensional supergravity.[6]

Here there is a totally enigmatic interpretation of Kaluza's theory of the fifth dimension and a mention of the quantum problem of eleven-dimensional supergravity. In spite of the fact that only a few theoretical physicists could have an idea of what is going on, these quotes constitute the backbone of the poem, because they are juxtaposed with a most natural kid's question about death and coming alive again. The obscure physico-mathematical sentences are used as counterpoints to the seemingly simple, but in fact also totally incomprehensible questions of ephemeral human life. Again, the only scientific trait pertaining to the quotes is the courage, or rather joy, in their use. Actually they operate like some kind of incursion of Chinese in the English text, but are still basically acceptable within the structure of the poem, as I know from readings and from the London Underground, where the poem was displayed for a week and the poor commuters had to read it instead of advertisements for laxatives. They did.

Nobody ever said that 'Spacetime' is a scientific poem. It was accepted as an amusing poem, as some sort of poetic fun, and I must admit that I prefer, even in poetry, fun to suicidal seriousness. The preference for fun, humour, irony, and above all self-irony may be a science-derived tool.

Next comes an example of a poem which I would regard as scientific, though it does not use science-derived terms and quotations. It is a new poem called 'Because':

Don't go to the mountain, the zodiac lions roar there!
    They will go anyway.
Don't crawl into holes, black gnomes pierce the souls with curved needles!
    They will crawl anyway.
Don't open the words, hopelessness is spelled into them!
    They will open them anyway.
Don't tinker with genes, a fragile aureola sticks to them!
    They will tinker anyway.
Because they are humans.

I regard the poem as 'scientific' because it is almost optimistic and certainly opposed to the routinely negativistic attitude towards science and technology in poetry which for 170 years follows the good and frank Edgar Allan Poe:

Science! true daughter of Old Time thou art!
Who alterest all things with thy peering eyes,
Why preyest thou thus upon the poet's heart,
Vulture, whose wings are dull realities?[7]

To indicate how my recycling of kinds of scientific images in verse has developed, I might turn to a poem of mine written many years ago, and often quoted in writings on Science & Poetry. The poem is called 'In the Microscope':

Here too are dreaming landscapes,
lunar, derelict.
Here too are the masses,
tillers of the soil.
And cells, fighters,
who lay down their lives
for all the world.

Here too are cemeteries,
fame, snow and spates.
And I hear murmuring,
the revolt of immense estates.[8]

Compared with 'The Rampage', this is a very lyrical poem, not a dramatic script with an unpredictable result. It is an almost obvious description of a microscopic still life, namely of a histological picture of chronic inflammation provoked by Freud's adjuvant in subcutaneous tissue. This was, incidentally, the theme of my first scientific paper, so 'In the Microscope' is also a very personal poem, almost a page of a diary.

Here again there is a leap from the microscopic to the macroscopic, from cells and tissues to humans and landscapes. But the poem deals with a far from unpredictable event. 'In the Microscope' is not an action poem, but a stationary poem on the state resulting from a battle. It is even sweetened by a rhyme (which vanished in the original old translation) and there are no technical or professional expressions in the poem. As a beginner, I didn't dare deploy these. Today, I would have fibrin fibres, interleukins, cellular stress proteins, and oxygen radicals included, because they are essential for the battlefield, because they are the driving force behind the apparently still life, because they are better known today, and because I am much less cautious now about the reaction of editors and reviewers who would regard fibrins and cytokines as a scientific arrogance and obfuscation, especially when compared to those oxymorons, metonymy, palimpsests, and reincarnations that must be familiar to any cultured consumer of poetry and poetics.

The development from the poem 'In the Microscope' to 'The Rampage' may be connected with my status as a so-called poet, not with the basic approach. I am afraid that my basic approach didn't change much over the thirty years between these two poems. I may just tend to be more dramatic and controversial, in the new conditions in my country where a rendering of a cellular process is not any more a subtle form of protests against the communist blockheads (like Lysenko and Lepeshinskaya) who would understand and support only some kind of scientific surrealism.

Today, I am more emotional, more angry, about the science–antiscience tensions, because these are generated not any more by the communist blockheads, but by supposedly normal intellectuals who admire and eloquently advocate of their own free will anything from metempsychosis and astrology to healing by 'magnetic water'. Paul Feyerabend once said that we should have a democratic right to accept or not to accept gravitation. I find it a very good idea for a surrealist poem, but not for a normal human practice. In my view, the poem would be very ironical, in other words related to a normal human life.

I was always ravished by surrealism, but my own surrealism is also a reaction against the reigning absurdity of Marxist ideology, or against the primitive allusions of present-day pseudosciences and spiritual profundities. There may be a basic difference between a literary surrealism and the inescapable surrealism of a dominant stupidity which may be counteracted by surreal irony. My image of a corporal who bans, under penalty of quartering, all numbers from three up, is a reaction against political pseudologic and has nothing to do with any mathematical background, despite the fact that the poem concerned was included in an anthology of 'mathematical poetry'. The poem 'The corporal who killed Archimedes' was in its time a very political poem:

With one bold stroke
he killed the circle, tangent, cotangent,
and point of intersection of parallels
in infinity.

On penalty of quartering
he banned numbers
from three up.

In Syracuse now
he heads the school of philosophers,
for another thousand years
squats on his halbert
and writes:

one two
one two
one two
one two[9]

In many other instances, of course, some kind of sober 'scientific' thinking was a great help in my way of resistance against the reigning myths. The conditions of life in Central Europe were—and still are—definitely a corroborating principle in my adherence to science and scientific evidence. And to a mild surrealism.

In my opinion, the scientific allusions in a poem like 'The Rampage' are some kind of anchors in the high seas of feelings, sympathies, hates, impressions, and memories. If the poem says 'the last time | something really won', referring to the cellular process of fertilization, it's a hard fact.[10] The poem is hitting a firm ground underneath the relativity of human winning and losing. The rampage of the cells, the cellular drama, represents for me even some kind of energy and spontaneity, as opposed to the intellectual and poetic attitude which I have defined in the poem 'Kuru, or the Smiling Death Syndrome' as a counterpart of a slow virus:

We aren't the Fores of New Guinea,
we don't indulge in ritual cannibalism,
we don't harbour the slow virus that
causes degeneration
of the brain and spinal cord with spasms, shivers,
progressive dementia and
the typical grimace.

We just smile,
embarrassed, we smile,
embarrassed, we smile,
embarrassed, we smile.[11]

In most poems I am going back and forth from the microscopic to the visible, from the exploding stars to human tenderness and fear, from the objective to the subjective, in order to get some temporary assurance. I am following William Carlos Williams's poem—'There is | the | microscopic | anatomy || of the whale | this is | reassuring'.[12] I may lack the poetic depressions and abysses, but I share the Sisyphus syndrome as interpreted by the Albert Camus who thought that one must imagine Sisyphus as happy.

In conclusion, I suggest (and this is a very scientific form of words) that a scientist, even writing poetry, is and should be and must remain a scientist: science has a deep influence on his personality, giving him assurance and relieving him from abysmal feelings. He is the member of the intellectual community who still has a deep and visible importance for the society and its everyday life. Science is nowadays the hidden and positive 'rampage' of mankind. Science in poetry is not the function of scientific terms, expressions, results, and technical ideas. It is the function of the scientific, hard-centred approach to reality and to comforting myths. It has its immanent optimism. The poetry of a practising scientist is basically a dialogue; consequently it should be clear enough to be understood and strong enough to lead somewhere in human terms. Science in poetry should shed some relatively new light. It is definitely not the post-romantic and postmodern poetic way of wearing dark glasses on a moonless night.

# As Above

Don Paterson

## With An Introduction

by Andrew Riches

### Introduction

Having read a few of Don Paterson's poems before I met him, I was aware of his craftsmanship with language, and the careful selection and juxtaposition of words in his work. For example, in his poem 'The Sea at Brighton' I was quite taken with the image of 'The bird . . . that skites over its blank flags', and in 'The White Lie' I liked 'nor could I put a name to my own face'. When I spoke to him I realized that I was ignorant of the strategies for a poem's construction. Don talked about rhymed monometers, riffs, and pararhymes which, for the initiated, form the framework on which some of his poems are built.

Our meeting started in my laboratory in the Bute Medical School at the University of St Andrews, where I introduced Don to the science, indeed the art, of cell culture. By growing human cells in the laboratory, we are able to treat them with substances that induce cancer and can then try to discover the changes that have taken place as the normal cell is converted into an abnormal cell in a defined manner in our cell culture flask. I find growing cells very satisfying, and I think Don responded to some of this enthusiasm. He was particularly taken with the molecular analysis we do to try and find the mistakes occurring in genes in the cancer cells. There are very powerful techniques available now for investigating chromosomes and DNA, and these methods give rather colourful and vivid images.

In the poem produced after the visit, Don has taken the idea of strings of genetic code which then deviate from normal to give rise to mutations, thus leading to erroneous replication—'bad code', as he describes it. From these general concepts, he has translated this theme into words using replication and erroneous replication in word form. He tells me this is pararhyme, where the consonantal pattern of the word stays the same but the vowels change, as in 'burst' and 'breast'. Clearly the poem does not move like a linear, descriptive tale. Instead, it captures images in short word bites. It also conjures up questions: who or what 'lapped | her breast | sky-blue'? Is it the reflected light through 'the naked | skylight'? Why would the 'I' of the poem blink 'for the crow | or rook'? Am 'I' waking up in the morning as the birds move and the 'foursquare | burst | of the dark' heralds daybreak? Or does it really portend something much worse? Perhaps I am trying to analyse too much like a scientist and should just breathe the word forms.

## As Above

*i. m. C. T.*

As she slept
late
below
the naked
skylight
I lapped
her breast
sky-blue

Had I blinked
for the crow
or rook
one foursquare
burst
of the dark?

# Poetry and Virtual Realities

Edwin Morgan

Links between poetry and science, far from being rare and strange, are actually quite hard to avoid, if one takes the whole history of poetry into account. Well-known names line up to be considered: Lucretius, Dante, Milton, Goethe, Shelley, Leopardi, to which you might add Omar Khayyàm, famous in the West as a poet but more famous in his own country of Persia as a mathematician and astronomer, and Virgil, whose *Georgics* is a fine poem but at the same time a manual of agriculture and animal husbandry, written by an author who was not a dilettante but himself a farmer. Virgil's overall title of the four-part poem, *Georgicon*, can be translated as 'works of earth': poet, farmer, and poem are all a part of nature and the understanding of nature and the transformation of nature. This poem looks back to Lucretius (whom Virgil admired) in being didactic. Lucretius' *De Rerum Natura* (On the Nature of the Universe) is first and foremost a great poem, but it has the purpose, as the author tells us himself, of being a sort of one-man Enlightenment, using science and philosophy to free people's minds from the shackles of religion and superstition. It has a remarkable (not to say epic) sweep of topics: cosmology, physics, optics, meteorology, language, sex, and the social contract. Is it dry? Is it dead? No, not really. Parts of it are hard going, and parts have obviously been superseded, but the atomic theory of matter which Lucretius uses chimes in well with modern thinking, and his passionate feeling for the grandeur of natural phenomena is not diminished by his desire to explain their workings. His is a living cosmos:

> semper in adsiduo motu res quaeque geruntur.[1]
> The whole universe is always in ceaseless motion.

It is also an unbounded cosmos:

nec refert quibus adsistas regionibus eius:
usque adeo, quem quisque locum possedit, in omnis
tantundem partis infinitum omne relinquit.[2]

It does not matter in what regions of the universe you set yourself: the fact is that from whatever spot anyone may occupy, the universe is left stretching equally unbounded in every direction.

Lucretius often uses highly descriptive or figurative language, but in the two passages just quoted he shows that statement itself, without any simile or metaphor, can be eloquent, if something large and visionary is being revealed. Perhaps because science addresses itself to fundamental questions of space and time, there is always a window open to the poetic imagination, though the poet must of course be capable of using that window. Dante and Milton are good examples. Dante was a visionary and Milton was an anti-visionary, but they both offer us a thrilling assurance that human fate, human events, human aspirations take place against and within a huge cosmic set or shell from which they cannot be detached; and it is therefore impossible for anything that happens to be truly trivial. Both poets knew about and used the science of their own time. They were not exactly 'learned' men in the full sense, but they shared the belief which was usual in the classical, medieval, and Renaissance periods that the best poets should be well-read persons, especially in non-literary subjects; they should have good general knowledge, of which science would be a part, science being itself simply *scientia*, 'knowledge'.

Milton's *Paradise Lost* (1667) is specially interesting because of its cosmology. Milton used the geocentric Ptolemaic universe for the setting of his poem, which would have been regarded at that date as a somewhat old-fashioned procedure. He did this, however, not because he was unaware of the new astronomy, which he refers to in the poem, but because a geocentric universe suited his subject, the Fall of Man. Most of the poem takes place in Hell and Heaven, but the action has finally to centre on the earth, where the climax is focused. It's fascinating to see how often, as if he felt guilty about it, Milton refers to Galileo, whom he had met in Italy as a young man and whom he obviously admired. Galileo is the only one of Milton's contemporaries to be mentioned by name in *Paradise Lost*, which is remarkable enough, but the poem also refers, at various points, to

Galileo's use of the telescope, to show how rough the surface of the moon was, or to study sunspots, or to discover the phases of Venus, or to trace the Milky Way. This knowledge, this *scientia*, is not paraded; it simply emerges from a well-stocked mind. But it signals very clearly that if you try to stuff the poem into the pigeon-hole of pure theology, you'll find that it won't fit.

In the other poets I mentioned, it's usually not hard to see the relevance of science. Goethe wrote on biology, anatomy, optics, acoustics, sometimes being perversely wrong, sometimes making genuine discoveries, but always believing that the most useful poets were never those who were only poets. Leopardi was the first poet, in a wonderful passage in 'La ginestra', to write about the distant galaxies which had recently been discovered. But Shelley, is Shelley not the odd man out? He was certainly an odd man! But he has his place too. When Carl Grabo's book *A Newton Among Poets* came out in 1930, it raised not a few eyebrows. Its subtitle is 'Shelley's Use of Science in "Prometheus Unbound" ', and its main claim was that the extravagant, almost surrealistic, often obscure imagery of the poem could be clarified and disentangled as reflecting Shelley's knowledge of various scientific ideas of his time. We know that Shelley was interested in science. He was familiar with the work of Humphrey Davy in chemistry, Erasmus Darwin in botany, William Herschel in astronomy. As a student at Oxford he filled his rooms with chemical and electrical experiments, as his fellow-student Thomas Jefferson Hogg recounted later in his biography of Shelley:

> He then proceeded, with much eagerness and enthusiasm, to show me the various instruments, especially the electrical apparatus; turning round the handle very rapidly, so that the fierce, crackling sparks flew forth; and presently standing upon the stool with glass feet, he begged me to work the machine until he was filled with the fluid, so that his long, wild locks bristled and stood on end. Afterwards he charged a powerful battery of several jars; labouring with vast energy, and discoursing with increasing vehemence of the marvellous powers of electricity.[3]

Hogg wrote rather mockingly of these student pranks, but in fact they were a sign of something that went deep into Shelley's mind and emerged with great force in the dramatic poem *Prometheus Unbound.* Prometheus, in the Greek legend, had stolen fire from the gods and given it to mankind, for which he was later regarded as the father of science and technology. He was chained to a rock by Zeus as punishment for his dissidence, and Shelley's poem deals with the moment of his release, which is both caused by and itself causes a huge emission of energy, partly subterranean and quasi-atomic and partly electric. The energy is symbolized by a sphere that rolls over the earth and contains within it many smaller revolving spheres and also a small child, curled up asleep but smiling; and the child sends out from its brow vast electric searchlights which whirl across, down into, and up from the earth, revealing, liberating, transforming. They stream out into space and give life to the moon, which is no longer a dead world but has an atmosphere, clouds, rain, trees and civilizations and extinct prehistoric creatures. The imagery seems devised to bring out how science can empower man, make him learn from the past and prepare for the future. As the Earth says in the poem:

> The lightning is his slave; heaven's utmost deep
> Gives up her stars, and like a flock of sheep
> They pass before his eye, are numbered, and roll on!
> The tempest is his steed, he strides the air;
> And the abyss shouts from her depth laid bare,
> Heaven, hast thou secrets? Man unveils me; I have none.[4]

Shelley, writing at the beginning of the age of electricity, was an optimist, and it was perhaps not too difficult for him to believe in progress, as so many of his Victorian successors did. The next poet I want to talk about, Hugh MacDiarmid, writing a century later, also believed in progress, but he had more than Shelley's galvanic battery to contend with, and his heroic struggles to prevent poetry and science from saying goodbye to each other were bound not to be plain sailing. Since we are now moving into a Scottish context, I'd like to say a word or two about John Davidson, one of MacDiarmid's forerunners in that struggle at the end of the nineteenth century.

Davidson was trained as a chemist, and had a keen interest in both science and technology. He wrote poetry about the Crystal Palace, one of the most advanced buildings of its time (he didn't like it but he saw its importance). He wrote about trains and cranes and the first motor-cars:

> For 'twas the freedom of the motor-car
> That showed how tyrannous the railways are.[5]

Changed days now! He was a convinced materialist, and wanted to show that matter, even if it became conscious through human beings and their activities, was still matter; everything from a stone to John Davidson was one stuff. To deal with this idea, he thought it was important to intertwine scientific and non-scientific discourse, something which later appealed to Hugh MacDiarmid. This passage from his poem 'Fleet Street' illustrates the method:

> The carbon, iron, copper, silicon,
> Zinc, aluminium vapours, metalloids,
> Constituents of the skeleton and shell
> Of Fleet Street—of the woodwork, metalwork,
> Brickwork, electric apparatus, drains
> And printing-presses, conduits, pavement, road—
> Were at the first unelemented space,
> Imponderable tension in the dark
> Consummate matter of eternity.
> And so the flesh and blood of Fleet Street, nerve
> And brain infusing life and soul, the men,
> The women, woven, built and kneaded up
> Of hydrogen, of azote, oxygen,
> Of carbon, phosphorus, chlorine, sulphur, iron,
> Of calcium, kalium, natrum, manganese,
> The warm humanities that day and night
> Inhabit and employ it and inspire,
> Were in the ether mingled with it, there
> Distinguished nothing from the road, the shops,
> The drainpipes, sewage, sweepings of the street:
> Matter of infinite beauty and delight.[6]

And the poem ends with a remarkable dialogue between the bricks of the London street and the fragments of rock in the rings of Saturn; the rings envy the bricks for their solid usefulness while the bricks admire the shining beauty of the rings. So Fleet Street, centre of worldly communication, has a hotline to the stars, even if it doesn't yet know it. But poets know it.

Hugh MacDiarmid was both moved and influenced by Davidson. He said Davidson's death affected him with unexpected force. He wrote in an essay:

I did not know him personally, but I remember as if it were yesterday how the news of his suicide by walking into the sea off Penzance in March 1909, when I was a lad of seventeen, affected me. I felt as if the bottom had fallen out of my world. Later I wrote of this:

> I remember one death in my boyhood
> That next to my father's, and darker, endures;
> Not Queen Victoria's but Davidson, yours,
> And something in me has always stood
> Since then looking down the sandslope
> On your small black shape by the edge of the sea
> —A bullet-hole through a great scene's beauty,
> God through the wrong end of a telescope.[7]

MacDiarmid used a scientific image, the telescope, to close that tribute to John Davidson. He was a strong believer in the unity of knowledge, and he refused to accept a split between the arts and the sciences. Unlike Davidson, he had no scientific training himself, but he was an extraordinarily well-read man who wanted to bring the fruits of his reading into his poetry, and that included many references to the sciences. Sometimes he put them in for their own sake, because he found them interesting; sometimes he used them as comparisons, analogues, similes; but he was never afraid to employ technical or specialized words, to the dismay of many of his admirers. He wanted it all: vocabulary, theories, facts. He sent it all out like an enormous undecoded but not undecodable letter to a bumbazed public. He had a large appetite for facts, and wanted to upgrade them, to make poetry

> A protest, invaluable to science itself,
> Against the exclusion of value
> From the essence of matter of fact.[8]

In following this out, he sometimes got rather carried away. In that same long poem, 'The Kind of Poetry I Want', he envisages how we shall have a poetry which

> Examines the statistics of North Atlantic air temperatures,
> Nile flood levels, wheat prices, winter in Europe,
> Tree-rings, sedimentary layers and lake deposits,

The dates of the sprouting and bloom of hawthorn,
Of the first cuckoo, of the beginning of harvest,
Of cattle products, herring and salmon catches, diphtheria,
Typhus and measles epidemics, prices of Consols,
Workers' wages, coal production, discount at the Bank of England,
British export trade, American wheat production,
Suicides and lynchings—and finds the eleven-year cycle in them all
And shows the connection between them.[9]

No doubt MacDiarmid is interested in the scientific possibility and implications of an eleven-year cycle which could embrace such a disparate array of events, but from the aesthetic point of view he simply enjoys the cumulative effect, the boisterousness of a list, an ancient device in poetry. He was always searching, and genuinely searching (as in 'In Memoriam James Joyce'), for

The point where science and art can meet,
For there are two kinds of knowledge,
Knowing about things and knowing things,
Scientific data and aesthetic realization,
And I seek their perfect fusion in my work.[10]

That fusion is hard to obtain, and often the scientific data stand out bald an unassimilated, gesturing towards nothing except some book he has read. But there are impressive victories, in poems which are not really very like anybody else's: the geology of 'On a Raised Beach' and 'Stony Limits', the mineralogy of 'Crystals Like Blood', and the zoology of 'To a Friend and Fellow-Poet (Ruth Pitter)'. The last two are the most concentrated, and perhaps come nearest to the ideal of fusion. 'To a Friend and Fellow-Poet' describes, in fascinated and almost horrified magnified detail, the parturition of a Guinea worm. The choice of Ruth Pitter as the addressee is not without interest, as several of her own poems, published in *A Mad Lady's Garland* (1934), explore similar territory: 'Song of the Virtuous Female Spider', 'The Bee Turned Anchorite', 'The Coffin-Worm', and especially 'The Heretical Caterpillar'. (She is not mentioned in Alan Bold's biography of MacDiarmid or in his edition of that poet's letters, but her relationship with MacDiarmid would be worth investigating.) The Guinea worm is a parasite which lives under the skin of various mammals, including man, and the poem describes how the female with her teeming progeny has to sacrifice most of her bodily organs till she becomes

> Little more than one long tube close-packed with young;
> Until from the ruptured bulla, the little circular sore,
> You see her dauntless head protrude, and presently, slowly,
> A beautiful, delicate, and pellucid tube
> Is projected from her mouth, tenses and suddenly spills
> Her countless brood in response to a stimulus applied
> Not directly to the worm herself, but the skin of her host
> With whom she has no organised connection (and that stimulus
> O Poets! But cold water!) . . . The worm's whole musculocutaneous coat
> Thus finally functions as a uterus, forcing the uterine tube
> With its contents through her mouth. And when the prolapsed uterus
> ruptures
> The protruded and now collapsed portion shrivels to a thread
> (Alexander Blok's utter emptiness after creating a poem!)
> The rapid drying of which effectually and firmly
> Closes the wound for the time being . . .[11]

And that's not the end of it. The process is repeated again and again, 'ejaculating another seething mass of embryos', until 'the entire uterus is expelled and parturition concluded.' The poem ends on the desired note of fusion, the worm becoming the poet, straining in the throes of the delivery of his or her art:

> Is it not precisely thus we poets deliver our store,
> Our whole being the instrument of our suicidal art,
> And by the skin of our teeth flype ourselves into fame?

Most of it is like watching the close-ups of a David Attenborough film, but MacDiarmid is careful to insert little parentheses which remind us that it's only half about Guinea worms—the other half is about you, Ruth Pitter, and me, Hugh MacDiarmid. The important difference between this method and (say) an epic simile in Virgil or Milton is that it's not a case of external matter being brought in to illustrate the higher-order aesthetic concerns of the poem; here, the reader is expected to enjoy learning something he probably didn't know before, as well as enjoy the analogy that's sprung on him.

The other poem, 'Crystals Like Blood', holds this balance or fusion of scientific and non-scientific in a more ambiguous but equally satisfying way. The speaker describes how he remembers walking in the countryside and picking up a broken rock which was a mixture of minerals and colours, limestone, quartz, brown, grey, green, not very interesting, but there inside the quartz something that suddenly caught his eye, 'veins and beads | Of bright magenta'—the crystals like blood of the title. This rouses another memory:

And I remember how later on I saw
How mercury is extracted from cinnabar
—The double ring of iron piledrivers
Like the multiple legs of a fantastically symmetrical spider
Rising and falling with monotonous precision,
Marching round in an endless circle
And pounding up and down with a tireless, thunderous force,
While, beyond, another conveyor drew the crumbled ore
From the bottom and raised it to an opening high
In the side of a gigantic grey-white kiln.

So I remember how mercury is got
When I contrast my living memory of you
And your dear body rotting here in the clay
—And feel once again released in me
The bright torrents of felicity, naturalness, and faith
My treadmill memory draws from you yet.[12]

This poem on the one hand gives an observed, technically described account of the extraction of mercury from cinnabar by an industrial process; on the other hand it's about the memory of some loved person who has died. Which, if either, is the more important? Is the shining silvery mercury only an image, a metaphor for the 'bright torrents of felicity and faith' which the treadmill of memory squeezes out in the poet's mind as he thinks about the dead person? That is what you might expect, i.e., that the poem is a sort of devious off-beat elegy. But then you notice that the poet doesn't say 'So I remember you when I think of cinnabar and mercury', he says 'So I remember how mercury is got when I think of you'—not quite so flattering to the deceased but surely a signal to the reader that the world of rocks, and the industrial world of man's processing of rocks, are not there to be downgraded in favour of the human emotion of overcoming bereavement. Whether the reader accepts this signal is a nice test of how we all stand in openness to the persuasions of science and fact.

I myself as a poet, born a generation after MacDiarmid, sympathized with what he was doing and I generally defended his scientific poetry when I was writing about him, but I was interested in the place of science in human culture long before I read MacDiarmid. I remember at school we were asked to write an essay on what sort of career we were attracted by, and I wrote about archaeology and/or astronomy. The former is probably to be explained by the fact that the 1920s and 1930s were one of the heydays of Egyptian archaeological discovery, and I had followed the accounts of this fairly vividly. The astronomy option came partly from my reading of popular science books by Jeans and Eddington and partly from my fondness for science-fiction. I recall that the teacher expressed some scepticism about me either scrabbling among the tombs or measuring the Milky Way, but in a sense I knew what I was doing and probably enjoyed his surprise. I was fumbling towards the idea that there really is only one culture, and when I took, as my four Highers, English, French, Art, and Mathematics, I was trying to make the same point, though it was regarded as an eccentric group of subjects.

When I gradually made my way into MacDiarmid's poetry after the Second World War—and it wasn't until 1955, when he published *In Memoriam James Joyce* as a book, that the full scope of his poetry of fact and science was revealed—I could see what was quixotic about his ambition: that no single mind in the twentieth century could have a grasp of the sum of knowledge as Lucretius and Leonardo da Vinci have had in their times. Specialization spreads from year to year. We have Professors not only of Biochemistry but of Nucleic Acid Biochemistry, not only of Oncology but of Radiation Oncology, not only of Parasitology but of Molecular Parasitology. And so it will continue. This means that almost all the information in MacDiarmid came at second hand, and could sometimes be wrong. He was not a man in a white coat. He had not, like Shelley, given himself electric shocks to see if his hair would stand on end (it stood on end in any case). What he did do, and I gave him credit for it, was gather together all the facts and theories and processes and discoveries that genuinely interested him and that might be deliberately—apparently!—off-centre, so that there was always something creative, something of the 'making strange', about his depredations and juxtapositions. I think he really did want to show that poetry and science could be brought together, but he could do it only on his own terms.

He had no interest, for example, in the development of computers and cybernetics in the 1950s and 1960s, even when it became clear that cultural ramifications, and not only scientific advances, were involved. The computer threw out challenges in many directions, in music and poetry, in chess, in cryptography, in linguistic analysis and translation. I myself was very conscious of this gap in MacDiarmid, since it was an area I was happily exploring. In an imaginary dialogue (written in 1957) between neurophysiologist Grey Walter and poet Jean Cocteau I envisaged a sophisticated robot as my interface between two strongly held divergent views of human creativity. Cocteau has no faith in the future of robotics:

> Poetry's like a gull, protesting, sheering off;
> It's a radio-star the telescope can't catch;
> It's an act of love with an angel in anger;
> It's a darkness for the searchlight of a question.
> The poet is invisible, he speaks in code
> Although the great cryptographers acclaim in joy
> His clarity extraordinarily pure.
> The creator's hidden, the conception's hidden,
> The statue moves, Hermione breathes. What is life?
> 'Like an old tale still, though credit be asleep'? Oh
> But the feigned statue becomes a statue by art
> And we share the miracle of the deceived king!
> The very untruth cradles the rapturous thing.
> What logic flashes through the seagull's sudden wing?[13]

But Dr Walter is quick to reply:

> Some logic, which human patience is approaching.
> You are not quite so invisible as you think.
> Even the unexpected has limitations;
> Machines can be persuaded to stumble on dreams—
> Except that it isn't stumbling and they aren't dreams.
> Why do you think I called this creature the Whittrick?
> The flash of imagination has been build in,
> Its logic allows the leap of thought. It's brooding,
> Ticking, scanning more myriads of possibilities

> Than those great heads that sought the words of the *Winter's Tale* or the *Principia Mathematica.*
> It must not only solve problems, but present them.
> Creation's as dear to me as it is to you;
> Babbage's dream and Bottom's dream begin to meet.
> You fear what I hope: the created may create.[14]

That poem expressed something of the 1950s new-toy optimism about computer potential. In other poems I allowed a fly of irony to settle on the interface. 'The Computer's First Christmas Card', 'The Computer's Second Christmas Card', and 'The Computer's First Birthday Card' all show the computer struggling to present messages which the human mind would regard as acceptable. 'The Computer's First Code Poem' combines a genuine, moderately difficult code with what is claimed to be a sort of poetry that could not be created in any other way, and the reader is invited to decide whether this is the case.

These were simulated and not actual computer poems. But although I was not using a computer, I was interested in the computer's creative possibilities. I have a 'Cybernetics' file of cuttings from newspapers and magazines which I started in 1949, at a time when computers were exploring cryptography and machine translation, both of which were areas that attracted me. I had contacts with MIT, with the Cambridge Language Research Unit, and with the Computing Laboratory at Glasgow University. I wrote articles and gave talks on what relations there might be between artistic creativity and high-speed computing. But when it came to poetry itself, I started off with pencil, pen, or typewriter, and made the poems a bridge, as it were, between traditional methods of composition and adumbrations of a future where human brain-circuits might be challenged. Since existing examples of 'computer poetry' were at best surrealistically quirky and at worst dully mechanical, I thought an imaginative, simulated approach could open up the subject and let it shake its feathers for general speculation.

Concrete poetry, insofar as it frequently makes use of structural elements of repetition, serial development, reversals and mirrorings, and precise counts of verbal or typographical or phonic components, has recognizable though not readily definable links with the cybernetic age, and the 'pared down to the maximum' character of much of its approach may well appeal to the scientific as well as to the aesthetic sensibility.

t e l f i s h
d o g s t a r
s a r p h i n
d o l d i n e
t e l w h a l
n a r s t a r
s a r d o c k
h a d d i n e
d o g w h a l
n a r f i s h
d o l d o c k
h a d p h i n
d o g d o c k
h a d f i s h
d o l w h a l
n a r p h i n
h a d w h a l
n a r d o c k
t e l d o c k
h a d s t a r
s a r w h a l
n a r d i n e
d o g p h i n
d o l f i s h
s a r f i s h
d o g d i n e
d o l s t a r
t e l p h i n
s a r s t a r
t e l d i n e
s a r d i n e
d o l p h i n
h a d d o c k
n a r w h a l
d o g f i s h
t e l s t a r[15]

When the first transatlantic telecommunication signals by satellite were received at Goonhilly in Cornwall in 1962, I thought the best way to celebrate the occasion, and its nicely named satellite Telstar, would be by means of a permutational poem using the elements of five names of sea-creatures combined with the elements of Telstar, to suggest the voyage of the signals across the Atlantic, the message becoming clear only at the end of the poem. In this poem, 'Unscrambling the Waves at Goonhilly', the interlacing of sea-creature and satellite in this way could be seen as a braiding of poetry and science.

In my poetry in general, I was more interested than MacDiarmid was in the workings of the imagination, and in how scientific facts and discoveries could be opened out fictionally within a broader context of human experience. And at times I would use science-fiction proper, in that the basis of the fiction would be something not yet discovered or materialized, or something thought at present to be impossible. The two approaches are not mutually exclusive, but an example of the first might be 'The Moons of Jupiter', which was started off in my mind when pictures of the extraordinarily varied satellites of Jupiter were published, and I imagined them being visited one by one by future explorers—something which might conceivably happen. An example of the second approach would be 'Golden Apples', where I imagine, as in Ray Bradbury's story, a voyage to the sun, but in my case using methods unknown to science.

> The craft must stand a million degrees, roughly.
> Roughly stand, or roughly a million? Both, with
> no guarantee! This is not science fiction.
> Lateral thinking scrubs refrigeration
> as the only hope. Phoenix and salamander
> hint heat is conquered by habitatizing,
> not fending off. What fish wear macintoshes?
> I can see navigators burning like poets,
> boiling like Picts without a stitch of armour,
> bolts from the blue that run into the unblue,
> themselves both it and not it, gold and ungold,
> not melted by but melting, staring, into
> groves of energy, billets of resurgence.
> And where else should they be, our navigators?[16]

A poem like that, in the poetry–science balance, obviously leans towards poetry, though it retains (in a passage not quoted) scientific terms such as *prominences, neutrinos, helium.* It's probably what you would call Promethean, reflecting my feeling that many of the things we call impossible will turn out someday not to be so.

There's a somewhat less improbable scenario in the untitled ninth poem in my 'From the Video Box' sequence. This floats the possibility of special TV programmes for the colour-blind. The Japanese Ishihara test for colour-blindness involves visual reactions to the splotches of colour on a card or page, and it convincingly shows up the difference between persons of normal vision and those who are colour-blind. So why not extend this in time, and make a movie which will tell two different stories to the two groups? I focused the poem on Neal Cassady, guru of the Beats, who was a red-green colour-blind and worked (of all things) on the railroad.

> We saw how he cheated at the Ishihara,
> got the job to show man can do anything.
> Well, that's all right. I don't admire him
> to distraction, but I do admire
> the secret film he made
> for his fellow colour-blinders. All you out there
> with your green green grass and your red red rose
> saw a conventional story,
> a bar, a shoot-out, a car-chase,
> as my friends tell me,
> but we saw something different,
> oh, very different, and it is something you will never know
> unless we tell you, because you cannot see it—
> it is the same film, but strain as you will,
> your lovely normal eyes will never figure
> that carpet, our carpet,
> rolled out from its orient.[17]

That poem involved an extension or projection of something already existing, and this is a method that appeals to me, partly in order to ask questions, both of myself and of the reader, in this case questions about human perception, and partly I suppose to show, to prove if proof should be needed, that the poet's mind can react positively to something that has emerged in the scientific domain. The scientific starting-point may be something relatively unfamiliar, like the Ishihara test card, and in that case the poetic context has a certain duty to make things clear, if not didactically spelt out. Sometimes as a writer you are not sure how familiar the fact is, and you have to take a risk. In a recent poem I referred to 'black smokers', and I remember when I was in the mid-throes of composition I had a nagging doubt at the back of my mind as to whether I should use a term that would be well known to oceanographers and zoologists but maybe not to the average chap who had never been to the bottom of the sea. Anyway, I did use the words, in a benignly educational spirit. You only have to look up the *New Shorter Oxford English Dictionary*, which defines a smoker as a 'hydrothermal vent from which water and mineral particles issue'. But that definition doesn't tell you the really interesting fact about the smokers—that hitherto unknown marine life clusters around these vents, living in what you would think were impossible conditions of heat and pressure and darkness. Philip Larkin once said that he couldn't stand 'anything to do with the wonders of nature'.[18] Well, I love the wonders of nature, and (as in my poem 'Submarine Demon') it's clearly one of the areas where science and poetry can come together.

> It's
> All alive! Mounds, columns, vents
> Pouring heat, pouring smoke, white and black,
> Sulphurous, greatly fierce, hundreds of degrees
> I reckon, cracks in the mantle, factories
> Of particles bursting and burning through the darkness!
> It's all alive I tell you!—such creatures
> Basking; large, coiling, uncoiling, unnamed,
> Snuggling round the black smokers, alive
> In these impossible degrees. My torch is off,
> The sun's not here, the sun's not needed, it is
> The earth itself that can't have enough of life.[19]

So far, the examples I've given have all been fairly definable in terms of space exploration, deep-sea exploration, or the testing of human vision. But we live in a world now where less definable influences from the sciences to the poetic art may be important. The 1980s and 1990s took us into the age of virtual reality, whatever that may be. There is nothing new in the idea itself, which goes back at least to Plato. For Plato, the true reality is the reality you can't see, the ideal template behind the poor worldly example, the bed you can't lie on even if it's a better bed than any you can lie on. But that's not quite what we mean today by virtual reality. You begin with plastic flowers and holograms; you move on to flight simulators for training airlines pilots; then you find yourself donning helmet and gloves like the Lawnmower Man who in the film of that name became addicted to sensual experiences more 'real' than those of ordinary non-wired-up life. This ability to deceive has been advancing rapidly on many fronts. A good example was the fact that in the film *Jurassic Park*, although models were used for some of the dinosaurs, by far the most convincing creatures were those that had been computer-generated, they were made of nothing, made of numbers, made of commands to a keyboard. The next stage, which is already being worked on, is the digital replication of dead actors (including their voices), so that new films could be created around them. John Wayne rides again—for ever. Those who work in the field do have occasional misgivings, though this doesn't stop them. Phil Tippett, from his own animation studio in Berkeley, California, has said:

> [W]e now have the ability and the technology to make things look photo-realistic using the computer. But this revolution is going to surpass the industrial revolution, and there's going to be a lot of blood on the floor . . . [T]he computer demands that you be very procedural and use specific language . . . It's not the same thing at all as having a relationship with materials. My concern is that . . . one can tend to lose touch and sight of the real physical world.[20]

As far as one can see, the general public don't share these misgivings. Should they? Remember how Dr Faustus in Marlowe's play asked to see and was shown Helen of Troy, embraced her, gave her a deep kiss, and uttered the famous line, 'Was this the face that launched a thousand ships?' Well, no: it wasn't. What he had in his arms was a spirit, a devil disguised as a virtual woman, and she wouldn't do him any good. Compare with the words of Othello to Emilia, after he has just strangled Desdemona for her supposed unfaithfulness:

> . . . had she been true,<br>
> If heaven would make me such another world,<br>
> Of one entire and perfect chrysolite,<br>
> I'd not have sold her for it.[21]

Unlike Dr Faustus, who was no longer able to distinguish between the virtual and the real, Othello would reject a whole artificial earth, a virtual earth of extreme beauty, shining as if cut from a single gemstone, if it meant giving up the reality of one woman, Desdemona.

I found myself writing poems all around this subject. I knew that all art is in one sense illusion. You can't smoke Magritte's pipe. You can't eat Burns's haggis, even though it's 'Warm-reekin, rich!'[22] On the other hand, it was believed in medieval times, especially in Celtic countries, that you could rhyme someone to death, kill an enemy by uttering ingeniously maleficent verses, and there are, if you want to credit it, recorded instances of this actually happening. We often speak about good poetry being powerful or having power. But does it also have, in a slightly different sense, certain powers? I felt that within such questions there were poems, lurking and waiting to be discovered. I wrote a sequence called *Virtual and Other Realities*, from which I shall quote some examples.

What is the reality of the fax? Fax machines are now so commonplace that they are taken very much for granted, but the invention remains a rather remarkable one. The lay mind, thinking about it, comes up with questions which of course have a ready technical answer, since otherwise the machine wouldn't work, but which tease and tantalize the imagination. What happens to the message, and it might be a poem, what status does it have, in the seconds between being sent out and being received perhaps thousands of miles away? It's no longer in words, far less in black marks on white paper. It has been converted into impulses that can be dealt with by the telephone system. If we could fix, not fax, that moment, would we say, That's my boy—or would we shake our heads and mutter darkly about the magic of modern science? This is from a poem called 'March':

A wilder March I never saw for sleet.
I feed my fax, and watch the whitening street.
I send the southern sun sheet after sheet.

The signals go, the page remains, the snow
the hail the ice dissolve, the driven show
shouts like a flare before it's forced below . . .

The fax
is in the land of numbers, covers its tracks,
its impulses like rations brought in packs

> across a thousand miles can only say
> the dialling hand is up and on its way
> braced by one raffish, restless, rude spring day.[23]

Realities of life and death are blurred in an electrical experiment said to have been carried out at the University of Glasgow in 1818. Although some aspects of the story have been argued, it seems to be reasonably well documented. Matthew Clydesdale, a miner condemned to death for murder, was duly hanged, and the body was taken to the anatomy hall for a scientific experiment:

> The professor-dissector
> gowns himself in white, bows to the theatre
> of buzzing tiers, introduces an experimenter.
>
> A Glasgow Frankenstein is Doctor Ure.
> The hanged man sits unbound in an armchair.
> His dreadful face faces the handsome professor,
>
> the avant-garde chemist, the galvanic battery. Air
> enters his lung, his tongue wags, eyes flutter,
> limbs convulse, he stands, amazed, aware—
>
> his death is not in order! In the uproar
> shouts, faintings, shrieks, applause conspire
> to let Professor Jeffrey lance the jugular
>
> with theatrical flourish. At his third death, the collier
> leaving the electric arms of his resurrector
> slumps in the blade-cold arms of his dissector.
>
> Clear the hall. Pity the executioner,
> pity the murderer, pity the professor,
> pity the doctor with his battery and his ardour.[24]

That medical experiment took place just a few months after the publication of Mary Shelley's *Frankenstein.* Maybe Dr Ure had read the novel, and was trying to make life imitate art?

In other poems I wanted to be more speculative and imaginative. In 'Early Days' I put forward the idea that the universe is not even in its infancy but is still gestating, working to emerge from some enormous womb. I sifted in, without emphasizing them, a few prime numbers to suggest irregular but steady growth:

Millennial rays
very gently warm the hedgeless maze:

the maze, the plot, the net, the knot, the heart,
the tuft, the beat, the loom, the thrust, the start
the grit, the silt, the salt, the shine, the chart,

the swirl, the sift, the two, the break, the three,
the surge, the drive, the five, the fire, the scree,
the gush, the crash, the roar, the gush, the sea,

the air and the eleven and the cloud,
the lung, the luck, the thirteen and the crowd,
the seventeen, the shrivelling of the shroud,

the tugging of the cord, but not in panic,
the peals, the nineteenth, throbbing but not manic:
until the prime cry tears out, weak, titanic.[25]

I felt I must somehow bring in William Gibson, virtual-reality-meister, author of *Neuromancer* and *Virtual Light*. I gave the real man a virtual adventure, taking him to the city of Glasgow, where he is buttonholed by a local person who knows his works and expatiates on them in the local patois. The communication, perfectly real to the Glaswegian speaker, would come across as largely virtual to the ear of Gibson. Despite this, there would really be no mistaking the message, which is wildly, virtually friendly:

Gibson Gibson Gibson Gibson Gib-son!
Hullo therr, goany geez a bliddy crib, son.
Dinnae wahnt some eejit tae gie ye a chib, son.

Ur aw thae radgie nuts in Cybernippon
guys an dolls yer hauns kin get a grip on,
an if they're no, whit screens ur they a blip on?

Is it blid, is it juice, is it a chairge, ur they randy?
Is their denner pretend-sampura wi trash-shandy?
Whit d'ye mean ye're no sure. That's handy![26]

But lastly, I go back in time to Giordano Bruno, the Italian astronomer and philosopher who was burnt at the stake in 1600 for various heresies, including his belief in the illimitability of the universe and in a multiplicity of worlds that harboured life just as the earth did. Above all, he stands as a martyr to potentiality, to the idea that the Cosmos is in ceaseless change and development, and holds almost unimaginable powers in wait for us if we can dare to search for them:

> Why would the lord of life confine his writ
> to this one ball of water, flesh and grit?
> You say it's special? Ah but transcending it
>
> are specks we see, and specks we cannot see
> but must imagine, in that immensity.
> It is reason sets imagination free.
>
> Configurations still unfigurable,
> visions and visitations still invisible,
> powers to come, still impermissible—
>
> these give the slip to my incarceration.[27]

## Grimoire

Michael Donaghy

## With an Introduction

by Kevin Warwick

### Introduction

From Puccini to Geri Halliwell, from Monet to David Hockney, from Delibes' music to jewellery that changes colour, my brush with art was sorted. Poetry was never high on the agenda, after I waved goodbye, at school, to the Assyrian's coming down and a fair measure of half a league, half a league. So the chance of meeting with a modern-day poet was a delightful injection of diversity.

Lunch with Michael Donaghy surprised me, with discussion ranging from my own Cyborg research, linking implants to my nervous system, through the everyday trials and tribulations of a contemporary poet's life to the ups and downs of our favourite soccer teams. We were, to all intents and purposes, merely a couple of guys chatting over a pint in the local hostelry. So what poetry could possibly erupt from such mundane beginnings? I awaited Michael's outpourings, like a nervous teenager waiting for A level results, excitement and anticipation ringed with nervousness and a smattering of foreboding. What would Michael make of the research that I was doing? Would he say what a great guy I was, or conversely paint me as an ogre and a tyrant? Most importantly, would I understand it at all?

The big day arrived and I tentatively opened Michael's email attachment to reveal the title 'Grimoire'. What the hell did that mean? A skimp through the verses themselves left me none the wiser. I understood most, not all, of the words, but making sense of the sentences was not an instant success. Clearly I needed to think about it all; it wasn't something akin to a Jeffrey Archer novel that I could spend five minutes on, use little brain power, and forget all about next time the phone rang.

For me it was rather like reading an academic paper: not an unpleasant thing but rather something to work on. I started by picking on islands of ideas and concepts within the piece, that I felt I understood, and ventured out from these safe havens into the work in its entirety in order to taste the full flavour of its intent; when I still had difficulty with one or two references I discussed them with others and we arrived at a consensus.

I guess as a scientist I had never before given art the time of day. Either it hit me full in the face or I passed it by on the other side of the street. But here, for the first time, I had to work at it.

Grimoire—a book for summoning up demons—for me brought to life in a rather melodramatic way, an important aspect of the research that I am doing, linking humans directly with technology in order to create super humans, Cyborgs, an evolutionary step forward. The reference to Zarathustra was clear and poignant.

I found 'Grimoire' dark and frightening, leaving me with a scary taste, the sort of feeling you get at the end of *Jekyll and Hyde*. Like a real-world Dr Jekyll, from the inside I never see my research as frightening. But, like Dr Jekyll, I will press ahead even if others are horrified.

I respect the fact that Michael expended a considerable amount of effort to understand my science; I trust that I have responded in a similar fashion towards his poetry. For me it was a deeply moving experience. Through Michael's words I was able to look at myself in a ten-dimensional space.

## Grimoire

An intervening object does not impede the vision of the blessed . . . Christ could see the face of his mother when she was prostrate on the ground . . . as if he were looking directly at her face. It is clear that the blessed can see the front of an object from the back, the face through the back of the head.

Bartholomew Rimbertinus, *On the Sensible Delights of Heaven, Venice, 1498*

1

An afterlife in the theatre:
'And this, gentlemen' (removes top of skull),
'is the principal sulcus of the dorsolateral prefontal cortex,
which manifests remarkable accord
amongst the senses, even in the sane.
The smelling salts for Mr Bohman, Sister.'

2

To speak aloud among the sober
of the sweet reek of bright green,
the soft hiss of yellow, the bitter shapes
of the sound of the space in which we speak,
their lavender numbers tasting of sesame,
is indiscreet. Make sense.
But only one sense at a time.
To remark on the silence breaking
on the facets of a word the way
light breaks across an oilslick
to the polyphonic iridescence
of simultaneous orgasm
betrays one to the panicked guest
whose eyes alert the host across the room.
Patience, children. Learn to hush your wonder.
Thus the Persian, weary of his wisdom,
began his long descent into the world.

3

Keep up! The argument has run ahead,
like an angry bearded black robed bishop
who leads us through a labyrinth of alleys
to Chloras, goldsmith, busy through the night
in his workshop of important toys.
Here, a monk that kneels at clockwork prayer,
here, a lady flautist trills and winks,
and here, his masterpiece, that nightingale
of hammered gold and gold enamelling.
It tilts its head, it whirrs, it clicks its wings
and—truly this the devil's work—it speaks,
*Keep up! Reach out! Your day will come,*
*Your fingers brush a face across the sea.*

4

At the commandement of the conjuror he dooth
take awaie the sight of anie one.
He is a great prince, taking the forme of a thrush,
except he be brought to a chaulk triangle
and therein he teacheth divinelie,
rhetorike, logike, pyromancie.
He giveth men the understanding of all birds,
of the lowing of bullocks, and barking of dogs,
and also of the sound and noise of waters,
he ruleth now thirtie legions of divels,
who was of the celestiall orders
and will possess agayne and rule the world.

5

Keep up. The argument will run ahead,
outstripping words, will tear down neural paths,
branching, recombining, out of sight
and far beyond your power to direct.
Upgraded man, who sees in the dark,
what you might tell us of the world beyond speech
no one, no, not even you, can say.

# Spirit Machines: The Human and the Computational

Robert Crawford

> Shortly before my father died, I began to use a computer for the first time. It was in my office at work, and I'm not sure he ever saw it. For over a year after it was installed I didn't do anything with it. Now at least I use it as a word-processor, and summon up one or two databases. Once, when it broke down, a technician came and prized open its casing, revealing drab chips and wiring. But when it is working in its closed body, it has its own sense of animation and activity. What appears on its screen appears tangibly present, yet has almost no being, seems part of a sensation connected both with faith and bereavement. I remember the last time I touched my father's body where he lay collapsed. I knew he was dead, but his face was still warm and stubbly, the essential face of a Dad. The computer after a little while gives off a mild, but unhirsute warmth. It is somehow akin to the machines which replaced my father, yet to which he is linked and I connect him through printing out this. Memories feed the machine, the machine holds memory. The machine too dies, is replaced—not a soul, but a body through which the spirit can be known. My father's lifetime saw the birth of these spirit machines.

Already we are coming to take the computer for granted. It is our twenty-first century familiar. Much of this essay, though, reflects the strangeness of its arrival, and draws on some poems written at a time when the computer was both fresh and alien to me, existing at once as virtual and as tangible reality.

Before it came to be used of a machine in the late nineteenth century, the word 'computer' had been used for two centuries to refer to people. In Jonathan Swift's *A Tale of a Tub* the 'very skilful *computer*' is someone who excels at arithmetic.[1] Sir Thomas Browne in the seventeenth century and Sir David Brewster, writing in the nineteenth about Isaac Newton, used 'computer' in a similar sense.[2] So when we think of such topics as 'the Renaissance computer', we should have an image of a human being, not just of a machine or an encyclopaedic book.[3] Around the same time as the word 'typewriter' came to denote a thing rather than a person, something similar happened to the word 'computer'. To recall and draw nourishment from such verbal recalibrations is part of the work of the poet as well as a job for lexicographers and historians of language, literature, or culture. The epigraph to this essay comes from a memoir of my father which I published in 1998.[4] I quote these sentences because they may help bring into focus some of my attitudes towards science. Contemporary science and technology offer the poet metaphors, sounds, and lexis for writing about experiences (some familiar and familial, some strange and estranged) in an idiom that is true to the grain of contemporary language and contemporary culture. Yet, used in a poem, these scientific elements may also be in contact with the kinds of etymological, magical, visionary, even religious experience that many poets tend to love. Paul Valéry wrote of the poet as carrying out the role of the scientist; T. S. Eliot was fascinated by the view that 'the pre-logical mentality persists in civilised man, but becomes available only to or through the poet'.[5] Both these perceptions are true, but they are truer still when each is in touch with the other. Images of the poet as scientist and shaman can be nourishing. Ultimately, though, poems emerge from words and the music of words.

Poets write out of an insatiable relishing of language and, for the most part, out of love, be it love of people, poetry itself, or country, globe, or universe. As a poet I have some interest in science and technology *per se*, especially when they reveal the marvellous articulatedness and articulacy of the universe, but I am no scientist. Indeed, it may be that I like the concepts of science far more than the practices, and I have an instinctive distrust of the dourly secular rationalism which sometimes but not always accompanies scientific mindsets. I like the science that fuels and is fuelled by the dream-mind. I love to think of poetry and science as kinds of discovery quickened by observation and imagination.

Science, for many poets, also has a more basic allure, which one might characterize as the allure of the dictionary. Scientists use good words. Take the word 'Heterojunctive', for instance. Its etymological sense (involving 'joining with the other') gives it an erotic patina, but also a sense of meeting the strange, the alien. To poets the etymological undertones and reach of language are often alluring; part of poetry involves reaching into the secret messages, implications, and undertones which words may have, may half conduct. Just as a poet may hear in cliché or dead metaphor something which could be revivified or brought into a new acoustic, so in the vocabulary of science there lie linguistic possibilities which may go unremarked in everyday speech or scientific texts. More and more of us now spend part of our day in front of a screen, and increasingly the language of science is part of our everyday linguistic clothing. It is part of the poet's delight, even duty, to use such words and experience in poetry. For poetry must always be open to the full spectrum of language, and just as the medieval poet William Dunbar relished a marvellous acoustic of aureate diction, so may the poet who makes meaningful music with the terminology of modern science.

Screens and words are enriched by being imbued with metaphorical resonance and possibility. Poetry will continue to be obsessed with sea and stars, love and death, but if it is not also alert to semiconductors and computers, windfarming and global warming, it will grow subtly untrue to the linguistic and cultural climate in which it is written. Poetry must be special (a 'holiday' in the sense of a 'holy day' at the heart of language), but if it ignores great areas of our contemporary experience, it will be 'special' in the wrong sense, a ghetto concern only. Often the life of a poem comes from the tension between its familiarity and its strangeness, between the elements that have wandered in from the street and those that have escaped from some secret chamber. Science can function in poems as familiar, as strange, sometimes as both at once. There is a particular formal challenge (and poets like formal challenges) in taking scientific material which might often be heard as 'cold', and deploying it alongside warmer, even erotic language and imagery; each element can lend to the other a peculiar and vivifying charge.

My family background in the 1960s made me aware of computers from an early age, not just when I played as a young child with punched cards given to me by one of my parents' friends, but when computers came to take over some of the tasks my father performed as a bank teller. My schooling made me aware that for poets such as

Hesiod, Virgil, and Lucretius scientific materials and information were part of the fibre of their verse. In a more nuanced, and increasingly reflective way, my Scottish upbringing and my work on Scottish literature have made me particularly aware that for over a century there has been a strong tradition of the convergence of poetry and science in Scottish writing: most excitingly in verse by John Davidson (1857–1909), Hugh MacDiarmid (1892–1978), and Edwin Morgan (b. 1920).

Writing about it in several books, I have tried to relate this tradition to an earlier and continuing preoccupation with eclecticism, encyclopaedism, and the dissemination of information in Scottish culture which goes back at least to the Enlightenment, if not to the Reformation.[6] Manifestations of this include the *Encyclopaedia Britannica*, the eager Newtonianism of the older Scottish universities, and the continuing 'generalist' structure of their degrees. My own taste for the eclectic, and for 'Informationism' in poetry (a label attached to a grouping of contemporary Scottish poets who use scientific and eclectic textures in their work) may belong to the shifting weather of postmodernism.[7] Yet it has particular nuances in a Scottish context—nuances associated with the polyphonic, polylingual nature of Scottish poetry over fifteen centuries, and with the plethora of cultural and often mutually aware value systems circulating in Scotland. Though I prefer terms such as 'eclectic' to 'generalist', there is surely a connection between the line of Scottish science-and-poetry writing over the last century and the generalist tradition (some might say empowering myth) of 'the democratic intellect'. Such philosophically underpinned Scottish academic generalism, taking in both arts and science subjects, is quite different from Snow's English 'Two Cultures' model, and was championed in two books which I read with excitement in the 1980s: George Davie's *The Democratic Intellect* (1961) and *The Crisis of the Democratic Intellect* (1986). Though I do not always agree with it, Davie's view of arts and sciences as united in one philosophical spectrum was certainly quickening for me, as it has been for other Scottish poets of several generations. Reading Davie's work at the same time as I was reading and publishing in *Verse* magazine poems by Michel Deguy, Miroslav Holub, Edwin Morgan, and others brought with it certain kinds of excitement and recognition that can help provide conceptual nutrients for the often intuitive acts of making involved in writing poems.

Such excitement and recognition can help clarify the process of structuring my first collection of verse.

That book, published in 1990, was called *A Scottish Assembly.* The title was in part a political one (the poems were written mainly in the 1980s when pressures for a Scottish Parliament or 'Assembly' were growing), but the title also denoted a eclectic gathering of Scottish materials (in the way that the General Assembly of the Church of Scotland gathers Kirk ministers), or an 'assembly' in the sense that machines may be assembled on assembly lines or one might speak of the assembly of an engine. A number of the poems concerned Scottish scientists and inventors—Clerk Maxwell and Logie Baird, for instance—and sometimes I was interested in the way these figures (like Scotland itself at the time) seemed perilously balanced between breakthrough and failure. Having grown up in the West of Scotland in the 1960s and 1970s, and having been involved in the search for paid academic work in the 1980s, I was also very aware of unemployment. A number of poems in the book are alert to new technologies not just as inventions but as innovations that sweep away earlier industries. In 'The Saltcoats Structuralists', the Empire's proud 'structuralists' working with railway lines and girders in the West of Scotland heavy industrial tradition are swept aside by an 'electronics revolution': 'They felt poststructuralism, tanged with salt.'[8] Just as waves of 1980s cultural theory were apparently overwhelming older university workers, so in the region where I grew up, the light work of electronics was replacing the heavy labour of shipbuilding or steelmaking. I was very aware that contemporary science and technology were bound up with such social turmoil. Later, in using computer imagery to elegize my father, I was also conscious that his job, that of a bank teller, was now often done by a machine.

When in the 1980s I wrote about Scotland as a 'Semiconductor country', I was drawing not just on some small scientific awareness, but also on personal circumstances. On the one hand, I had been living and working in Oxford for several years and, though the experience had helped educate and mature me, I was desperately keen to get home to Scotland (which I loved in all sorts of ways, and regarded as more 'democratic'), if only I could get a job there. In Oxford I had been in love with a semiconductor physicist who was a political refugee and came from a very different culture. This had made me think hard, among other things, about what it meant to me to be Scottish, and had encouraged a nascent fascination with science which had started not at school (where I found physics and chemistry utterly boring and dumped them as soon as possible for Latin and Greek) but at Glasgow University where I had begun to read the poetry of Hugh MacDiarmid as a result of being tutored in my second year by Edwin Morgan. Poems are often merciless in the way they fuse elements in order to be born. I was reassured, for instance, to know that the verse of the Gaelic poet Sorley MacLean had drawn on the experience of several love affairs to produce the composite figure of 'Eimhir', because I felt some (but perhaps not enough) embarrassment at drawing on more than one relationship in writing such poems as 'Photonics' and 'Scotland'.[9] In 'Photonics', a poem looking forward to my marriage to Alice Wales, I remember the poem being sparked by a photograph in a Sunday newspaper of a computer system that ran only on light. Later a television science documentary gave me some vocabulary that seemed as immediately appealing as some of the Scots words in Jamieson's Dictionary. 'Photonics' begins,

> We're a new technology, a system that weds
> Lasers; no electronics; no gob-drops
> Of glass fibre to be teased and spun; just conjugate-phasing
> Turning constant signals into rings of light,
> A burgh packed with brilliant marriages.[10]

Around the same time elements from my personal life fused with other concerns to produce what is for me a kind of love poem addressed to Scotland in one of two poems from the same book which share a common title. 'Scotland' uses imagery of semiconductor manufacture (then emerging as a dominant economic force in 'Silicon Glen') and aerial photography to speak of how I love the combination of languages, cultures, landscapes, and other elements in such a supposedly small country. In some ways the internationalism of its scientific terminology has made it easily translatable for non-Scottish and non-English-speaking audiences. Yet there is also a love of placenames and local cultural details; this habit is strong in Scottish poetry, especially perhaps in Gaelic. In drawing on it and redeploying it in a poem that sounds a clear note of late-twentieth-century 'post-modernity', I wanted the local, national, and international to be bonded in a way that exemplified what I came to call my poetic ideal of 'Cosmopolibackofbeyondism'.[11]

Scotland

Semiconductor country, land crammed with intimate expanses,
Your cities are superlattices, heterojunctive
Graphed from the air, your cropmarked farmlands
Are epitaxies of tweed.

All night motorways carry your signal, swept
To East Kilbride or Dunfermline. A brightness off low headlands
Beams-in the dawn to Fife's interstices,
Optoelectronics of hay.

Micro-nation. So small you cannot be forgotten,
Bible inscribed on a rice-grain, hi-tech's key
Locked into the earth, your televised Glasgows
Are broadcast in Rio. Among circuitboard crowsteps

To be miniaturised is not small-minded.
To love you needs more details than the Book of Kells—
Your harbours, your photography, your democratic intellect
Still boundless, chip of a nation.[12]

There may be local meanings stashed in this, but I hope the poem is not incomprehensible to a wider audience. The western Scottish *polis* of East Kilbride functions here as a new town, juxtaposed with and linked to the much older east-coast town of Dunfermline just as, on a larger scale, the air-archaeologist's or air-photographer's age-old 'cropmarked farmlands' are fused with the complex patternings of a semiconductor. Poems often signal in related microscopic details what they also communicate on a more macroscopic level—an aspect of their behaviour which may make Alice Fulton's idea of the 'fractal' poem useful.[13] Though some may regard the semiconductor as somehow an unpoetic image, I don't see it that way. Rather I view it as hoaching with promise, partly because it is so etymologically and imagistically resonant, and partly because it can come fairly fresh to poetry. I love the way Robert Fergusson uses the term 'surd roots' in a tonally complex eighteenth-century Scots elegy, and how MacDiarmid uses 'musculocutaneous'—in each case, surely, for the first time in a poem.[14] The contemporary French poet Michel Deguy remarked once in passing how 'Semiconductor' would be a great title for a poetry magazine. Though it has become a knee-jerk reaction in literary criticism to mock the earlier twentieth-century English 'Pylon poets' who tried to make poems about such new technological landscape features as electricity pylons, I have always had a soft spot for such an impulse, and even for Stephen Spender's 'The Pylons' (with its images of electricity pylons as 'nude, giant girls that have no secret') which, for all its awkwardness and political incorrectness (and maybe because of those things) has stayed with me ever since I read it at the back of the sniggerably named *Poet's Quair* anthology we used at school in Glasgow.[15] That impulse to bring pylons into poetry is surely consonant with one of the famous passages of the Preface to *Lyrical Ballads*, which Edwin Morgan quotes in one of his fine essays on MacDiarmid's later poetry, and which is worth restating here as a kind of (to some 'unWordsworthian') credo. After affirming that 'Poetry is the first and last of all knowledge . . . is as immortal as the heart of man,' Wordsworth (who took it for granted scientists were chaps) continues:

> If the labours of men of science should ever create any material revolution, direct or indirect, in our condition and in the impressions which we habitually receive, the poet will sleep then no more than at present, but he will be ready to follow the steps of the man of science, not only in those general indirect effects, but he will be at his side, carrying sensation into the midst of the objects of science itself. The remotest discoveries of the chemist, the botanist or mineralogist will be as proper objects of the poet's art as any upon which it can be employed, if the time should ever come when these things shall be familiar to us, and the relations under which they are contemplated by the followers of these respective sciences shall be manifestly and palpably material to us as enjoying and suffering beings. If the time should ever come when what is now called science, thus familiarised to men, shall be ready to put on, as it were, a form of flesh and blood, the poet will lend his divine spirit to aid the transfiguration, and will welcome the being thus produced as a dear and genuine inmate of the household of man.[16]

I think that we are now living in such an age, and it is the job of both poetry and science to acknowledge that. This does not mean that poetry should sound conventionally Wordsworthian; indeed, as Wordsworth might have been the first to realize, twenty-first-century poetry in English must sound unWordsworthian if it is to follow Wordsworth's precept as set out above. It must contain within it a note of scientifically inflected modernity, as well as being attuned to what Wordsworth terms the 'divine' and 'the heart of man'.

In a book called *The Modern Poet*, I have argued that an interaction with academia and knowledge, often scientific knowledge, is almost inescapable now, and has been bound up with the cultural role of the poet (and with poetic practice) since at least the mid-eighteenth century. Here I will just say that poets are likely to be conscious of sounding, and wishing to sound that note of scientifically inflected modernity even as they write of what might seem archetypal events. This sort of impulse informs 'The Handshakes', a poem about the birth of our son in my collection *Masculinity* (1996); written in a much plainer diction, 'The Handshakes' again contains some 'scientific' or technological specifics. The 'reflex action' was explained by the midwife. The poem is in part about the pain of childbirth, and a male sense of helplessness in the face of that, but it is about other things too, kinds of bonding (female, male, and female–male) that are both inclusive and exclusive. The use of the etymologically rich word 'Entonox' gives, I hope, a flash of scientific modernity to the poem, siting it in our age when anaesthetic gas is manufactured to be available to women in a technologically equipped 'Labour Suite':

> I flinched at the handshake of a woman in labour
> Through mid-contraction when you pushed our son
>
> Down towards the forceps.
> Soon his fingers curled
>
> Possessively around my index finger
> And then round yours,
>
> Welcoming us with a reflex action
> To take your hand beyond yon Labour Suite
>
> Where you clutched me as you breathed the Entonox
> And called for your own mother, who is dead.[17]

This is a poem that tries to get in touch with what Wordsworth calls 'the heart of man', but is aware of a world of gynaecology, science, and sensibility rather different from the early nineteenth-century Wordsworthian one. Again, though it sounds scientific notes within its vernacular music, this poem is a love poem. The MacDiarmidian cosmological sweep, the colossal possibilities of science excite me, but it is in its metaphorical potential for intimate revelation that science may be strongest in verse. This is evident, say, in MacDiarmid's own Scots lyrics such as 'The Bonnie Broukit Bairn' or 'The Innumerable Christ'. Often, to work best in a poem, scientific knowledge should have its own lexical allure and/or may contribute towards a sense of something both 'more distant than stars and nearer than the eye' as Eliot puts it in some of the most wonderful words of 'Marina'.[18]

That is why, though, like other poets of my generation I grew up fascinated by the poetry of Miroslav Holub in English translation (and can remember discussing with Edwin Morgan around 1981 Holub's work and his loyalty to his country in times of political difficulty), I disagree with Holub's apparent insistence in this present book that poetry should not use science for its own metaphorical, unscientific, imaginative purposes. Unlike Holub, I am no scientist. To some extent that may be disabling. Yet in other ways it is surely liberating, because it gives the poet the freedom to treat science as poets might treat other areas of experience: as material to serve the ends of the medium of poetry, rather than as something which poetry must follow. Poems come from language, and the poet aims to be in intimate communion with language, to sense its peculiar quirks and grain, to sound it and be sounded by it. In seeking and making (to use Wordsworth's phrase) 'the pleasure which the mind derives from the perception of similitude in dissimilitude', language, metaphor, and poetry must take precedence over science and scientific reasoning.[19] The point is not so much that the poet courts the irrational (though many poets have a hankering after the supposedly 'shamanistic' which can shade into the religious), as that poetry is the poet's medium and has its own requirements, just as prose, numbers, and equations exact their own demands of the scientist. There may be points of contact between poet and scientist: both use imagination and observation, for instance; poets and scientists may be dreamers as well as readers of reference works. But each operates in a different medium, and each, to do the job properly, owes an ultimate loyalty to the medium which he or she has chosen. That is why it will always be rare to find a scientist who is also a poet, and even rarer to find a really good scientist who is also, like Holub, a superb poet. Ultimately to make fine use of science in his or her work, the poet needs to be a poet, but not necessarily a scientist.

Most of us encounter science through technology. There is a tendency sometimes to view this technology as cold, inhuman, clever but emotionally impoverished and unresonant. So I think an important function for modern poetry is to discover metaphorical resonance in technology, letting it speak to us about our deepest concerns. Inevitably, those concerns include both birth and death, absence and plenitude. Poets, more than scientists, tend to sing the plenitude of existence, but science, surely, is also potentially filled with that refrain. An attunement between the plenitude of revelatory science and the exfoliatory plenitude of poetry is called for. In trying to write about my father, his death, and my experience of bereavement there were personal reasons but also, if you like, aesthetic principles which led me to write about him in terms of computer technology. Intuitively (for I had not looked up the *OED* at the time), I was trying to put in touch with each other the older and the newer senses of the word 'computer'.

Perhaps the most striking aspect of bereavement is an apprehension of simultaneous absence and presence; there's a sense of the dead person as intimately with us, ghosting our thoughts and actions, yet that very sense of haunting is also an indicator of absence: the person is intangible, gone, flickering. For a long time I've been fascinated by the work and phenomenon of Ossian, those post-Culloden 'translations' from a prehistoric Gaelic whose 'originals' are 'somehow reported missing'.[20] Ossian's is a great poetry of mourning since (and some people hate it for this) there is a constant sense of at best a flickering and perhaps a non-existent world beyond the text. Because of all the uncertainty about lost originals, Ossian may depend on something, or on nothing; it is very much a music of echoes and loss. This Ossianic ghostliness has a rather fey, tissue-thin quality which is accentuated further in the later writing of the 'Celtic Twilight'.

Scotland is a much ghosted country, and the international movement that was the Celtic Twilight drew a kind of drained energy from that. In Ossian and much Celtic Twilight work the solid becomes weightless, the words a rather fey, thin skin beyond which little seems to exist, a ghost-writing. All this seemed to me close to the sensation that I had as a recent computer user. I had felt that sense that the new user feels of wanting to reach into the machine, touch the text and move it around; but I had come to be more adept at the controls and had realised that I must subject myself to the discipline of using the symbols rather than any greater physical pressure to summon up what was cut off from me beyond the screen. If Ossian and the Celtic Twilight seemed to be about a kind of dematerialization of reality, then so did the computer; it was part of the material world, yet also presented a kind of constant simulacrum, something mundane in our screen culture, yet also intermittently striking—the way people used to talk about 'the paperless office', defining the office not in terms of a new presence but an absence, a loss. It's a common sensation among new computer users to see the computer both in terms of an amazing, apparently inexhaustible profusion (it holds so much), at the same time as feeling there's virtually nothing there. It's not real. Just virtual.

'Deincarnation' in my 'Spirit Machines' sequence tries to talk about that sense of ghostliness, of clearance, of lost solidity that accompanies bereavement and is part both of the Ossianic/Celtic Twilight Highlands and of a computational, virtual reality world. So it talks about laptops siphoning off the glens, about great, granitic mountains becoming weightless, losing substance; and it brings to the Highland Clearances in a slightly comic, but also menacing way 'shrewd pioneers of computing'. The computer is, metaphorically at least, both a means of remembrance, preservation, and a kind of estrangement, a screening out of the muddily or bloodily tangible. 'Deincarnation', like the landscapes of Ossian and the Celtic Twilight, offers cyber-Highlands, Never-Neverlands, images of an uncertain otherworld. The computational and the spiritual/religious both feed off and clash with each other. All this was coming out of the kind of 'Informationist' writing that I was used to practising, stealing from informational, scientific, and quasi-academic texts and modes, though mixing this up with emotion and with visionary as well as comic material. But such techniques had a new necessity for me as I tried to memorialize my father.

> Each daybreak laptops siphon off the glens,
> Ada, Countess of Lovelace, Vannevar Bush,
>
> Alan Turing spectral in Scourie,
> Babbage downloading half of Sutherland

With factors and reels, inescapable
Whirring of difference engines.

Inverailort and Morar host
Shrewd pioneers of computing.

Digitized, blue, massive Roshven
Loses its substance, granite and grass

Deincarnated and weightless.
Shaking hands with absentees,

Beaters, gutters have their pockets emptied
Of any last objects, even a nanomachine,

A pebble, a lucky coin.
Skulking on Celtic Twilight shores,

Each loch beyond is cleared of itself,
Gaelic names, flora, rainfall

So close, the tangible spirited away,
Cybered in a world of light.[21]

Searching through the prose poems of Fiona Macleod, that figure so spectral that the Ossian-tinged name itself tends to appear in inverted commas, hunting for some work that came close to convincing me, I found a prose poem called 'Nocturne' in 'The Silence of Amor'.[22] Like one of Whistler's 'Nocturnes', Macleod's poem is a vague wash with pinpricks of light. Its rather bodiless tone made me think of the dematerialization of money involved in such processes as electronic cash transfer and the late-capitalist rush towards 'branding' and image, away from chunky manufacturing substance; so the first sentence of my prose poem 'Exchange' is 'Promising always to pay the bearer, money aspires to the condition of purest spirit.' Macleod's Celtic Twilight 'prose rhythm' has almost vanished in my prose poem 'Exchange', but fragments of it and of other Macleod poems survive in my prosthetic rewriting. There are perhaps unsettling congruities as well as incongruities, so that the poem involves materiality, materialism, and the dematerialized as well as the spiritual.

It might be said that what I tend to use here is technology rather than science, but I have little interest in differentiating between the two; they are surely bound together, as the technology of the printing press was bound up with the scientific breakthoughs of an earlier period. Particularly in our 'information age' the distinctions between 'science', 'technology', and 'culture' all seem oddly artificial. If a poem codes information and involves delicate balances, so does an equation, a formula, or a gene-string, and so does a computer; that is not to say a poem is a gene-string, or a computer; nor is it to say that a poem or a person can be reduced to the computational, but all may be related, fused in new ways. Poems, like gene-strings, are all about 'strands' and have their molecular repeats, complex internal bondings, and minute, intricate refrains.

Science and technology excite me most as metaphors. To restate, re-express spiritual and religious values in an age dominated, or at least processed by machine intelligences, is surely an exciting task. There is no reason why the visionary imagination (which, after all, produced these machines) should not be expressed through them; why the computer should not act as a way of figuring bereavement, the human and the computational reconnected; or why the multiplicity of the Web should not be a metaphor for or articulation of the many mansions of the Kingdom of Heaven.

Bound up with the sense of bereavement is the act of remembrance, the impossible longing to remember every moment of the loved one's life. Remembering becomes a kind of love and nourishment, a way of using memory as a memorial against absolute loss. Acts of recording, from names and dates on gravestones, to talking about or writing about the dead are natural, but the very word 'recording' carries with it for us now connotations of science and technology. Often 'recording' happens today through photography, or through digitization. If one thinks of the great digital collections and encyclopaedias being assembled by various computer companies, these are like sacred archives, designed to ensure the imperial 'capture' of all that is deemed valuable in the world; the digitized body leaves the actual body behind; almost extinct species are kept alive in the digital record, ruined buildings are digitally frozen through a kind of cryogenic impulse to preserve what is fading away. Yet to preserve everything as part of a huge photographic or digital mausoleum would be to overwhelm our own lives, overloading them with information from the dead: listing, listing, and listing the lost. Such an infinite recall would be both bewitching and stifling. Loss may be essential to salvation.

The final poem in the 'Spirit Machines' sequence is called 'Alford', named after the village in Aberdeenshire where my father lived in his teens in the 1920s and early 1930s. It uses the figure of the Internet as one which liberates the imagination, allowing the presentation of a kind of visionary poem which also makes sense in terms of the technological world as it is now evolving. Again, there is a kind of impulse to run together the religious, the scientific, and the technological. The poem is written in three-line stanzas, a kind of abashed wink to Dante reinforced in the opening lines with their '*Nel mezzo del cammin*' sense of being rather lost in mid-life.[23]

Just as the computer produces endless lists (delightful to poets, as Auden and others have remarked), so this poem lists of kinds of poultry, drawn from one of the few books I inherited from my father, the wonderfully titled *The Poultry-Keeper's Vade Mecum*. In 'Alford' the listing and the 'surfing' from time to time are, if you like, 'justified' by the use of the Internet as a framing device, one that liberates the imagination. As the Internet telescopes geographies, times, recorded incidents, so does the mind in acts of remembrance, and does the dream-mind that produces poems. While there is a certain playing off of the scientific material against the more conventionally elegiac or lyrical, there are also ways in which these are operating in tandem. In terms of the poem's wordscape, I was certainly excited to put together such elements as 'Tibberchindy' (pronounced 'Tibberhinny') and 'Virtual reality', to juxtapose Scots elements ('presses' means cupboards, though if English senses of the word intrude, they are welcome) with a bit of Greek, giving the poem a certain discreet 'speaking in tongues' quality that is both very true to the grain of Scottish poetic tradition and also seemed to fuel the religious dream and design. The sense of history as a pained but also benign labyrinth in which all histories might co-exist seemed to marry well with the apparently endlessly capacious Internet and the notion of Heaven as containing many mansions as it is expressed by Christ in the Gospel according to John. I wanted a poem that could move easily between the familiar name of the Aberdeen paper, the *Press and Journal*, and the rather strange-sounding (though translated) New Testament Greek of the final stanza, just as it could slip easily between the human and the computational. 'Alford' is about a kind of translation from and of this world into another. Both the Internet and 'virtual reality' seemed suitable metaphors for that, though (as the poem may suggest) metaphors that fall somewhat short of the eventual magnificence of the kind of translation envisaged.

Blearily rummaging the internet,
Aged thirty eight, not knowing where I was,
I found a site designed as an old harled manse,

Sash windows opening on many Scotlands.
Through one surf broke on the West Sands, St Andrews,
And through another Glasgow mobbed George Square.

Templeton carpets fluttered up and clucked:
Crevecoeurs, La Fleches, azeels, minorcas,
Cochins, Langshans, Scots dumpies, Cornish game.

The hallstand's canny, digitized gamp
Pointed to fading pixels; when I touched them
I felt *The Poultry-Keeper's Vade Mecum*,

Though in the next room, where a bren-gun spat,
Its title changed into *King's Regulations*;
Tanks manoeuvred round the hearth and range,

Smashing duck eggs, throwing up clouds of flour.
Fleeing the earth-floored kitchen, an ironing table
Hirpled like girderwork from bombed Cologne

Into the study where my Aunt Jean studied
How not to be a skivvy all her life,
While my dead uncle revved his BSA,

Wiping used, oily hands on Flanders lace.
Ministers primed themselves in Jesus's Greek.
Bankers shot pheasants. Girls sang. My father

Walked me through presses with a map of Paris,
Though all the names he used were Cattens, Leochil,
Tibberchindy, Alford, Don Midmill.

I understood. 'Virtual reality?'
I asked him. In reply he looked so blank
His loved face was a fresh roll of papyrus

Waiting to be made a sacred text,
Hands empty as the screen where he projected
Slides of our holidays at Arisaig,

His body fresh cotton sheets from the best bedroom
Of his boyhood home before he was a boy.
Waiting here, he waits to meet my mother,

For a first date at St Martin in the fields.
Here, his own father, Robert, catches light
On his own deathbed, pipe and *Press and Journal*

Combusting in a way none can control.
Manse rooms huddle, fill with shetland ponies,
London tubes. There is no here. Here goes.

*En te oikia tou Patros mou monai eisin:*
In my Father's house are many mansions:
If it were not so, I would have told you.[24]

Since writing that concluding poem of *Spirit Machines*, and since grieving over my father's death, I have felt a returning sense of the plenitude of the physical world and wished to signal this in poems that speak less of deincarnation and the mechanical than of bodily presence and vitality. So a more recent poem such as 'Fiat Lux' may use such scientific terms as 'holophotal lenses' or 'retinal cone', but does so in a context of delight in the abundance of creation, its fractal-like or liturgical repeats, and its verbal and physical fullness.[25] If the title *Spirit Machines* looks towards the computational, while being alert to the human, the title of the succeeding collection, *The Tip of My Tongue* (2003) has a more immediately human, bodily ring to it, something picked up on in many of the poems. One of these, 'Double Helix', uses the DNA pattern to create a new poetic form. 'Fiat Lux', 'A Moment of Your Time', 'Credo', and other poems are often celebratory, but pieces such as 'The Bad Shepherd', 'Planetist', and 'Acceptance Speech' are also alert to environmental precariousness. I find myself drawn more to sciences that let me speak of creation, environment in the widest sense, and of our part in that environment. An awareness of science and technology, in their lighter and darker manifestations, continues to be important to me as a poet. It may be that one of the greatest desires for both poets and scientists is simply to develop, to mature as a creative organism—with all the loopings, rhymings, and tergiversations that development may involve—and to do so with a full sense of recall and of exploration, yet without ever quite repeating ourselves.

# Biology

Robert Crawford

## With an Introduction

by Rona R. Ramsay

### Introduction

The day I received Robert Crawford's poem, my initial impression of 'Biology' was that it lacked logic, the essence of science. The lack of logic made it alien to me as a written communication. It would never get past peer review by a picky scientist. Alienation came too from the use of words out of context, 'lost in translation' from science to poetry. Words such as 'carnitine', a specific recognition molecule in the cell, jump out from amongst the non-specific terms around them; abstruse nomenclature and central themes of molecular biology are mixed at random.

Scientist and poet in this project were given the impossible task of sharing, over one lunch, the sense of mystery and challenge of science and the sense of music and ideas in poetry, each in their own particular style. The time was much too short and our conversation could easily have stretched over several meetings when the opportunity to focus on issues and clarify connections would have been possible. I had expected the language of science to be a hurdle, as it is to students new to biology, but Robert took the dialect in his stride. When I explained the object I had brought with me (an automated pipette) as a symbol of measurement and precision, Robert likened it to a pen. On my side, I learned that the mystery of poetry is that the connotations of words can be different for each reader, evoking different pictures from the same music.

So, on re-reading six weeks later, I found the literary logic. The poetry is there for me as a scientist, although perhaps in a different way from the general reader for whom the words do not evoke the associations and memories, the joy and challenge that science has given me over the twenty-five years of my adult life.

Not only have I learned from the poet–scientist discussions, but Robert Crawford has produced from the discussions a love poem for science. The words speak for themselves, evoking 'recognition scenes'. My research seeks to explain how the three-dimensional shapes of small molecules fit together with large enzymes for recognition and affinity. In the end, 'deft, intermolecular embrace' sums up what my science is all about.

## Biology

*for Lewis*

Our days and ways, our chromosomes are numbered,
Lettered, making up a long, tagged story,

A still unfolding Book of Genesis,
But one, like poetry, lost in translation,

So most of us, to find the original sense,
Must call to mind some song our mother sang,

One taken in with nursery rhymes and milk,
Then dream we come to love strange dialects—

From *zymogens* to *Avogadro's Number*—
Whose folktales speak in strands of narrative,

Dense, trailing clauses scribbled by pipettes,
Enzyme legends, each a secret pathway

Through tiny mitochondric organelles,
Where carnitine, the label proteins read,

Acts out unseen, wee recognition scenes,
Atom-fine get-togethers, microbondings,

Pos and neg held in a cyclic shape,
And there, in trees, in cats' or human kidneys,

Articulates a sort of Word made flesh,
Goes recognized, unspoken, joins together

Mice, people, choughs, so colourlessly proving
Gut feelings true, that all are held in one

Genetic myth, one Loch Ness-deep, compelling,
Deft, intermolecular embrace.

# Testament and Confessions of an Informationist

W. N. Herbert

## I

I am one of those unfortunate souls who hear voices, usually indistinct, opinionated ones, which assail me when I wake up. My radio alarm afflicts me with a particular kind of information: the incessant voices of Middle Britain, for some years well exemplified by the writer and broadcaster Melvyn Bragg on his BBC Radio 4 programme *Start the Week*. Not so long ago I heard him yet again setting scientist against religious commentator whilst reserving writer (in this case Will Self) to throw in the cultural kedgeree. It was the usual scientist's argument that science is based on facts whereas religion is based on ideas, while Will Self claimed that his fiction occupied a parallel realm entirely. Listening dejectedly, I concluded that science appeared to be a bleak and doctrinaire dimension, populated by those so sure of their own rightness that they feel no need to pause and consider whether a fact is in fact all that different from an idea in the first place.

Had I, though, come to all that much of a conclusion, or did the conclusion simply arrive, predictable as the morning post, given these circumstances? The adversarial debate favoured by the BBC in these kinds of situations encourages listeners to take one or the other side of arguments to which we may prefer to have more complex responses. The media in general seems keen to promote a suppression of our subconscious life or individual inclinations in favour of some grand gesture of inclusion in a culture. More accurately, perhaps, the media strives to include us in their less than fully conscious agenda for a culture. We learn to endure this as we endure each morning's loss of the contradictory world of dream, and so our responses may become as passive as those of the Radio 4 scientist who uttered such a troubling banality—or those of Will Self himself who, for all his efforts at *épater*, was reduced to just another course in the British breakfast of ideas. Shall science and logic be forever at war with religion and metaphysics while literature stands around, concerned in the way a rodeo clown is concerned, to entertain us whilst separating wild steer from unsettled cowboy?

Shortly after listening to that radio debate, I was driving through the Lake District and found myself almost involuntarily in receipt of a broadcast from Lyric FM, better known as the Preface to *Lyrical Ballads:*

> If the labours of Men of Science should ever create any material revolution, direct or indirect, in our condition, and in the impressions which we habitually receive, the Poet will sleep no more than at present, but he will be ready to follow the steps of the Man of Science, not only in those general indirect effects, but he will be at his side, carrying sensation into the midst of the objects of Science itself.[1]

The concept of 'sensation' has little value for the sort of methodological essentialist who occasionally broadcasts on the radio. Yet, perversely, as a poet who has been described as a 'Scottish Informationist', it is always this sort of figure—the scientist compromised by belief or the believer compromised by science—that I am most drawn to write about.

Stephen Prickett in his excellent study of this tension between belief and science, *Words and the Word*, describes it as follows: 'The principle assumes the possibility of knowledge of "things-in-themselves" once they have been laid bare by the march of knowledge.'[2] It is this attempt to show the literalness of a truth that has no literal basis that I admire in, say, the writings of the nineteenth-century Reverend Thomas Dick, for whom the heavens were so vast and beautiful it seemed obvious that the reason we had an immortal soul was that it enabled us to become astronomers in the afterlife.[3] And it is this laying bare of an otherwise covert belief structure that draws me to examples such as the following from Prickett's book:

> In 1688 John Wilkins, then Dean of Ripon and a Fellow of the Royal Society, as a 'digression' in his *Essay Towards a Real Character and a Philosophical Language* offers an exact reconstruction of Noah's ark from the information and dimensions given in Genesis vi–viii, showing that it was seaworthy and would hold all the animals then known and later discovered plus precisely

the right amount of foodstuffs—including an appropriate surplus of sheep (1888 all told) to feed all the carnivores on the forty day voyage.[4]

It is wonderful what you can do with figures. Or perhaps I should say that it's terrible what, supposedly, you can't do without figures, as Wordsworth's other lyrical dictum suggests:

> The Poet writes under one restriction only, namely, that of the necessity of giving immediate pleasure to a human Being possessed of that information which may be expected of him, not as a lawyer, a physician, a mariner, an astronomer or a natural philosopher, but as a Man.[5]

This sounds dubious to me, though it perhaps contains more of a hidden appeal to common sense than a desire not to alienate the ordinary reader. It would certainly appear to make it difficult to employ scientific or other jargons. I rather prefer Coleridge's views on the abstruser vocabularies:

> The mere man of the world who insists that no other terms but such as occur in common conversation should be employed in a scientific disquisition, and with no greater a precision, is as truly a pedant as the man of letters who either over-rating the acquirements of his auditors, or misled by his own familiarity with technical or scholastic terms, converses at the wine-table with his mind fixed on his museum or laboratory.[6]

Really, being in the stomping-ground of the Romantics only meant that the same issue that pestered me awake in the ambit of Radio 4 was continuing to afflict me. Can poets write meaningfully about science, or are they instead limited to writing poetry that employs scientific terminology? Should they write about science? And are they called upon or do they feel drawn to intervene in the great debate between kinds of knowledge? And do Scottish poets have a particular engagement with all of these issues?

## II

In September 1892 in *The Bookman*, W. B. Yeats remarked,

> A friend of mine is accustomed to say that there is poetry and there is prose, and there is something which, though often most interesting, and even moving, is yet neither one nor the other. To this he applies the curious term 'noetry'; a word ingenious persons derive from the Greek word *nous*, and

consider descriptive of verse which, though full of intellectual faculty, is lacking in imaginative impulse.[7]

This comment may have a supercilious tone, but I have to admit to a certain satisfaction with it as a dismissive pseudo-definition, because formally, if not in terms of content, it is a pretty good definition of Informationism. *The aesthetic of the definition* would be my first stab at describing what I'm after on one of those admittedly rare occasions when I feel like an 'Informationist'. But in order to be more precise I must take issue with Yeats's highbrow attitude.

Highbrow is all about shibboleths: it's about the unspoken aesthetics behind gastronomy, opera, and Radio 4. Its codes have the same unquestioning rigidity as a doctrinaire scientist's concept of facts. Its world is always dividing into Greeks and barbarians, prosecution and defence, U and non-U, and its main *raison d'être* is to end up on the right side of the fence, even if that involves moving the fence posts. It's about the empty rituals of manners rather than politeness. Above all, it is jealous of what it thinks of as its secrets. Poetry is one of its little gewgaws, and remarks like Yeats's seem designed to placate the bourgeois sensibility that requires that Highbrow art remain a matter of 'impulse', reassuringly ineffable and necessarily imprecise. Highbrow hated Modernism, for instance, because Pound and Eliot and Wyndham Lewis immediately declared themselves to be 'Even More Informed than Thou', and left folk staggering for their Quiller-Couches all over the Home Counties.

But of course the pursuit of cultural information in the standard Modernist manner is also slightly risible; witness any real, snot-blooded academic taking Pound or MacDiarmid's 'learning' to pedantic pieces. As the British satirist Chris Morris has demonstrated the absurd conceit of the media, so the Informationist declares the absurd conceit of the broader fields of political discourse, cinema, scientific, academic, and philosophical jargon, history, and, of course, cultural kitsch and detritus of all sorts, from 'popular' music to advertising. We don't want to claim the higher brow. Except most of the poets I could define as Informationist—David Kinloch, Alan Riach, Peter McCarey, Richard Price—are after something more than post-modern jocosity.

If, in Pound's grandiose but rarely examined phrase, ' "Literature is news that STAYS news" ', then perhaps literature ought to be at least interested in the format of news broadcasting, since that is the closest thing to Bible truth our culture seems to have.[8] If, as is increasingly the case, a good deal of poetry seems a lot more transitory than the news, then perhaps people need to be told that 'bible' is another word for the third stomach of a ruminant, because it has many folds like the leaves of a book. If that particular lump of noetry is 'lacking in imaginative impulse', then I'll call myself Aengus and wander round looking for silver apples.

The ability to negotiate between jargons is of increasing importance in our culture. The ability to take aesthetic pleasure in this verbal diplomacy is what distinguishes the Informationist as a dedicated Jargonaut, ready to take oar against an ocean of syntax to seek out the Golden Interface. The ability to turn this pleasure to positive ends, to be informative, to provide a post-Poundian communal *periplum*, is what the quest is all about.

Although Informationism is just something everybody does, particularly all writers, the Informationists as a unit are Scottish, male, and generally suffering from Post-Academic Trauma (not so Post-, in some cases). So that means we Informationists have a particular heritage, and a particular agenda. The heritage is, in a nutshell, John Davidson, Hugh MacDiarmid, Edwin Morgan: poets who all establish that it is as important to know as it is to feel, and that it is vital to examine what we mean by, as well as what we feel about, knowledge. Generations of Scottish thinkers, sceptics, and scientists stand behind that trio: George Davie, Patrick Geddes, J. G. Frazer, J. F. Ferrier, Hugh Miller, Thomas Reid, David Hume—all the way back to John Mair and Duns Scotus; but our specific poetic agenda, I'd argue, is largely shaped by these three poets.

Davidson laid down that agenda in his *Testaments* and in his magnificent posthumous volume of 1909, *Fleet Street and Other Poems*: an urban poetry, a scientific poetry, a poetry that engages with contemporary metaphysics, and a poetry that can manipulate a prose voice. Consider 'The Wasp', in which a wasp flies into a train carriage in which the poet is riding, and is momentarily baffled by the opposite window before escaping. The situation recalls Bede's image for human life, of a bird flying through a lighted hall, but the immediacy of the context and the precision of Davidson's central observation take that idea into a proto-Modernist existential realm that anticipates Edwin Morgan's Glasgow poems of the 1960s:

Perplexed now by opacity with foot and wing
She coasted up and down the wood, and worked
Her wrath to passion-point again. Then from the frame
She slipped by chance into the open space
Left by the lowered sash—the world once more
In sight! She paused; she closed her wings, and felt
The air with learned antennae for the smooth
Resistance that she knew now must belong
To such mysterious transparencies.[9]

What MacDiarmid adds to this viewpoint is a sense of the primacy of discourse. Whether in Scots or English, he is always language-led, almost to the swamping of his individual 'I'. In fact, MacDiarmid rarely cares whether he 'really' did some of the things his plagiaristic eye claims for his verse; to lie, after all, is part of an odyssey like MacDiarmid's *Mature Art.* What interests him is that little space in which we believe him enough to accept a new (and often ridiculous) possibility. For this he must claim shibboleth after highbrow shibboleth:

Apart from a handful of scientists and poets
Hardly anyone is aware of it yet.
(A society of people without a voice for the consciousness
That is slowly growing within them)
Nevertheless everywhere among the great masses of mankind
With every hour it is growing and emerging
Like a mango tree under a cloth,
Stirring the dull cloth,
Sending out tentacles.[10]

This is vintage MacDiarmid, rattling away like a Pathe newsreel about 'the great masses of mankind', and entirely forgetting to tell us what 'it' actually is. It's . . . it's, you know, that important thing that's exactly like a mango tree under a cloth. Who put that mango tree under that cloth? Not MacDiarmid, surely, but just for the moment, the authority of the image has us feeling our way with our 'learned antennae' like Kafkaesque forkietaillies, reaching into a free space we did not know we possessed.

Occupying that free space through judicious manipulation of language is what Edwin Morgan's poetry is all about. From 'Pleasures of a Technological University', with its paired lists of educative terms, its nodules of modules: 'ergs and Bacon', 'stichomythia and feedback', and 'copula and cupola', where one begins to experience puns and anagrams as tonal qualities; to 'from *The Dictionary of Tea*', a prophecy of Informationism in its format and its spoof definitions: '*teafish*: bred by the Japanese in special fish-farms, where it feeds on tannin-impregnated potato extract, this famous fish is the source of our "instant fish teas", tasting equally of fish, chips and tea.' From the gentle dismissal of Ashbery's endless play of signifiers in 'On the Water' ('There is something almost but not quite | beguiling about the thought of houseboat days') to the harsh but ecstatic realism of 'Death in Duke Street' ('These were next to him when he fell | and must support him into death'), and above all in the clear-eyed constant search for a language that can convey multiple levels of truth, geological as well as lyrical, Morgan opens the field of our kinds of concerns, as in 'Trilobites':

> A grey-blue slab, fanned like a pigeon's wing,
> stands on my record cabinet
> between a lamp and a speaker.
> Trapped in a sea of solid stone
> the trilobites still almost swim;
> the darker grey of their backs,
> thumbnail-sized and thumbnail-shaped,
> gives out a dull shine as I switch on the lamp.
> I have eight of them; half are crushed, but
> two are almost perfect, lacking nothing but the antennas.
> My fingertip, coarse and loutish
> tracing the three delicate rows of furrowed plates,
> tries to read the paleozoic braille
> as vainly as the blast of Wagner at their ear
> searches for entrance five hundred million years
> and a world of air too late. But I would not trade
> my family torn by chance from time
> for Grecian urn or gold Byzantium.[11]

I think that refusal to sail to Byzantium would stand for most of the Informationists. We've too much cultural reclaiming and historical recontextualizing to do on our mapmaker's circumnavigation of Scotland. We'd much rather keep our antennas intact and extended, watching for dolphins of found material, stopping off at islands of specialisms for fresh buckets of discourse, and, of course, extending metaphors so far they begin to groan under the steam of testing. So we're not 'really' Informationists, not all the time, not with manifestos that we have all po-facedly signed. But the idea will hold water, just for the moment, just for long enough to quote Thomas Mann on the real reason we must write 'noetry' as well as 'poetry'; because we don't know what we'll need to meet what's coming next, and must include, can't afford to exclude, any medium:

> That the writer (and the philosopher) is a reporting instrument, seismograph, medium of sensitivity, though lacking clear knowledge of his organic function and therefore quite capable of wrong judgements also—this seems to me the only proper perspective on writing.[12]

## III

The basis of Yeats's somewhat strident faith in poetry is, of course, to be found in his Romantic roots. Many of Wordsworth's propositions (and Coleridge's subtle counter-propositions), as Stephen Prickett establishes, are derived from the eighteenth century's reclassification of poetry as a quasi-religious discourse.

John Dennis, in his essay 'The Grounds of Criticism in Poetry', referred to Longinus' comment on the sublimity of the opening of Genesis, then went on to state 'the greatest sublimity is to be deriv'd from Religious Ideas' and concluded that 'Poetry is the most natural Language of Religion'.[13] This had been cited by various Scottish thinkers by the end of the eighteenth century, among them Hugh Blair and Dugald Stewart. My friend and fellow-Informationist, the poet and critic Robert Crawford, has written persuasively about how influential the Scottish academics of this period were in setting up the discipline we now think of as English Literature.[14] It is equally true that Blair in particular was an influence on one of that discipline's favourite subjects of study, namely Wordsworth. When Blair writes that poetry is 'the language of passion, enlivened imagination', Wordsworth replies, 'all good poetry is the spontaneous overflow of powerful feelings', and both men assume the passions and feelings have a distinctly high moral cast derived from the Biblical sublime.[15] This is not the rapture of the football fan, for all Wordsworth's appeals to the transformation of the ordinary. The crucial point here is that poetic language has acquired the particular authority we associate with religious utterance and revelation. It is a vehicle for stating a certain kind of truth antithetical to fact and observation according to scientific method.

For Coleridge too poetry had this revelatory quality, and for him the aesthetic qualities of poetic language were the complicating factor: 'A poem is that species of composition which is opposed to works of science by proposing for its immediate object pleasure, not truth . . .' But, to reflect this argument back on its origins, this would be a very odd way to describe the Bible unless the concept of truth is modified to encompass pleasure, or is at least capable of being reconciled with pleasure. The ability of poetry to harmonize in just this way turns out to be, for Coleridge, one of its most powerful effects: 'This power . . . reveals itself in the balance or reconciliation of opposite or discordant qualities.'[16] A version of this supposition, that poetry has a role in reconciling opposites such as revelation and scientific discovery, is at play in both Wordsworth's original pronouncement, and in *Start the Week*'s deployment of Will Self (the famous poet).

That the qualified, quasi-religious revelation, if not the reconciling of opposites, is a continuing thread in poetic thought is clear from the prose of one of our most authoritative authors, Seamus Heaney. In his piece from *Preoccupations* on Mandelstam, 'Faith, Hope and Poetry', even his title is clearly playing with this idea, while the text goes even further: 'Art has a religious, a binding force, for the artist. Language is the poet's faith and the faith of his fathers and in order to go his own way and do his proper work in an agnostic time, he has to bring that faith to the point of arrogance and triumphalism.'[17] Certainly this was MacDiarmid's response, as one of the most profound believers in the power of language. MacDiarmid's career follows a pattern of acquiring one significant vocabulary after another, extracting all the juicy shibboleths from them, and inserting them into poems that began strange and grew even stranger. Hearing voices indeed.

His first victim was the Scottish dictionary, which he shook by the scruff of the binding until it yielded some of the finest Scots lyrics since Burns. However, this was an enterprise fraught with Wordsworthian difficulties. Since he was employing words that were sometimes rare, sometimes obsolete, and that were neither part of his use vocabulary nor that of any Scot living at the time, he raised a spectre familiar to readers of the *Biographia Literaria*: what is 'a selection of the real language of men'? Coleridge objects there to an idealization of language, though he might as well object to the way this enables Wordsworth to take possession of his subject, to claim authenticity.[18] For authenticity is the very issue raised by MacDiarmid's acquisition of dictionary Scots for literary purposes, and when he goes on to acquire the jargons of science or critical theory and to employ found material from these disciplines, we begin to see how significant this concept of authenticity is.

Heaney's original assessment of MacDiarmid, somewhat but not entirely mitigated by his lecture on him as Oxford's Professor of Poetry, turns on an apparent distinction between the early and late work. He states,

> He set out not so much to purify as to restore the language of the tribe, with a passion that was as philological as it was poetic. Dictionaries are necessary to his diction. Lallans, his poetic Scots language, is based on the language of men, specifically on the dialect of his home district around Langholm in Dumfriesshire, but its attractive gaudiness is qualified by the not infrequent inanities of his English, for he occasionally speaks a language that the ones in Langholm do not know . . . There is an uncertainty about language here, peculiar not just to MacDiarmid, but to others who write generally in English, but particularly out of a region where the culture and language are at variance with standard English utterance and attitudes.[19]

It is this uncertainty which, for me, marks out MacDiarmid as the most significant Scottish poet of last century, the first post-modernist, and the only writer who suggests a cultural agenda in which poets are not on the epistemological sidelines, running out to sponge down a battling bishop in his hopeless fight against scientific orthodoxy. Because Heaney's appeal in this piece is to his faith in language in the Wordsworthian sense as revelatory, the issue of authenticity, the fact that MacDiarmid would not naturally use a scientific vocabulary, is revealed to be an issue of authority. Heaney is suggesting that poetry may go so far, but no further. He is declaring the lyric mode with a pastoral vocabulary as a specialism. But of course the authenticity of MacDiarmid's early Scots poetry is as problematic as Coleridge found the 'real' language of *Lyrical Ballads* to be. And perhaps the authenticity of poetic utterance, this issue which stems from its identification with the authority of Biblical language, is the real problem.

The issue for contemporary poetry is exactly this: lots, perhaps even most, of us *are* displaced from any concept of a poetic diction that is at once authentic, authoritative, and mutually comprehensible. Basically, we are uncertain. Lots, perhaps most, of us are decentred by race, gender, sexuality—even the centre is pretty decentred by its own mainstream conservatism, which places poetic authority firmly in its past, and cultural authority—the capacity to make meaningful contributions to scientific debate, to ethical or political discussion—firmly in the hands of the relevant specialism. So where does this leave us?

To provide an answer I will have to turn back briefly to the Scottish academics and philosophers of the nineteenth century, with reference to the twentieth-century analysis of George Davie. I would like to compare the general cast of Davie's argument with a particular point in it, in the hope of arriving at a position which explains why I feel so devolved from the poetics of, say, Seamus Heaney, and why I feel a corresponding freedom to engage with science and the language of science as an ordinary subject for poetry. Davie argues in *The Democratic Intellect* that the characteristic Scottish mode of approaching an academic subject was through philosophical discussion, what we today might consider to be an approach steeped in theory, and he contrasts this with the Oxbridge mode in a manner that again bears comparison with our protagonists of the Radio 4 airwaves. Essentially, Davie argues that the Scottish mind has a certain resistance to specialisms:

> It was apparently this predominance of philosophy over the other subjects that made the educational system in Scotland so different from that found in England. In England, where philosophy, far from being compulsory, was hardly an academic subject at all, the attitude to classics was largely philological and literary and the attitude to mathematics largely technical and specialist. In Scotland, on the other hand, the national taste for philosophy, aided by a fairly thorough training in it, coloured the whole approach of the native classical and mathematical Professors to their respective subjects, and gave their reading . . . a characteristically humanist flavour. As is testified both by textbooks and accounts of the spirit of the teaching, it was usual in Scotland, in teaching mathematics and science, language and literature, to

give an unusually large amount of attention to the first principles and metaphysical ground of the disciplines.[20]

In his subsequent book, *The Crisis of the Democratic Intellect*, Davie argues that the war fought in the universities in the nineteenth century between Scots and English methodologies was re-fought in the twentieth century in the secondary schools, and, far more crucially, that the banner of generalism was taken up by the poets, particularly Hugh MacDiarmid. In other words, MacDiarmid's use of scientific language, as with his use of dictionary Scots, was part of an endeavour found also in the works of John Davidson or indeed Edwin Morgan not to exclude from the creative mode of thought the topics and language of broader cultural issues such as science. Having said that, Davie does agree with Heaney when he says MacDiarmid's earlier use of Scots touched on interesting philosophical ideas, whereas his use of science is somewhat superficial: 'in his poetic defence of the progressivist idea in *Lucky Poet*, [he] does not bother to think out the fundamentals of the position for himself, but instead puts it over by means of appeals to scientific authority.'[21] In other words, MacDiarmid's intention is a kind of concession to scientism.

But intention is not necessarily equivalent to effect. The effect of MacDiarmid's poetry in this later mode is extraordinary in its liberating potential, and this liberation is induced principally through its language:

> With each of these many essences culled
> From the vast field of life some part of one's own
> Complex personality has affinity and resembles
> When climbing on to the ice-cap a little south of Cape Bismarck
> And keeping the nunataks of Dronning Louises Land on our left
> We travel five days
> On tolerable ice in good weather
> With few bergs to surmount
> And no crevasses to delay us.
> Then suddenly our luck turns.
> A wind of 120 miles an hour blows from the East,
> And the plateau becomes a playground of gales
> And the novel light gives us snow-blindness.
> We fumble along with partially bandaged eyes
> Our reindeer-skin kamiks worn into holes

And no fresh sedge-grass to stump them with.
We come on ice-fields like mammoth ploughlands
And mountainous seracs which would puzzle an Alpine climber.
This is what adventuring in dictionaries means,
All the abysses and altitudes of the mind of man,
Every test and trial of the spirit,
Among the debris of all past literature
And raw material of all the literature to be.[22]

And did MacDiarmid ever travel in such territory? Only by analogy. And did he know precisely what a 'nunatak' was (if not an assault by a nun)? Perhaps not, but he knew it sounded good. The system of thought here is acquisitive and accretive, it is endlessly analogical. If it accedes to scientism, this is only to absorb the authority of scientific utterance alongside the other authorities MacDiarmid claims and proclaims. In other words the writing is profoundly relativist in its methodology, and generalist in its approach. In this it harks back to the terms of a specific debate George Davie cites in *The Democratic Intellect* as the 'great and undeservedly forgotten controversy between Francis Jeffrey and Dugald Stewart between 1805 and 1810.'

The keynote of this Northern controversy concerned the pragmatic, utilitarian value of empirical science. One of the prime issues was whether in respect of utility a sharp line should be drawn between the science which involved experiment proper and the science which rested on observation, especially visual observation. Francis Jeffrey argued that an experimental science, because of its involving actual manipulation and control of its objects, necessarily led to a command over nature, whereas an observational science, because of not being able to manipulate its objects, did not give power over matter. On the other side, Dugald Stewart refused to regard the distinction as important, and pointed out that an observational science like astronomy, though it did not give command over the bodies observed, was nevertheless practically useful by its contribution to navigation and measure of time.[23]

This argument feels rather reminiscent of all the debates I've alluded to in the course of this essay: the scientist for whom the idea of a fact was more powerful than the idea of an idea; the poet for whom the revelatory power of words debars the use of non-authentic language; the university for which the generalist approach was vague and unscholarly—these are all types of the debarrer, the enforcer of specialisms as a means of limiting endeavour rather than opening it to what Wordsworth referred to as 'sensation', and to what MacDiarmid referred to as

> A poetry in which all connections will constantly render such services
> As the protest of the nature poetry of the English poets
> Of the Romantic reaction on behalf of value,
> On behalf of the organic view of nature,
> A protest, invaluable to science itself,
> Against the exclusion of value
> From the essence of matter of fact.[24]

Grand stuff, but I have to make a confession. For me 'value' in this context, like 'sensation' or indeed 'authority' or especially 'authenticity', is just a remnant of a supposed power, once ceded to poetry from religion and now apparently languishing unused by science. They are all inadequate terms for the event that happens in a fine poem, or the sensation we experience when confronted by its scientific equivalent—MacDiarmid's poetry of facts, Wordsworth's 'impassioned expression which is in the countenance of all Science'. My own version of the event of poetry stands in relation to the scientific experiment rather as Dugald Stewart's analysis of the utility of observational science stands in relation to Francis Jeffrey's suggestion that manipulation leads to power.

I have to confess I have an unsystematic, unscholarly, unscientific, and rather uncertain mind. I never paid attention during chemistry classes. I may dislike radio, but I love TV, which has possibly the most insidious agenda of all: to echo Tristan Tzara, 'the universal installation of the idiot'.[25]

I have to confess that science, the media, critical theory are of equal interest to me, are all voices, but that I have an anarchic reluctance to be fully fluent in their systems of thought. I do not consider the theoretical impasse to equal the resolution of a problem, and I believe that the naive approach of the inexpert occasionally produces workable combinations impossible for the specialist. Essentially the value system which privileges one discourse over another in our culture does not apply in the cognitive freefall which is creativity, reassert itself though it must via the ripcord of reason if we are to land safely.

When I engage with any supposedly 'foreign' material it is always in a randomized manner: I allow issues to approach me, to signal their relevance by chance encounter and coincidental reinforcement. I do not pursue issues—however relevant they may be to what I think of as my interests—which do not present themselves in this way, unless an irrationally strong impulse to do so intervenes. I disdain the powers of memory, preferring a goldfish-bowl-type amnesia in which all linguistic traces rot down to a potentially useful mulch. I do not recall like a folk musician, I improvise like a jazz player. I do not remember poems (including my own) in a bard-like manner, and when I encounter those who do I am reminded of being told of the director Mark Rydell's somewhat dodgy statement about John Wayne: 'Wayne was no dummy—he could quote Shelley for half an hour.'

When I write I am conducting an experiment that combines a putative subject and a tentative vocabulary with an expected condition—some version of inspiration—and a number of variables, including how this process will make me feel when I am engaged in it. What occurs during the process of waiting to write, writing, drafting, and redrafting, is at least two revelations. One is that the experiment is shared, not only with previous and fellow writers, but also with events—the appropriate newspaper article, the synchronicitous collision with a seagull, whatever the mind perceives is good for the mix. The second is that the result is never, in a successful poem, what you intended it to be: it is always the appropriate coalescence of all the intervening events plus your attention. In this it is both like and strikingly unlike an experiment: in an experiment the hoped-for result is prepared for and the procedure changes only to help bring it about; in writing the procedure is observed to be inflexible and the result changes to accommodate this realization. Of course there are a number of instances where it is the unintentional discovery, as of penicillin, which turns out to be the more desired result. At such moments the scientist and the poet are far closer than Radio 4 would give us to believe.

For me, to observe the process of creativity, and the unpredictability of its efforts, is to recognize with Dugald Stewart that there is no reason to draw distinctions between disciplines on the premise of power; that a poetic or scientific discovery need not be submitted to such an assessment, since it is capable of surviving on its own terms;

and that these terms, 'poetic' and 'scientific', are merely different, not actively inimical.

I'm told there is an Inuit word, 'Inukshuk', which describes a construction of stones, one piled vertically on another and held there by snow. It means 'You can live here'. My reaction to the endeavours of the Romantics, to the Scottish tradition, and to MacDiarmid and Edwin Morgan, is to look on a vast territory of subjects and hear a vast range of voices, including the media, literary theory, and science, and recognize that, as a poet, I can live here.

# The Working Self

W. N. Herbert

## With an Introduction

by Martin Conway

## Introduction

Images of the self exist in every memory. The analogy between memories and a hologram is a good one, although what is seen through the shards of mental glass that are memories is not only something from the past but also something from the present. The rememberer exists now and the memory is constructed from different fragments glued together by more abstract knowledge of one's life, reflecting a self that is past and a self that you may or may not like to meet again. Discrepancies between what we were then, what we are now, and what we may become drive our use of memory, a use that often lies outside conscious control—which is why a poem can surprise us with what it makes us feel and what memories those feelings may be based on.

But poetry, other types of art, and, indeed, everyday experiences, can only be emotionally responded to and brought together with our past when memory and the self are not too discrepant. Consider a young man with the narcissistic delusion that he is a famous rock guitarist. A belief he holds even though he knows he cannot play a guitar. He is deluded because although in some sense he knows his belief is 'wrong', that it is contradicted by his memory, for him memory no longer carries the weight it once did in anchoring the self in reality, in a remembered reality. Consider too the patient with brain damage to the frontal lobes who confabulates a past consisting of fragments of memories but now configured or 'glued together' in ways wholly incorrect. The confabulations of such patients are sometimes referred to as 'honest lies', they are not delusions but rather attempts to make sense of reality after one's ability to manipulate knowledge into self-coherent forms as failed.

Extreme cases? Maybe. W. N. Herbert's poem catches neatly the idea of discrepancy, the idea of all the selves we're not and all the selves we are. Memory is the database of what we call the 'working self': a repository of currently active goals, models of the self, and beliefs about ourselves, what we are, what we want to be, and we ought to be. The working self and knowledge of that past are locked together in a dynamic embrace that when broken, in pathology, brain damage, and dementia, releases a self set free from the past. But when the self is not anchored in the past there is no tangible future, the goal structure falls apart, and the discrepancies between the different domains of the working self dissipate. When memory is negated, when it becomes 'is not' rather than 'is', the self can be anything.

## The Working Self

the naked man with briefcase
descending three flights of lighthouse stairs
his neckmuscles held by a hatstand of stress
and a new version of the *Inferno* blackening his cerebellum
in which the only dead are his poetic texts
and those of all the writers he has ever loved
wanting to be asleep with all the fervour of the truly middle-aged

is not

the naked man running into
the midnight sea at Teignmouth
with the surprisingly large-breasted girl
he will not sleep with later in the sand
all the car-load of friends all following *The Wedding Present*
from gig to gig all stoned and half-undressed and
sleepily silenusian in the cold cupping sand

is not

the student standing with a white-furred uvula in
the campanile of his newly-smoking throat
before the galvanised facade of Milan cathedral
on his first morning in Italy, before visiting the Brera, the Uffizi,
focusing on the lens as it falls from his spectacles and smashes

on the delicious pasticceria icing of the paving stones
is not
the seventeen year old staring at Rossetti's
loganberry compote of a dream of Dante and the corpse of Beatrice
remembering the final cold corner bust up by the bridge
by the Post Office where he stood for hours knowing
she would never feel the need to come back
not knowing that he would never speak to her again or know
her whereabouts or children or the moment of her death
is not
the boy visiting a grandfather
he hadn't seen so long he almost had begun
to think of him as dead and dreamed about it endlessly
after the rapidly-following death
the slow hand touching the bandaged throat, the querulous witty
voice
the dark conspiratorial spectacles, always
not dead after all but still with him, talking
is not
the boy who dreamt that all his classmates sat in darkness in
a circle and the circle was so large it seemed to contain
all the people of the multis at Trottick, all the people in Dundee
perhaps all the people in Scotland and in the centre was a figure,
cowled like a monk, rotating in the darkness with an index finger
pointing and revolving like a planet in an orrery
and when the figure pointed straight at him
woke up in the dark moon-streaked fourth-floor bedroom for the
first time
clearly alone

# A Science of Belonging: Poetry as Ecology

John Burnside

A small fishing town on the east coast of Scotland: November, 2002, the first day of the (pagan) year. The night was stormy and this morning the wind is still high; lines of townsfolk have formed at the breakwater to watch the great waves smash against the wall, coming out from rooms haunted by television and muzak, bringing their children to see, bringing cameras and binoculars, a little awed, in spite of themselves, at this great spectacle of *the real*. I am taking my son on our usual walk to the lighthouse at the end of the quay, past the boats moored in the inner harbour, past the stacks of creels and old fish-crates on the dock, out to where the crab-boats come in, on finer days than this. My son is two years old and *here* is his favourite place: he likes to watch the gulls sail overhead and, in season, he tracks our summer visitors, swallows tracing the line of the breakwater at low tide, catching the flies that are drawn to the tumbles of weed on the shore, Arctic terns hovering over the shallow water, searching for food in the clear light they follow from pole to pole with the changing seasons. Most of all he likes to see the crabs, to exchange a few words with the 'crab-man' and loiter a while for the five-fathom scent of the creels and the massed colours of the catch, the black and orange bodies packed into old boxes dripping with hairweed and a greeny deepwater-light. This is what we know of life: sea birds, caught fish, the odd twenty-foot wave flaring against a wall, the dark scent of unknown waters—and, though sometimes we are embarrassed to say it, what we need to say, what we need to remember above and beyond all our other concerns is that this is the real world, this is our enduring mystery. Nothing virtual, nothing managed can replace it. We can tell ourselves other stories—history, politics, advertising, entertainment—but this is the basic ground of our being. 'It is not *how* things are in the world that is mystical, but *that* it exists', says Wittgenstein and he adds, 'We feel that even when all *possible* scientific questions have been answered, the problems of life remain completely untouched. Of course there are then no questions left, and this itself is the answer.'[1] It would be too simple to say that the work of science is to investigate how things are in the world, and the work of poetry is to remind us of this separate mystery—the fact of a world, the sense of wonder that anything exists at all—but it would not be entirely mistaken. At the same time, it would be absurd to suggest that the scientist is always a scientist, the poet always a poet: we all have to deal with the *how* and the *that*. Knowing the *how*, and celebrating the *that*, it seems to me, is the basis of meaningful dwelling: what interests me about ecology and poetry is that, together, they make up a science of belonging, a discipline by which we may both describe and celebrate the 'everything that is the case' of the world, and so become worthy participants in a natural history.

There is another way of understanding, or rather, failing to understand, our place in the cosmos. We call this method 'history', but it is a method that frequently loses its place in the book of life, a description of being that assigns far too great importance to human affairs. In its purest form, such a history might usefully contribute to our understanding, but our experience has shown that it is too malleable, too reductive, too innately humanistic in its approach. This is a history that repeats itself, something natural history never does; it even seems capable of coming to 'an end', as Francis Fukuyama and others have suggested. In other words, official history fails us as a discipline—or rather, it fails the wider community of life, what some philosophical ecologists refer to as 'the more than human'—by allowing itself to become reductive, almost behaviourist and, worst of all, superstitious in its description of the world. 'As a simplistic, linear, literal account of events and powers as unpredictable as parental anger,' says Paul Shepard, 'history is a juvenile idea'—and, like all juvenile ideas, official history lends itself to manipulation and misuse.[2] At present, the version of history we are encouraged to consume is one that suits big corporations and their employees in our state governments. It is a history of conflict and consumption, of production and power that denies us elements of our very nature, as human animals.

This version of history—told selectively and endorsed by the most suspect of interests—would have us believe that, even if the good were not always as good as they might have been, the bad were visibly so from a long way off. We forget the glamour of Nazism in its most public forms, the apparent vigour of Mussolini's fascists. Of course, this is part of the overall scheme: the powers that be would not want us to learn any but the most obvious lessons from history. So it is that the new fascists are difficult for the ordinary consumer to recognize, because the new fascism is different from the old fascism, just as the new issues are different from the old. The new fascism is corporate and wears a smily face, and because its public (Entertainment) wing has been careful to ensure that as many of us as possible have zero knowledge of our (natural) history—or indeed of our own local cultures, as opposed to that we've been sold by the snake-oil dealers in Tinseltown—it contrives to go about its ugly business, while enjoying the minimum possible disruption and the maximum possible profits. On the way, it has redefined what most people mean when they use the word 'science'.

It is not necessarily the work of the writer to point any of this out. Art is neither a political pursuit, nor a historical event, in the juvenile sense of the word. However, to live one's whole life in the pursuit of such a spiritually rewarding discipline as poetry, while failing to suggest some possible alternatives would seem, at best, ungrateful. Indeed, it would be impossible—for all good poetry is political to the extent that it insists upon the actual and so opposes those who would blind us to any telling of history other than their own. As a poet, I want to suggest the importance of those elements of life that have hitherto been considered minor, commonplace, even trivial. The beauty of the real, as opposed to the virtual. The starlit darkness of the actual night, the salt and physicality and achieved grace of real bodies, the pleasure of walking as opposed to driving. A view of identity that sets terrain and habitat before tribal allegiances, the integrity of place before the idea of nation or state, the pagan calendar before the atomic clock. A philosophy of dwelling that includes all things, living and non-living, and informed by the principle of *ahimsa*, of doing, if not no harm, then the absolute minimum of harm. At the beginning of a new century, I am interested in finding what Heidegger called a new way of thinking, and to propose that art contributes, in subtle but cumulative ways, to the examined life.

Is this too ambitious a project for a poet, given a small embattled readership and the hostility of a wider society hooked on three-minute diversions best suited to the proverbial and probably excessively maligned goldfish? Of course it is. The great thing about being an ecological poet is that one is utterly inconsequential and so entirely free to propose anything. Even the impossible.

That (official) science is on the side of the good has always been one of the tenets of our official, essentially positivist, history. That view is especially popular in the West, and in the USA in particular. It is in the interests of the corporations to propagate a fairly unquestioning view of (their version of) 'science' as good, beneficial, and life-enhancing, because it helps them sell products that might otherwise seem entirely suspect to us. Like GM foods. Or ill-tested and carelessly manufactured vaccines. Or 'beauty products' that, without the veneer of 'scientific research', would be seen as so much obvious snake oil. Governments like science too, because they can shift the blame for their mistakes to other shoulders: 'It wasn't our fault, we just did what the experts told us to do.' Or they can cover up their failure to tackle root problems like poverty, exploitation, and environmental degradation with 'scientific' fixes and programmes, like mass inoculations or GM-tainted food aid. None of this is science, of course. It's business—which is why the new thinking must address the main social and political problem relating to science: that of its definition.

How to begin? One of the confusions surrounding science is its separation from other intellectual disciplines, the more readily to deify it. Yet at root, science and technology are, or should be, part of a wider intellectual enterprise. We see this immediately, when we examine the etymology: *technē*, Greek: skill, craft, art. It's an interesting idea, this view of technology as art or craft. It suggests something human and holistic, rather than the mechanical and reductionist: know-how, gumption, savvy, skill. The Latin word *scientia* suggests something similar: knowledge, yes, but the heuristic, questing, sometimes intuitive knowledge by which we come to an understanding of—and *with*—the world, and of our place in it. From the first, humans have used *scientia* and *technē* to navigate the world—not just in the fight for survival, but also in the quest for beauty and a sense of the authentic.

Of course, this is a writer's way of looking at things, a concern with language and concepts, rather than an appreciation of method or mathematics. Yet I think of my own work as a discipline as much akin to *scientia* as it is to rhapsody, because I consider it to be ecological in the broadest philosophical sense—in other words, I think of the discipline of poetry as a slow, lyrical, and fairly tentative attempt to understand and describe a meaningful way of dwelling in this extraordinary world.

This is not to say that I wish to nominate the brand of philosophical ecology I study as a science, in the usual sense of the word. I know it will never be accepted as such, because it will never make money for the corporations, or political capital for the men in Greyhall. But I would say that this discipline, this 'poetry as ecology' is, for me, a form of *scientia*, a technique for reclaiming the authentic, a method for reinstating the real, a politics of the actual. A poem (or drawing or song or dance movement) that reclaims membership of a wider, more-than-human world is as necessary an enterprise as any I can think of—and I have no doubt that we need this form of ecological *technē* as much as we need any other (which is not to dispute the value of any *technē* which adds to The Good, to the overall well-being of the wider, more-than-human world).

All of this is fairly obvious: there are times when stating the obvious seems necessary. It will also be obvious, and may also need stating that, while science at its best seeks to reduce our ignorance, it cannot—and should not seek to—eliminate mystery. The more we know, the more the mystery deepens. If poetry has a role in relation to science, it is to remind science of that universal truth. In this, it is also an essentially ecological discipline. It teaches us part of the duty of dwelling, it teaches us a necessary awe. This awe is central, is vitally necessary, to any description of the world. A description that lacks this awe is, in truth, a lie.

A digression: there is no such thing as Artificial Intelligence. We can make a machine clever, we cannot make it intelligent. Intelligence is wet, contingent, and grounded in a true awareness of others.

Towards the beginning of *Underworld*, Don DeLillo describes a group of student volunteers, working with an artist in a desert where the US tested its war planes and developed its nuclear arsenal, as 'burnt-out hackers looking for the unwired world'.[3] Towards the end, in the very closing pages, DeLillo invokes 'things in the room, off-screen, unwebbed, the tissued grain of the deskwood alive in the light, the thick lived tenor of things'—and it is here, at the close, that we understand, that everything falls into place, not just the aesthetic experience of a finely crafted novel, but a philosophy, a new way of thinking, a vision. DeLillo is, in my opinion, the finest and most troubling narrator of this new vision, but he is not alone. Many writers today—most, not surprisingly perhaps, in the United States, where the real, the unwired, the thick lived tenor of things is most threatened—feel the need to explore, and perhaps to reassert the authentic and the given in the face of a society whose main credo is that we can be or do or have whatever we want (that is, whatever the corporations tell us we want), if not in the actual, then in some virtual world. I honour these writers, and can think of no better way to demonstrate my regard than to try to learn from them. Their work is ecological, in the broadest sense, for they investigate the science of belonging, the science of dwelling. As an example, I shall cite another of these writers, the poet Mark Doty, writing in what is, for me, one of the key texts of this new century, *Still Life with Oysters and Lemon*:

> That there can never be too much of reality; that the attempt to draw nearer to it—which will fail—will not fail entirely, as it will give us not the fact of lemons and oysters but this, which is its own fact, its own brave assay toward what is.
>
> That description is an inexact, loving art, and a reflexive one; when we describe the world we come closer to saying what we are.[4]

Here Doty is considering a still life by Jan Davidsz de Heem, but he is also talking about all our descriptions, all our attempts to know ourselves and the world. What lies at the heart of this attempt, he says, echoing Gaston Bachelard, is *intimacy*. Poetry restores to our investigations the intimacy they lack, when we think in terms of subject, object; of self and other. We know ourselves by knowing the world: 'looking outward,' he says, 'we experience the one who does the seeing'.[5] In our moments of intimacy we see that reality is continuous, seamless, and inclusive, and that the world is both given and imagined.

At some point in any consideration of any art, we come to the question Tolstoy asked, the question of what is to be done. How do we oppose the degradation of our shared environment, the obscene power of the corporations, the cheapening of our shared experience? (My inner life may be rich, but how do I share it with my neighbour if all we have in common is bubblegum 'culture' and a rather desperate sense of irony?) It's a big question—too big for this essay—but I will make one small suggestion in the space that remains—a simple, banal, absurdly unambitious suggestion about walking. It is a suggestion about the role poetry can play in the way we experience the world, but it is not a matter for poets alone (as works of visual art by Hamish Fulton, say, or Richard Long, illustrate). What I want to suggest is that, on foot, we all become artists to the extent that, while walking, we have the potential to attune ourselves to 'the song of the earth'.[6] What I would also suggest is that, on foot, we become ecologists because, walking, we have the potential to see the world as it is, not in virtual glimpses through a VCR or a car windscreen, but as the here and now, the immediate, the intimate ground of our being. (As the poet Jack Collom writes, 'The word ecology means literally "knowledge of the house". In the sense that our house is now the entire world, the study of ecology has come to be a comprehensive study of the relational'.[7] How can we study the relations between things if we flash past them in motorized non-time, distracted by our mobile phone, our car radio, or cut off from the scent and sound and feel of them by a windscreen?)

If all of this sounds far too fanciful (or grandiose), that's fine: just stop reading here and go out for a walk. In fact, stop reading and go for a walk anyway. Why read about it, when you can do it?

South Africa: 1990. The pictures were seen all around the world: as he emerged from prison, Nelson Mandela left his car and began what would become famous as 'the long walk to freedom'. That he should choose to walk seemed not only politically astute, but also inspired—for is not a man walking, out in the open, vulnerable and free, the very model of human dignity? Actually, as Mandela himself notes, the walk was suggested by a television presenter:

> There was little time for lengthy farewells. The plan was that Winnie and I would be driven in a car to the front gate of the prison . . . At a few minutes after three, I was telephoned by a well-known SABC presenter who

requested that I get out of the car a few hundred feet before the gate so that they could film me walking toward freedom. This seemed reasonable, and I agreed to do it . . . Shortly before four, we left in a small motorcade from the cottage. About a quarter of a mile in front of the gate, the car slowed to a stop and Winnie and I got out and began to walk toward the prison gate.[8]

Mandela may not have known it at the time—though one suspects he was more astute than he pretends here—but this image of a man walking from his prison would become iconic, just as, only a year before, the image of a protester in Tiananmen Square, opposing a tank with nothing but his body, would attain a mythic resonance for the politics of our time. For myself, the decisive image of my formative years was of a line of armed men advancing towards a group of students, not much older than myself, and being met with the same gentle resistance, the resistance of the human body, people standing or walking in an open space—in this case, carrying flowers, which were placed, with due tenderness and piety, in the barrels of the soldiers' guns. And today, now, even as I write, Palestinian boys resist the might of Israel's occupying forces, veritable Davids opposing the loathsome power of an arrogant, ruthless Goliath with nothing more than their tender, indispensable bodies.

Even if we set aside these extreme examples, however, I would maintain that the very fact of walking—or rather, of being a human body exposed, moving or standing in the open—is an essentially *ecological* act, part of the provisional and continuing science of belonging, an act that is both deeply significant, and desperately urgent, in an age when the destructiveness of the mounted, environmentally careless man–machine amalgam—the car, the truck, the tank, the tractor, the earth-mover—is emblematic of a whole society's disregard, not so much for 'Mother Earth' as for the future of its own children. In such a climate, walking takes us away from the machine and back to the world, and so to the real.

Two hundred years ago Coleridge wrote his 'Dejection: An Ode', an expression of the anomie that sent him out walking again, in search of that elusive true self, 'the natural man'. Here is his description of that disconnected quality:

> There was a time when, though my path was rough,
> This joy within me dallied with distress,

And all misfortunes were but as the stuff
Whence Fancy made me dreams of happiness:
For hope grew round me, like the twining vine,
And fruits, and foliage, not my own, seemed mine.
But now afflictions bow me down to earth:
Nor care I that they rob me of my mirth;
But oh! each visitation
Suspends what nature gave me at my birth,
My shaping spirit of Imagination.
For not to think of what I needs must feel,
But to be still and patient, all I can;
And haply by abstruse research to steal
From my own nature all the natural man—
This was my sole resource, my only plan:
Till that which suits a part infects the whole,
And now is almost grown the habit of my soul.[9]

What Coleridge meant by the 'natural man' is, of course, open to discussion, and it must be seen in the context of his times. In a contemporary context, however, the idea of natural man (or woman) is well expressed by Harald Gaski:

Even though the Sami probably are one of the most modernised indigenous peoples in the world, their role as communicators between an ever more estranged 'Western' conception of Nature and the indigenous peoples' preferred holistic view expressing the statement that all creatures are fundamentally dependent on each other, is important and steadily growing. This is the time to utilise the benefits of belonging to the affluent countries of the world, and also to benefit from a modern education system that enables the Sami of today to assume the position of mediators: advocating the view of the 'natural man' to the international society of the UN and the IMF, and, at the same time, convincing the indigenous peoples about the importance of letting one's voice be heard by the international community. This is the test and the challenge of modern natural man, still hearing and obeying the heartbeats of the Earth itself, imparting its message through the most modern mediums to an increasing number of serious listeners.[10]

For a modern poet whose predicament is at least similar if not identical to the one Coleridge identifies in 'Dejection', poetry itself can be seen as a means—a discipline, a spiritual path, a political-ecological commitment—to wholeness and reconnection with the earth itself. For an ecologically-*mindful* poet, the task is one of reconnecting, of rediscovering, as it were, one's own nature through connection with a wider reality, with the more-than-human. Following Gaski's logic, the works of indigenous artists become exemplary to those of us who struggle to find ways of reconnecting to the fundamental reality of the earth—and, to this end, we need to learn to appreciate the works of those 'modern natural' artists, such as Gaski's fellow Sami, Nils-Aslak Valkeapaa, who are rooted in an oral tradition and connected to a terrain and a way of life that respects 'the heartbeats of the Earth itself'. Reconnection is a continuous enterprise: just as Wordsworth and Coleridge learned from the life, work, and speech of 'the middle and lower classes of society' a language and a narrative with which to attempt 'a natural delineation of human passions, human characters and human incidents', so the modern poet, by experiencing the work of indigenous writers and thinkers, becomes the privileged apprentice to a way of thinking about the earth and other life forms that our corporatized society seems determined to eradicate.[11] By learning about the myths, cosmology, fairy tales, and folk wisdom of these peoples, we rediscover connections to our own (pagan, magical, myth-making) history, again, a history that the corporations want us to forget.

We are not confined, however, to studying the work of indigenous artists, if we would find models of ecologically sound poetry and prose. Given his concern with a restoration of the natural man, Coleridge's walks of 1802 and 1803 can been seen as having many parallels: Wordsworth, Clare, Dante, Mandelstam, Whitman, Thoreau to name but a few. Poets—especially lyric poets—have seen walking as a natural element in the composition process—poets who compose while walking will describe their method as working 'on the lips' (Mandelstam) or poetry of 'the way' (compare Machado's 'Yo voy sonando caminos'). These poets know that, when a person dies, his soul does not rise to heaven, but walks away in the sunshine, to become an other. One may compare Lorca's 'Despedida' ('Farewell'), from the 'Trasmundo' ('Afterlife') series in *Canciones* (1927):

Si muero,
dejad el balcón abierto.

El niño come naranjas.
(Desde mi balcón lo veo.)

El segador siega el trigo.
(Desde mi balcón lo siento.)

¡Si muero,
dejad el balcón abierto![12]

If I die,
leave the balcony open.

The boy is eating oranges.
(From my balcony, I see him.)

The reaper is cutting the wheat.
(From my balcony, I hear him.)

If I die,
leave the balcony open!

Thus, while walking, or being out in the open, has a fundamental influence on the form and music of poetry, it is not merely a matter of compositional method that drives poets out into the open. It is both a recognition of the spiritual importance of connection with the earth and the political importance of *being* open, of being on foot. There is a difference between the way a person on foot—a *peon*, as it were—and a mounted or driven figure—the *caballero*—experiences the world. This is not only a difference in status, but also in connectedness, both to the earth and to duration. This has always been recognized in ritual and initiation: for example, maze and labyrinth symbols in places as far apart as Malta and the Arctic Circle suggest that walking a maze or labyrinth was an essential part of a young person's initiation, not so much into tribal or clan tradition, as to belonging in a world. The walked maze alters the walker's perception, not only of place, but also of time: it is a way of becoming rooted in a locus, a way of connecting with the genius of a place, but it is also a way of shrugging off the necessary human constructs relating to time—clock time, calendar time—in a recognition of the momentary and eternal nature of *durée*, of which Bergson writes in *Time and Free Will*. A walking human—or, for that matter, any human being standing in the open, exposed, aware, at risk, untrammelled—is able to attune him or herself to the rhythm of the earth, the feel of a place, the presence of other animals, the elements, sidereal time, the divine. To be exposed in such a manner is, of course, dangerous—witness the myth of Euripides, who is supposed to have been killed by hunting dogs on a visit to Macedonia—but it is also essential to being human.

Paul Shepard makes an important distinction between the 'hunter-gatherer' mentality and that of the 'peasant', the peasant being the property-obsessed, resentful, nature-fearing human who is still the model for our society, in a consumer culture. I want to stress this: by peasant, Shepard means *us*, or at least the property-owning, hierarchical, monotheist traditions to which we belong. This peasant mind sees 'heaven' as otherworldly, a city in the sky, or in some abstract place—a city society is based on the placing of everything into an ownership context—land, spouse, children, ideas. The peasant also has a weak sense of himself, and of his place in the world:

> Men may now be the possessors of the world's flimsiest identity structure, the products of a prolonged tinkering with ontogenesis—by Paleolithic standards, childish adults. Because of this arrested development, modern society continues to work, for it requires dependence. But the private cost is massive therapy, escapism, intoxicants, narcotics, fits of destruction and rage, enormous grief, subordination to hierarchies that exhibit this callow ineptitude at every level, and perhaps worst of all, a readiness to strike back at a natural world that we dimly perceive as having failed us. From this erosion of human nurturing comes the failure of the passages of the life cycle and the exhaustion of our ecological accords.[13]

The hunter-gatherer mind, on the other hand, cannot imagine land as property, and sees ownership as a provisional thing: food and other provisions are shared, not as a matter of ideology, but as a fact of life, a strategy for survival. For this reason, the demand for immediate satisfaction inherent in consumerism seems to the hunter-gatherer absurd. To the hunter-gatherer mind—and I am not necessarily referring to a traditional way of life here as a mind set—the terrain is real, it has its own identity and energy, it is a living thing. The song of the earth is not a metaphor, but an actual sound, one that can be listened to. I tried to explore this idea in the following poem, written in Finnmark, northern Norway, in May, 2002:

*By Kautokeino*

I walk in a shower of ice
on the *Finnmarksvidda*:
freezing rain, not snow; hard pearls of ice,
stinging my face and hands as I make my way
to the frozen lake.
No sign of life—just scats and moulted hair;
but something calls from far across the water,
some elemental, lost beneath the sky,
darker than flesh and blood when it calls again
then waits, as if it wanted me to answer

and snow begins to fall—huge, sudden flakes,
drifting between the birch trees, blurring the moss,
as if some festival had been resumed,
the ceremony of another season.
Down in the village
they're coming away from church:
mothers and fathers, grandchildren, second cousins,
the blue-eyed girl I saw on the road to Avze,
the man in the tourist cafe
with his perfect English.
New wives stand in their kitchens
preparing *bidos*,
a pair of ducks go walking on the pond,
crossing his garden, an old man stops to acknowledge
the heartbeat under his feet, and the veins of thaw
far on the *vidda*, a music he hears in his sleep
through the mumble of ageing.

Out in the snow
I am making a landmark of bones,
a ring of scat, an avenue of lichens.
They say, if you make your camp
at the Pikefossen,
the girl who drowned there centuries ago
will wake you in the small hours, as her screams
unravel from the slow roar of the waters;
but surely there are other sounds to hear,
the subtler frequencies of earth and sky,
dead generations buried in the sand,
feeding the ling, feeding the birch trees and willows,
reindeer and Arctic fox and unnumbered men

who made a living here with skill and patience,
their works provisional, their dreams immense,
their children raised in memory and song.

Down in the village
they're drinking the sweet white coffee,
talking or falling silent, reading the paper
or fixing a broken sled
in a cluttered yard.
The blue-eyed girl I saw on the road to Avze
is turning aside from her book
to consider the future
when something gives her pause—a cry, a rumour,
the animal keening that hovers against the walls
of a quiet house;

and, setting her homework aside,
she stops to listen,
alone in herself, and thinking in the lull
of all her future lives: newlywed; old,
or travelling on somewhere
to a fresh beginning;
abroad in the world and singing a favourite hymn,
or here in the same bright house
with her kinfolk around her.
She turns to the open door, when a voice she loves
calls from the other room, to say 'It's nothing'
though nothing could explain the quiet song
that bleeds through the net of the wind
and the sound of water.
Nothing explains the pull and lurch of the sky,
how, sooner or later, each of us goes to answer;
no logic stills the heartbeat in the earth:
it never stops, it knits within the bone,
a world around the world we understand
waiting to be recovered and given names:
this gravity, this lifeblood in the thaw,
this salt of love, this mercury in absence.[14]

What I wanted to emphasize here was the sound of the Arctic north, and the deliberate, conscious work of attuning one's art to the song of the earth. To do this, it seems, the contemporary poet in a consumer culture needs to step outside that culture, to step away from the narrowly human realm—as delimited by consumerist mores—and connect with something larger and wider, with the more-than-human. Part of this poem's work is to remind us that human beings belong to the earth in the most fundamental way. For example, gravity is part of what makes us human, as we know from space travel research, which indicates that long periods in zero or low gravity conditions lead to disease, e.g. osteoporosis—and walking upon the earth is what we evolved to do. In his poem, 'Hamlet', Pasternak quotes the old Russian proverb 'to live is not as easy as crossing a field', but to live is, nevertheless, a journey, a journey ideally conducted for the most part on foot, a life long walk.[15] On this walk, we encounter the others—the animals, the birds, plant life, the elements. As walkers, out in the open, we are capable of restoring our ecological accords.

But what does this have to do with changing the (human, social) world (and it is my purpose, as a descendant of Shelley, to contribute in some tiny way to changing that world)? Well, at the most basic level, to sing the praises of anything, even an act so mundane as walking, is to remind others of its value—and this, in itself, is a political act. *Walking* is a political act. If I walk to the beach, I do not drive there. At ground level, at walking pace, out in the open, I participate in the world as it is, in the real. I get warm, or wet. I smell the wind. I taste the starlight.

In this sense, walking proposes a new politics; more importantly, it reminds us, as we experience the ground level reality of being human, that the *caballeros* who run the corporations have become disconnected from the earth. We—and they—are indoors too often; our shared animal life is confined to pets and domestic creatures; we kill what we do not know and so cannot trust; we fear the earth and its creatures (or we despise them). At one level, ecological art is intended to address this problem, to restore that mystery, to put us back into the open, to make us both vulnerable and wondrous again—to reconnect us. Such a reconnection seems to me the basis of a new way of thinking, a way of thinking that, with a little luck, may give birth to a new science of belonging that, in turn, may change the way we dwell in and with the rest of the living world.

In this sense, walking is the basic discipline of science of belonging, for this is a science based almost entirely upon field work. On foot, we are able to imagine an accord between poetry and ecology, a full-scale and rounded knowledge of what Gary Snyder calls the 'Earth House Hold'.[16] To achieve such a rounded science, we must set aside some of the errors we have grown up with and embark upon a new way of thinking. Imagine the science (and the poetry) that might have grown up in a society that was not rooted in a hostility to, or a romanticization of, the natural world. Imagine a science that had no preconceived ideas about 'objectivity', a pagan science in which no crude 'order' was projected upon the world. Imagine the description of the world that might have been accomplished by a society where reverence for life *really did* lie at the core of its value system. Imagine where we might be now if, as scientists and artists, we refused to put our understanding and imagination to work for corporations, or empires, or salesmen. Imagine poetry as ecology, ecology as poetry. Imagine a science of belonging.

## Steinar Undir Steinahlithum

John Burnside

## With an Introduction

by R. M. M. Crawford

### Introduction

Finding a human settlement, dead but not yet buried, is comparable to discovering an uninterred corpse. The photograph of one such rural Icelandic settlement which I gave to and discussed with John Burnside raises questions which his poem implicitly answers. How did it come to be here and how did it die? What drove people to settle this place and why did they trail 'out through the mist | to try their luck elsewhere'? The abandoned farms of Iceland are but the tip of an historical iceberg. A mere thousand years separate these denuded soils and mire-filled basins from a land that once had forests to the water's edge. The bogs of the North Atlantic isles have within them endless 'households and fiefdoms laid down in the dirt', buried landscapes that testify to the hopes of Norse settlers that set out from their sheltered fjords over a thousand years ago, west over the ocean to wrest a living on oceanic islands from the Hebrides to Iceland. What did they seek? Was it green pastures, where spring came early and where in favoured places sheep and cattle could winter outdoors? Or was it the freedom of new lands, where pioneers could stake out holdings according to their needs? They all must have shared hopes of a better land as they migrated to the seemingly benign bays and dales of the Atlantic seaboard.

All were successful for a time, especially when herds of milking cattle could be over-wintered. Making cheese and butter doubled the energy and protein that meat alone provided from a single beast. Populations grew, and demanded meal which also could be grown, thanks to the hardy bere-barley that flourished on the hillsides despite the Atlantic storms. Not that farming was easy. In the isles of the North Atlantic the coming of spring was always uncertain. Summers were doubtful, and when Hekla erupted harvests failed for years, all the way from Iceland to the Hebrides. The warmth of the ocean that gave them their winter pastures, also brought the rain that washed their soils for twelve months in the year, rendering them even poorer in nutrients. The forests that once clad the hillsides soon vanished and with them the thin soils eroded to deserts of stone and gravel. For these farmers their endeavours, their 'registries of blood', as John Burnside eloquently writes, were 'abandoned to the depths, time without end, | with all they might have been, could they have stayed'.

A people whose population has so often risen, then plunged to the verge of extinction and back, does not readily disappear. These folk may at times have 'trailed out through the mist | to try their luck elsewhere', but they still survive. I find Burnside's poem intensely sympathetic as it conjures their hardness and tenacity to the land with their farms, perched between the mountains and the sea—an awe-inspiring model of human resourcefulness and courage in maintaining a light in the darkness of the boreal night.

## Steinar Undir Steinahlithum

*Nature offers no home.*
*James P. Carse*

Each day the evening was smaller;
and what they left behind, dimmed lamps and sheets,
figments of glass and tinder, what they used
to build these narrow houses on a marsh
they thought had reached a standstill, all the goods
and movables they prized were filmed with peat
for weeks, before they trailed out through the mist
to try their luck elsewhere.
They should have guessed
how earnestly the land conducts itself
and how it longs for stories to contain:
households and fiefdoms laid down in the dirt,

the thumbprint on a harness or a knife,
a cotton doll, a candy-coloured skirt,
gas-stoves and ledgers falling through the earth
as softly as a snowflake falls through light.

The flood they knew from reading in The Book
was sweet with God's intent, and crystal clear:
the quiet man, his face turned to the dark
above his head, his mind a sieve of doubt,
and how his neighbours wondered, when they caught
the smell of fresh-hewn wood, cedar or pine,
where, two by two, the creatures probed the air,
near panic, as they sensed the storm's descent.
The whole house slept on deck, beneath the moon,
the younger children leaning from the Ark
and peering down through fifty feet of rain
to where the grass had filmed with roe and spawn,
another Eden, undeserved, yet claimed
according to a stranger's covenant.

But this was something else: a slighter thing
and less precise: surrender to new mire,
a failure in the science of belonging,
an aberration, fading on the air.
No rainbow issued from the Father's hand,
only the small abandonment of fire
and something hidden, rot-cold in the land:
their loves and fears, their registries of blood,
abandoned to the depths, time without end,
with all they might have been, could they have stayed,
prosperous cities, scribbles in the mud,
unnumbered children, tarnish on a blade.

# Modelling the Universe: Poetry, Science, and the Art of Metaphor

Simon Armitage

> Here are the skies, the planets seven,
> And all the starry train:
> Content you with the mimic heaven,
> And on the earth remain.
>
> A. E. Housman

Housman might have been wrong about the number of planets or he might have been anticipating the debate over the actual status of Pluto, but he did have something to say about imitation, and I'll come back to that 'mimic heaven' later in the day.

At the University where I once taught Creative Writing, the Physics Department offered a course known in the common room as *Astronomy for Poets.* Being somewhat interested in both subjects, I got very curious when I heard about *Astronomy for Poets*, and phoned up the admissions secretary, who sent me a glossy full-colour brochure, much of it written in Day-Glo yellow, like the wording on the packet of an improved biological washing powder. It included the following bullet-points:

- Discover the secrets of pulsars and black holes.
- Follow the evolution of the Universe from the Big Bang.
- Visit a radio telescope and study Hubble space telescope pictures.
- Investigate the births and deaths of stars and the origins of life beyond Headingley.

For anyone not clear about the significance of that last statement, Headingley is a constellation situated towards the outer edges of Leeds, whose points of interest include a concentrated cluster of student and staff accommodation, and the collapsing star of

Yorkshire Cricket Club, still operating as a test match venue but rapidly becoming something of a nebulous object below the tenth magnitude. Mention of it was clearly meant to make the module more attractive and approachable to a wider number of students from across all disciplines. Accordingly, *Astronomy for Poets* was an introductory option for all those with a developing curiosity about the night-sky or a long-standing romantic relationship with it. But more to the point, this was a course for people who couldn't add up. *Astronomy for Poets*, or *Physics 1141 Unravelling the Universe* as it was more properly known, was a hitchhiker's guide to the galaxy to suit all students with no knowledge of calculation. In the top left-hand corner of the handout came the all-important tag line, 'electives without maths'. In other words, 'poet', in this context, was a euphemism for a fairly familiar character. Star-gazer might be a kind way of putting it. Amateur might be another. But above all, the word implied the inability to engage with the subject at the approved and accepted level.

It isn't unusual, as a poet, to be associated with all kinds of scientific incompetence, the most obvious example being the well-travelled notion that poets can't drive. Statistically, I doubt that this has ever been proved, and annual income rather than hand–eye co-ordination might well be the causal factor if it were found to be true. But as someone who drives over twenty thousand miles a year and has three speeding endorsements to his name, it isn't a caricature I recognize. From time to time, it's given me no end of small-minded pleasure to arrive at a venue in Exeter or Canterbury or Glasgow or even Paris by car, only to hear that the organizer is waiting for me at the railway station or airport. Just to indulge in a little discrimination of my own for a moment, it seems that if there really is a technologically and mechanically inept body of people, it's the Arts Administrators. I'm talking about those organizers of readings and festivals, people who Hugo Williams once described as, 'men with eyes red from crying, women with garlands in their hair—they have just taken over from someone who committed suicide, or are trying to pass the job on to someone whose sanity is still intact.'[1] It's the Arts Administrators, who, under the flimsy pretext of owning a current driving licence, have threatened the lives of many a poet during the short journey from the station to the venue, usually in a borrowed car with windows steamed over through the heat of embarrassment or nervousness.

Coming back briefly to Leeds University, the School of English has a long-established and well-respected Icelandic Studies Department, which as well as teaching some of the oldest literature in the world offers a module in Icelandic Language. One of the staff from that faculty told me that two students from the Maths Department turned up one year and expressed an interest in the course, but were discouraged after the first session when they were presented with something called a 'reading list'. Rather than text-books or even dictionaries, it contained the titles of a couple of dozen books of a literary nature—novels, poetry, and the like. It came as a big surprise that such reading could actually play a part in the understanding of an academic subject. In fact they were more than surprised—they were suspicious. I understand they scurried away across the quad, or the precinct as it might more accurately be described, to the safety of their algebraic equations.

Presumably not all scientists think of poetry as ineffectual, effete, and useless. And it's likely that the bedtime reading of maths students extends far beyond Pi to 30,000 places. The perception that all things mathematical must express themselves as a number must be a great frustration to mathematicians; it's the same for poets whose works are expected to add up to a single and precise meaning. And although I've begun with anecdotes that suggest friction between science and the arts, what I want to go on to suggest is that poetry and science, for all their perceived differences, might well be attempting to accomplish the same thing and through remarkably similar means. And because I'm a writer, I want to do this by drawing on further parables from personal history.

I was ten or eleven when a gang of us found a tractor tyre on the moor and decided to roll it down into the village and burn it. We were Pagans back then, or it was bonfire night. In the poem, I tell of how the tyre gained an unstoppable momentum as it careered down the road towards the village, and how we lost sight of it as it headed for destruction and carnage. But when we arrived in the village, the tyre was nowhere to be seen. Nobody had even heard of it. And because science—or what knew of it at the time—had failed us, we were left to invent some other explanation.

Being more in tune with the feel of things
than science and facts, we knew that the tyre
had travelled too fast for its size and mass,
and broken through some barrier of speed,
outrun the act of being driven, steered,
and at that moment gone beyond itself
towards some other sphere, and disappeared.

I suppose what I'm trying to convey at the end of the poem is the sense of endless possibility that comes naturally to all children, just as it powers the imagination of most poets. At age ten or eleven, if a tyre mysteriously evaporates into nothing, the laws of the universe aren't suddenly thrown into confusion—it's perfectly acceptable. I'm not advocating a belief in fairy stories, mumbo jumbo, or even magic, but I am carrying a torch for that time of life when instinct and intuition still hold sway over logic, reason, and law. And I'm putting my faith in a way of describing events in terms of how they feel, metaphorically, rather than giving an incident its scientific sub-title. Science, it seems to me, is besotted with the issue of prediction. The possibility of an event happening again on the grounds that it has happened before in the same circumstances. Poetry might seem to be in conflict with that position, since it goes out of its way to describe every occasion in a new and fresh and surprising way. But in fact it attempts the same thing, albeit through sensation rather than understanding. The reaction a poem provokes is presumably a response by chemical and electrical components within the body to a set of external stimuli. There are, presumably, an infinite number of ways of describing how a large, inanimate object such as a tyre can go missing, and presumably and infinite number of reactions. But a successful poem brings about a kind of animal comprehension rather than its theoretical explanation, and comprehension comes from a common pool of experience. Some of us hope to remain open to that type of perception.

School is the place where very quickly we are shown how to predict the energies and forces of this world, and where possibility is sidelined into the shunting-yard of literature and art. I've rewritten many of my experiences in the physics lab or the chemistry lab not to the point of fiction but to the point where they have started to make sense. It wasn't long after the episode with the tyre when our eccentric science teacher asked myself and another boy to go outside and measure the size of the human voice. The school had very little in the way of scientific equipment, which was just as well because we weren't sure whether we needed a tape recorder or a tape measure. In the end, we decided to start shouting at each other but at the same time moving further and further apart. The size of the human voice would be the distance between us when we could no longer hear each other. Unfortunately, the village we lived in wasn't very big, and at some point the other boy fell over the edge. Into Lancashire, maybe. At least, that's how I remember it after almost thirty years, and it's when the science (or what little of it was present) breaks down that I try to get poetry to rush in and fill the gap. They say that every sound ever made is still reverberating through the universe, however quietly and however distant.

### The Shout

We went out
into the school yard together, me and the boy
whose name and face

I don't remember. We were testing the range
of the human voice:
he had to shout for all he was worth,

I had to raise an arm
from across the divide to signal back
that the sound had carried.

He called from over the park—I lifted an arm.
Out of bounds,
he yelled from the end of the road,

from the foot of the hill,
from beyond the look-out post of Fretwell's Farm—
I lifted an arm.

He left town, went on to be twenty years dead
with a gunshot hole
in the roof of his mouth, in Western Australia.

Boy with the name and face I don't remember,
you can stop shouting now, I can still hear you.

I was sixteen when I tried to measure the 'swing' of a cricket ball by catapulting it into the air using a length of wooden gutter-pipe and the spring from a second-hand chest expander. My first mistake was to try and embark on an O Level Physics project that did not meet with the approval of Mr J, head of physics, who would have preferred me to measure the conductivity of pencil lead. A low mark was the end result—twenty-two out of a hundred. Mr J, tall, bearded and ginger, said to me, 'What are you going to do about it? Cry?' I think I probably was, until he said that. My second mistake was to confuse a serious scientific investigation with cricketing folklore, such as the importance of rubbing one side of the ball on the inside of the thigh between deliveries. If only I'd have listened to Fred Trueman, the Yorkshire and England fast bowler, and his comment, 'We didn't have metaphor in my day. We didn't beat about the bush.'

I was seventeen when I measured, this time with the blessing of Mr J, the conductivity of lead graphite across a range of pencils for my A Level Physics dissertation. Result—about sixty percent I think. 'What did I tell you?' said Mr J, tall, bearded and ginger, prediction and outcome being two of his principal concerns. I failed the exam in the summer.

I was twenty-one I wrote my first poem about science, or using science as its subject I should say, in which I reflected on some of the happenings in the school science lab and its hinterland. Colne Valley High School had an electric fence, not just for keeping its pupils within the school grounds but for stopping the herd of school cattle coming marauding across the tennis courts and the bus bays. It was common knowledge that if a long line of kids held hands and one of them took hold of the fence, the person at the far end of the line was the one to get the electric shock. I say it was common knowledge, but most people found out the hard way. Then there was the Van de Graaff generator, which I remember as some huge belt and ball arrangement for the generating of industrial quantities of static electricity. Any person touching it became a local sub-station in their own right. It also allowed its supercharged subjects the opportunity of shaking hands with their worst enemy and blowing them away into the middle of next week. Then there was the gold-leaf meter, which measured ... what? ... microscopic amounts of static, and registered the charge through a strip of gold-leaf that curled upwards, erotically, when stimulated. Then there were the two pupils who went their own way through junior and secondary school, and who are the main personnel of the poem. Names have been changed, not just to protect the innocent but because not everything in this world comes with the right label attached to it. Part of the poet's job is to make those adjustments when necessary. A very glib explanation of the poem is that I wondered if Newton's Third Law—that every action has an opposite and equal reaction—could be applied to a social situation as well as a scientific one.

### Newton's Third Law

By the second year they were worlds away,
teasing knots from each other's hair at break
instead of baiting the school's mascot pig
or hauling first years through the long-jump pit.

They were peas in a pod, two blue-eyed blondes
who cocked a snook at Phyllis and Simone
as they were unaffectionately dubbed,
and held hands on the furthest playing fields

till the third year came and they shed their shells.
Once, two fifth years, having heard what they were
had them brace the back of a human chain
that was poised to touch the electric fence.

They jumped like salmon in a landing-net
but must have kept the taste. Geordie Jobson,
Head of Physics, burst a lung the day he
caught them through the prep-room keyhole, testing

their charge on the gold-leaf meter after
kissing the Van de Graaff generator.

And I was thirty-something when I found myself in a small, back-street shop in Stockport buying a telescope. It led to a series of poems called *The Whole of the Sky*, eighty-eight set-pieces, one for every constellation, although my motivation in embarking on that series had as much to do with the process of creativity as it did astronomy. I wanted to write a poem every day, to try and get to a point where writing poetry felt very natural—a first language—rather than the stuttering, stammering affair it can become if left for too long. My technique was to select a constellation, absorb as much scientific and mythological information as I could during the hours of daylight, then study it through the telescope after dark, weather and latitude permitting. I'd sleep on it, then come downstairs next morning and begin the poem, trying to work with the first image or idea that came to mind. The closest way of describing the technique is to recall the psychology exercise in which the analyst speaks a word and the subject responds with the first thing that comes into his or her head. I wanted it to be as instinctive as that, practitioner and patient at the same time. One other thing about the creative side of this project: I'd recently started playing the guitar and it suddenly occurred to me that I was attempting to make intricate shapes and movements with my left hand for the first time in my life. The fingers were forming patterns, like constellations. Before that, the dumb thing that dangled off the bottom of my left arm like a mitten on a piece of string had only been engaged in forking food towards the area of the mouth and steadying the top half of a cricket-bat handle. If different sides of the body are controlled by different areas of the brain, maybe I was opening up some parts of the grey matter that had previously been closed—like rooms in a mansion locked with the key on the inside, as Ted Hughes would say. Maybe it is possible to regenerate some of the circuitry in the right hemisphere of the mind, where other communication facilities might be packaged. Furthermore, many of the constellations include animal forms, and another part of my thinking at the time was to try and get much closer to such beasts than is possible by visiting a zoo or taking a safari in Kenya via CD ROM. I also wanted to initiate some kind of relationship with the animal kingdom that extended beyond the natural history version or the kind of animal-intimacy that we're most familiar with—that of carnivory. Those earliest animal paintings on the walls of caves are too esoteric, to my mind, to be simple doodles by bored and increasingly dextrous Homo-sapiens. They imply the first acts of self-consciousness ever undertaken on the planet, and their design and execution indicates an enquiry into the nature of the universe through art and ritual. Resonance with the world, rather than measurement of it, is what those paintings suggest. I suppose I wanted some of the constellation poems to be ritualistic in the same way—in the writing of them and in their reading.

The stars have always been the parish of poets. It would be boring to run through the number of poets who have made the heavens the object of their writing, and quicker to say that very few authors throughout the history of poetry have failed to include the stars and planets within their repertoire. Those points of light in their minutely adjusted positions have been part of the human ceiling since we slimed our way out of the water. Their patterns have been imprinted in our minds since the morning we opened our eyes, and have always represented the far limit of our consciousness, the edge of our ability, and the place of our dreams. Their designs are encoded in our brains like pictograms in a prehistoric alphabet, part and parcel of our subconscious. The stars themselves remain gloriously unavailable except as things to look towards, guess at, and wish on.

I wouldn't go as far as to say that in writing the poems I was trying to free the sky from the strait-jacket of science, or liberate the stars from the flea-circus of science fiction, or uncouple the buckled wheel of the ecliptic from the axle of the zodiac. Neither was I joining Whitman in his staged walk-out, 'rising and gliding' out of the lecture room into the 'mystical moist night air' to look up 'in perfect silence at the stars'. But one of contemporary poetry's greatest attributes is the ability to make points about the universal out of the particular, and in gazing into deep space, who can help but be ordered back to the fine detail of their own life. And that's exactly where I wanted to be, amongst the rummage and jumble of everyday living. Another thing I realized very quickly after pointing the telescope into the night was the great paradox of sky-watching. Looking into deep space isn't at all futuristic. To look into space is to look into history, and that's exactly how I wanted to see things, the modern world illuminated by billion-year-old light. To quote Ted Hughes again, 'The laws of Creation are the only literally rational things, and we don't yet know what they are. The nearest we can come to rational thinking is to stand respectfully, hat in hand, before this Creation, exceedingly alert for a new word.' And this is what I was trying to do I suppose, standing outside a cottage on the Yorkshire moors in the dead of winter, under a crystal clear sky with the door of the universe wide open, trying to peer as far back as I could. In my case, though, I had my hat firmly pulled down over my ears, not just because of frost-bite nibbling at the lobes, but because the words I was listening for were going to come from inside, a kind of echo-sounding from the deep of the mind, and I didn't want those words to be drowned out by the traffic. To read the increasingly flaccid and flowery

*National Geographic* is to appreciate that there are fewer and fewer territories to explore, stick a flag in and spoil. The regions that remain elusive are usually reckoned to be the far reaches of space, the far depths of the ocean, and the inner levels of matter somewhere below the subatomic. I would add to that list a fourth region, which is the dense, elastic knot of the brain, with its infinite number of threads, connections, crossovers, and ties, very few of them unravelled or stretched. Perhaps it is poets, rather than neurologists, who are best equipped for that journey.

The 'mimic heaven' was how Housman put it. Well over two-thousand years before him, when Aristotle used the word mimetics, he was talking about humanity's love of mimicry—the inclination to practise it, as well as our facility for such aping. He used the word with specific reference to poetry, and at some fundamental level, I believe his thesis still hold true, that poetry mimics the universe, and that the action of a poem intends to mirror the action of life as we understand it. I also believe this to be true of science. What science does is ventriloquise the universe in a very specific and logical way, though its main method is essentially a poetic one, that of metaphor. When Eliot described the evening 'spread out against the sky I Like a patient etherized upon a table' he conjured up an image of dusk which is full of connotations and sub-conscious connections yet one which appeals and makes fundamental sense to almost everyone who reads it. When Mr J, head of physics, described a model to explain the way electricity functions, he was doing pretty much the same thing. Electricity, he said, was a ball running down a slope; voltage was the height of the hill and therefore the steepness of the slope; an increase in amperage was an increased number of balls, and resistance was friction caused by the surface of the slope and its degree of roughness. Whatever gave energy to the system, such as a battery or generator, was a little man collecting the balls at the bottom of the slope and running back to the top to let them go again. This analogy might have been personal to him and shared only with us as a group, but essentially he was following the practice that physics has adopted over centuries—that of mimetics. There is no such thing as an atom. But in about 400 BC there was something like an invisibly small particle without sweetness, bitterness, or colour, according to Democritus. By the nineteenth century there was something that looked like a billiard ball, and by 1913 there was something that looked like a scale model of the solar system. By 1916 there was something that looked like the drawing of a clutch of ant eggs orbited by half a dozen flies, and by 1926 there was something that looked like a soft-focus target with fuzzy outer zones and a darker, harder bull's eye. And this is what science is—an ongoing refinement of metaphor. There is no such thing as a molecular structure, only a little model of Ping-Pong balls held together by pipe-cleaners to help us believe in it. Not statements of fact, but examples and illustrations that are comfortable and acceptable and convenient and comprehensible to the human brain. There is no such thing as nuclear fission, but there is a process by which certain phenomena can be made fathomable and by which its actions might be predicted, utilised, and explained, and that process is language. This is what science does; like poetry, it deals in likeness, similitude, and equivalence. If you're gambling with the world and its actions, science gives you better odds, because its logic is linear, whereas the logic of poetry is radial, or at its very best, entirely spherical. Life, as we know, imitates art, and science, I believe, imitates life. I don't suggest that as a hierarchy of importance, but to reinforce the interconnectedness of the two disciplines through the intermediary of the human presence. In placing this kind of importance on poetry, I'm asking it to come forward and be congratulated for its achievements, but also to take responsibility for the error of its ways. Science didn't take man to the moon. It might have worked out the trigonometry, but it was a poetic dream that propelled us into the heavens to set foot on the lunar mass which has pushed and pulled at us from before we had eyes to see it. But science didn't drop the bomb on Hiroshima either. It was a poetic nightmare-vision of hell-fire discharged into the infrastructure and flesh of an unsuspecting city that opened the bomb-hatch over the Ota river delta on 6 August 1945, even if science guided it down to its target. And the ego of poetry erected the World Trade Centre, just as a suicidal glimpse of poetic paradise brought it down again. Poetry proposed the existence of the DNA double helix with its eye for detail, and poetry postulated the theory of relativity with its penchant for cryptic crosswords, and poetry produced the first light bulb because of its fear of the dark, and poetry learned how to create fire from friction because of its grumbling dislike of the cold and its fascination with the supernatural effects of combustion. By the same token, poetry's mean-streak designed the rack and the whip and the cattle-prod and the stun-gun, and the devil in it pumped poison gas into the Tokyo underground, and its rhetoric took a million people into the killing fields, and its sense of worth went about slaughtering indigenous populations across massive proportions of the globe. Wondering if there could be any more poetry after Auschwitz doesn't take into account the part that poetry played in the visualizing of a holocaust. Genocide is not simply a meeting place between biology and calculus, it is conceptual art of a kind we would prefer not to think about.

But despite arguing the case for similarities between poetry and science, and for a kind of wholeness of approach, I'm not proposing a call for unification. I'm not going to say that nuclear physicists and slim-volumists everywhere should throw their arms around each other like long-lost Siamese twins separated by the scalpel of Hippocrates. As someone who believes first and foremost in difference and variation, I uphold the right of those who want to make sense of the world through statistics and calculation to the same extent as I defend the practice of exploring the circumstances of life through words and phrases. And in certain other respects, poetry and science must keep their distance, even go their separate ways. For example, the apparently exponential developments in technology over the past fifty years have left poetry with an important, adversarial role, that of getting beyond the high gloss and instant gratification of our contemporary world. The dominance of electronic means over mechanical and the preference for digital rather than analogue devices has eventually put the installation, maintenance, and even operation of many everyday contraptions beyond the understanding of most of their users. The most obvious example is the computer. If the new Packard Bell utterly refuses to comply with instructions, there are relatively few of us in this world with the know-how or the qualifications or the appropriate insurance policy to try and put it right. The same wasn't true of the abacus or the pen. A friend of mine recently bought a new MG, which upon closer inspection turns out to have nothing in the boot and nothing under the bonnet. All the workings are slung underneath, and the only toolkit supplied with the vehicle is a telephone number to call in case of difficulty, whereupon the makers offer a replacement vehicle while the other is spirited away to be mended. Keep up with the warranty payments and don't meddle—that seems to be the message. In that world, I think the role of poetry is one of insubordination; not to be seduced or bewildered or fobbed-off by technology, but to challenge it as the thing that can make us, if we're not careful, sloppy, accepting, lazy, subservient, cosseted, and cut off. Language can provide a bridge with the vitality of the world, keep open that channel of communication when double glazing, central heating, screen savers, and pot-noodles conspire to disconnect us from it. Poetry can be part of the campaign to stop reality becoming entirely virtual.

# Circadian

John Glenday

## With an Introduction

by Eric Priest

## Introduction

Joining John Glenday for lunch was a real privilege, which was much more a meeting of minds than a clash of cultures. I described what it is like for me to go about making scientific discoveries, and he did the same for constructing poems. It was amazing to find how close the two activities are.

John seemed to have a keen awareness of and care for the world around him and a desire to understand what is going on in depth and then to wrestle with ways of communicating his insights in new and pithy ways. For me as a theoretical solar physicist there is a strong desire to understand the enormous complexity and subtlety of the many processes going on in the Sun.

Stimulated by observations of the Sun, lots of ideas are continually floating around in my conscious and subconscious mind, and occasionally, when I wake up in the morning or am walking in the hills or working in the garden, one of them will take on a life of its own and crystallize. I then know in general terms the way I want to go, but have to spend many weeks discovering the detailed steps, using all the skills and mathematical techniques at my disposal—and often I will be led in unexpected directions on my journey to a fuller understanding. Indeed, the creative process for John seemed very similar, including the initial spark of inspiration, the hard work (often taking a couple of months!), and the sense of the poem taking on its own life.

Reading John's poems afterwards was also a great delight. His words are carefully weighed and full of new and subtle meanings, often surprising and only revealing themselves after pondering and re-reading. Many of them are concerned with life and death and with time.

So I waited expectantly for a poem to arrive by email—and was not in the least disappointed. It is clearly in John's style and has many of the common features of his earlier poems. At first I was surprised at how unscientific it is (wilfully so, as John remarked), but I do like it a lot. The Sun, not even mentioned in the poem by name but clearly its theme, has captivated me for my whole scientific career. The poem has a much more positive feel than many others that John has written in response to the real difficulties of modern life. While not denying the reality of those hardships, this poem reflects to me the importance of humanity and the daily support we are given.

The poem is short—but the words are precious and economical and I enjoyed savouring the depths of meaning and implication (not unlike the mathematical equations that describe the Sun). It is a combination of a love poem and a religious poem, with a hint of myth thrown in. I liked the idea of the one who is always there even though not seen and the thought of being ferried back to the beginning, to the start of a new day or to the source of life.

## Circadian

Rise over me
in the morning;

lay yourself under me
as the darkness breaks;

then ferry me like death,
like sleep, like memory,

back through the hidden
workings of the night

to a place where everything
lies buried, and begins.

# Astronomy and Poetry

## Jocelyn Bell Burnell

> The radiance of that star that leans on me
> Was shining years ago. The light that now
> Glitters up there my eye may never see,
> And so the time lag teases me with how
>
> Love that loves now may not reach me until
> Its first desire is spent. The star's impulse
> Must wait for eyes to claim it beautiful
> And love arrived may find us somewhere else.
>
> Elizabeth Jennings

In spite of a good education I came to appreciate music late in life, and to appreciate poetry even later. The turning point can be identified: I had done a talk on astronomy for a group of women, showing slides, explaining the size and scale of the universe, and how long it took light to travel the huge distances. Afterwards, Jennifer, a friend in the audience, gave me a copy of Elizabeth Jennings's poem 'Delay', and its power and its appropriateness immediately hit me.

I have given many talks on astronomy to lay audiences; I believe I make the subject accessible, explain things clearly, and hold the audience's interest. In such talks it is easy to play the wow, gee-whiz element of astronomy, it is easy to raise the hairs on the back of the neck talking about our place in the universe and the origin and future evolution of the universe. And there are photos of many wonderfully beautiful galaxies, nebulae, and groups of stars to give visual impact. As a woman I probably seem more approachable and less threatening than a male speaker, and I certainly get lots of very interesting questions on all manner of topics after each talk (provided the Chair does not get twitchy and close it down!). To draw others, especially women, into science, I would like to give fair space to the human side of science, but lack vehicles with which to do so in these talks. So I have always been left a little unsatisfied by the exclusively scientific content of my own talks.

Elizabeth Jennings's poem (which opens her 2002 Carcanet *New Collected Poems*) is not only powerful and appropriate, it is brief as well—just eight lines long. As such I could quote it in its entirety in one of my talks. And more and more I have done so, and included other non-scientific pieces of writing in my talks. I suspect the more 'nerdish' members of my audience do not know what to make of these pieces but, consistently, female audience members will come up to me afterwards and speak appreciatively of their inclusion. Such material should help the non-scientists in the audience relate to the topic, may woo those who are suspicious of science or scientists, and demonstrate that astronomy is part of our cultural heritage.

From those eight lines has grown a whole new interest, and a new dimension to life. I started 'collecting' poetry with an astronomical theme to use in my talks, and found it was speaking to something in me. The collecting acquired its own impetus. I compared my collection with those of others, and at tense times (such as waiting for the outcome of a job interview) when I could not concentrate on work, found that the poetry soothed and steadied me. I have always loved words and have always appreciated the richness and diversity of English vocabulary. Rhythm has also always appealed to me—expressed usually through dancing—so perhaps it is no surprise that poetry appeals.

The collecting has been quite challenging. Some poets (Robert Frost, Carl Sandburg, Diane Ackerman, for example) frequently write on astronomical themes, but the majority appear only to write one or two poems, and my impression is that those one or two are rarely included in general anthologies or selections. Word of mouth and casual references have led to research on the World Wide Web and the tracking down of many poems (blessings be to Google!). Tracking down the full reference has been as much work again!

Science is great—I would have difficulty living without it, and yet I could not live by science alone. There are other dimensions to life, other ways of thinking and behaving besides the scientific that ideally I need in my life in order to feel reasonably rounded. I like poetry because of its complementary nature, because it is so different from doing science. In saying this I do not want to give the impression that science is totally aseptic, mechanistic, and lacking in imagination. I have long argued that the scientific method as currently taught to our students underplays the role of imagination, synthesis, and creativity; we focus on how hypotheses and models, once created, are tested, and do not give enough attention to how they are created. Scientists do not always recognize the imagination needed to be a good scientist!

I also appreciate poetry for its healing properties, and clearly am not alone in this. It was striking how, in the days following September 11, people were turning to poetry, sharing quotations with each other, displaying snippets of verse and using them as memorials. But what is this healing? I believe it is more than giving comfort, in the sense of easing or making comfortable (although it does that too). It is closer to the original meaning of comfort—making strong. It strengthens because it recognizes and articulates hurt that many of us experience but may not be able to express. That recognition, that confirmation that others have similar experience, is reassuring. This is the start of the healing.

Behind the complementary nature of science and poetry there is of course a divide. My computer's 'spell checker' symbolizes that for me. Spell checker does not like abbreviations like 'o'er', it does not recognize classical illusions, it prefers a capital letter after a line break, and it desires verbs at regular intervals. It is methodical, consistent, and logical—and most of the time I am grateful for that. But we lose a lot if we can only express ourselves in spell-checker-approved language; we lose the less tangible, the phrasing and breathing, the rhythms and urge and patterns and shape, some of the allusions and illusions, indeed the very power of poetry. Poetry addresses the heart as well as the head, the emotional as well as the rational, and seems to me to do so better than prose. It reaches where no other words can reach; and the assiduous spell checker is blind to its nuances.

Modern astronomy started after World War II, when technologies such as radar and rocketry, developed during the war, were applied afterwards in the expanding field of astronomy. Our vision widened as the new astronomies, especially radio and X-ray, enabled us to see not just in visible light, but in other wavebands as well. Radar quickly became radio astronomy, often using actual radar dishes and reflectors as well as many of the same techniques. In Britain V2 rockets developed into the Skylark rocket programme, through which small pieces of equipment could be given brief flights above the Earth's atmosphere. The rockets then became the launch vehicles for artificial satellites. These launch vehicles opened up the far infra-red, ultra-violet, X-ray, and gamma-ray astronomy bands, which are normally blocked for us by the earth's atmosphere. The intellectual stimulus was huge. It was fuelled in the late 1950s by the Soviet launch of the first artificial satellite, Sputnik, the realization by the West that we had fallen behind, and the consequent emphasis on science.

I have taken 1950 as the start date for this essay. Since then astronomers have discovered quasars and pulsars, black holes and brown dwarfs, dark matter and dark energy. We have come to accept that there was a Big Bang, and have detected microwave radiation left over from that explosion. The size of the universe is appreciated (although we still have trouble envisaging such large scales) and we have an understanding of how stars are born, live and die. We can predict the future of our Sun, although are on less certain ground when we try to predict the future of the Universe.

Gathering and reflecting on one hundred and twenty or so post-1950 astronomy poems it has become apparent to me that while radio telescopes feature in several, none of the other new wavebands do. X-ray astronomy which, arguably, has had as much impact on astrophysics does not get a mention, although objects like black holes discovered by that branch of astronomy do. Why the distinction? Perhaps it is because radio telescopes are on the ground while most of the telescopes that operate in the other new wavebands have to be launched into space. Furthermore, radio telescopes are frequently big structures, like Jodrell Bank, and highly visible, whereas telescopes to be launched by rocket have to be compact (or fold up compactly). We are familiar with tuning into the radio waves broadcast by a particular station, but understand less well that similarly we can tune into other wavebands. So perhaps the choice of subject for poetry reflects visibility and familiarity.

Though their work predates the period covered by this essay, it is worth remarking that Thomas Hardy (1840–1928) and Robert Frost were keen amateur astronomers, each possessing a telescope. Highly developed skills in poetry and in astronomy are rarely found in the same person, but there have been some noteworthy familial links between poets and astronomers. Robinson Jeffers had a brother,

Hamilton, who was an astronomer at Lick Observatory, California, and Hilda Doolittle (1886–1961) was the daughter of an astronomer; her father was Director of the Flower Observatory, University of Pennsylvania. Percival Lowell, the astronomer who founded the Lowell Observatory in Arizona, was a distant cousin of Robert Lowell (1917–77), but died the year before the poet was born. The dedication of Gwyneth Lewis's (1959– ) book *Zero Gravity* reads, in part, 'to commemorate the voyage of my cousin Joe Tanner and the crew of Space Shuttle STS-82 to repair the Hubble Space Telescope'. Rebecca Elson (1960–99) was of that rare class—a professional astronomer who wrote poetry. Why, one wonders, are there not more Rebecca Elsons? I know scientists who paint, sculpt, dance, sing, play musical instruments, and one or two who write science fiction, but Rebecca apart, none who write poetry (or will admit to it). Why? Most of my collection of astronomical poetry is written by non-scientists.

When I first read it, I thought Frederick Seidel's poem 'The New Cosmology' was referring to a major new array of millimetre radio telescopes about to be built in Chile (called ALMA—the Atacama Large Millimetre Array). However, having checked the date of publication (1989) I suspect Seidel is referring to an earlier Swedish–European telescope. His poem will get even better with time, for ALMA will have many 'dishes' and will look more of an invasion, perched on a high plateau. One plan is to have the telescopes arranged in a spiral pattern on the ground, which will look intriguing to God or anyone else viewing from above.

> Above the Third World, looking down on a fourth:
> *Life's* aerial photograph of a new radio telescope
> Discolouring an inch of mountainside in Chile,
> A Martian invasion of dish receivers.
> The tribes of Israel in their tents
> Must have looked like this to God—
> A naïve stain of wildflowers on a hill,
> A field of ear trumpets listening for Him,
> Stuck listening to space like someone blind . . .[1]

The poem concerns the imaginable and the unimaginable, and how the latter is ousting the former; it is about how our growing knowledge is demolishing myth, and there is a touch of the classic science and religion debate here too. Seidel struggles to take all these in, but gives up and lapses into silence. Silence is an appropriate response in such circumstances. While it is always nice to have a positive, well-turned ending, an unresolved, open, searching end is nearer where we, the astronomers, are. Arguably it is where society should be too.

The theme of listening is one which might well appeal to poets tuned in to the precise calibrations of language, but radio astronomers also 'listen'. Diane Ackerman puts this elegantly in her poem 'We Are Listening':

> As our metal eyes wake
> to absolute night
> where whispers fly
> from the beginning of time
> we cup our ears to the heavens.
> We are listening
>
> on the volcanic rim of Flagstaff
> and in the fields beyond Boston,
> in a great array that blooms
> like coral from the desert floor,
> on highwire webs patrolled
> by computer spiders in Puerto Rico.
>
> We are listening for a sound
> beyond us, beyond sound,
>
> searching for a lighthouse
> in the breakwaters of our uncertainty
> an electronic murmur,
> a bright, fragile *I am.*
>
> Small as tree frogs
> staking out one end
> of an endless swamp,
> we are listening
> through the longest night
> we imagine, which dawns
> between the life and times of stars.[2]

What wonderful use of language, and what fun for the professional astronomer to be able to recognize and see afresh each of the telescopes she alludes to! The somewhat Churchillian 'We are listening | on the volcanic rim of Flagstaff | and in the fields beyond Boston', with its echoes of his proclamation 'We will fight them . . .', contrasts wonderfully with the faintness of the whisper of a signal that is being searched for. Diane Ackerman writes confidently and authoritatively on astronomical subjects. As a Ph.D. student at Cornell she wanted to work with the arts and the sciences, so on her doctoral committee had both a poet and the astronomer Carl Sagan. She later worked as a researcher for his 'Cosmos' TV series. The arts–science divide is not something she admits to, and her work combines superb imagery, excellent use of words, a sense of wonder and scientific accuracy. She is perhaps best known for an early book of astronomical poetry, *The Planets: A Cosmic Pastoral*, which included accurate and up-to-date material on the planets, often presented in a novel way (see, for example, her 'Saturn').[3] We don't have to listen that hard to hear the existential questions. Ackerman does not seem too bothered by them however, but is prepared to work with them rather than strive to have dominion over them and find 'solutions' that might be premature. As Rilke said in a letter of advice to a young poet, she is prepared to live the questions.

Miroslav Holub's 'Night at the Observatory' contains one of the earliest references to a radio astronomy observatory. It forms an atmospheric background for a courting couple. Gradually the 'camera' pulls back from the couple to note their surroundings, and then pulls back even further to consider the on-going-ness of the universe, independent of life. For me the most telling line in Holub's poem is 'Above the fields the wires hissed like iguanas.'[4] A purely descriptive line, what is the attraction? It is the identification, the articulation of something I knew but had never managed to express—for me that is a large part of what poetry is about. As one who spent most of her graduate student years in a cold, windy field surrounded by the posts and wires that formed a radio telescope (and did some courting there), I can affirm that that is exactly how it sounded. Neither the sound, nor the phrase, is an obvious one, so he must have been writing out of experience; I wonder which observatory it was that he visited? But you and I are dated, Miroslav. They no longer make radio telescopes from strands of wire—they've gone sophisticated, up-market, with dish-like structures, and it doesn't sound the same!

'Jodrell Bank' by Patric Dickinson starts confrontationally, with echoes of the Old Testament God's challenge to Job 'Where were you when I laid the foundations of the earth?'[5] The poem is somewhat anti-science, or at least directed against the arrogance of scientists. Dickinson feels that science has blown our comfortable world apart, destroyed our myths, and, in presenting 'spaces beyond the span | Of our myths', revealed our loneliness for what it is.[6] In certain ways his poem continues a note heard sometimes in Victorian poetry where astronomy could be seen as what Tennyson called one of the 'Terrible Muses', but other more recent poets have sensed an excitement in the science and its revelations.[7] The radio astronomy theme is continued by Adrienne Rich in her 'Planetarium'. This poem has the lengthy subtitle 'Thinking of Caroline Herschel (1750–1848), astronomer, sister of William; and others', and I have to declare an interest, since I suspect that as the female radio astronomer who discovered pulsars I might be one of the 'others'. This poem was apparently written in 1968, the year the discovery of pulsars was announced, so it was based on very topical material. It is said to have been written following a visit to a planetarium, hence the title.

Heartbeat of the pulsar
Heart sweating through my body
The radio impulse
pouring in from Taurus

I am bombarded yet I stand
I have been standing all my life in the
direct path of a battery of signals
the most accurately transmitted most
untranslatable language in the universe
. . . I am an instrument in the shape
of a woman trying to translate pulsations
into images for the relief of the body
and the reconstruction of the mind.[8]

There is a progression through the poem from the first two lines, 'A woman in the shape of a monster | a monster in the shape of a woman' to 'an instrument in the shape of a woman', and from 'a woman' and 'she' to 'I'. It moves from holding at a distance women doing unusual or peculiar things like science (monsters) to affirming them at the end; arguably it moves from a male perspective to a female one. Given the author's feminist track record, one half expects this; however, 1968 was early in the feminist movement, even in the USA.

Linking Caroline Herschel with a monster has other resonances for me. I was one of several female astronomers trying to ensure that at least one female was included in a series of lectures about famous astronomers; we proposed Caroline Herschel. We lost the argument, on that occasion, because it was judged the only surviving picture of her was not flattering—she looked ugly! I would agree; it is not a flattering picture. As a young girl she had been told by her father that since she was not pretty and the family was not rich, she should not expect to marry and should resign herself to being housekeeper to one of her brothers. A woman of lesser character would have curled up and died. She became housekeeper to her brother William. On nights when he was away on business and she was left on her own, she used a telescope he had given her to search the sky for comets, discovering eight in total! Living at a time when women were not always recognized, she was eclipsed by the male astronomers in her family, her brother William, and his son John.

She has been rehabilitated in recent years, and is being written back into history, as well as into verse. I am reassured that this process is an ongoing one, for not only is there Adrienne Rich's poem about Caroline Herschel, Jennifer Clement has a recent one too, 'William Herschel's Sister, Caroline, Discovers Eight Comets'. Adrienne Rich implies that the body senses the signals from space; Jennifer Clement is more direct: 'I feel the dust tails | hear them rustle | in my fringed sleeves.'[9] More humorously, as we shall soon note, Michael Longley picks up similar vibrations in his poem 'Halley's comet'.

At least since Sappho and Hesiod poets have responded to the stars, but there are two astronomical phenomena which are so spectacular that they will grab even the modern, academic astrophysicists and get them out there, under the sky, looking upwards. These phenomena are comets (well, some of them!), and total eclipses of the Sun. Only if one can travel each time to that small patch of the earth where there will be totality does one see many total solar eclipses; for most of us they are rarely or never experienced. So, not surprisingly, there are few poems about eclipses; however, Simon Armitage has written a complete poetic drama, 'Eclipse', set in Cornwall at the time of the 1999 solar eclipse.[10]

Comets are more widely seen, and can be wonderfully spectacular; they have found their way into contemporary poetry. Halley's comet is a periodic comet, returning every seventy-six years, and is the subject of several poems. Its 1910 apparition was remarkable and remembered by many. Its 1986 apparition, especially for those of us in the northern hemisphere, was extremely disappointing. As Sheenagh Pugh puts it in 'The Comet-Watcher's Perspective', 'look as he might, it was just a blue smudge.'[11]

The poor show in 1986 to a degree wrong-footed people like the poet Kenneth Rexroth who, having seen 'that long-haired star', the glorious comet in 1910 (when Rexroth was aged five), pictures its next return. But whether it actually happened like that or not, his description of a great comet, 'its plume over water | Dribbling on the liquid night', is magnificent. At the same time he confronts his own mortality (the theme is similar to that in Hardy's 'The Comet at Yell'ham') and there is an interesting mix of the cosmic perpetual and the human temporal. Rexroth's poem is addressed to his children, and by having children he is saved the full agony of his own death and can ponder the continuation of the human race as 'vessels' of a 'billion-year-long | River'.[12] Where Patric Dickinson sees astronomy as destroying myths, and so as threatening, Rexroth regards it as consonant with great rhythms of the universe which scientists, poets, and all humans may sense, and in which they participate.

Stanley Kunitz, born the same year as Kenneth Rexroth, lived long enough to see both apparitions of Halley's comet, and after the second wrote a charming poem recalling the first. In his 'Halley's Comet' he recalls his boyhood self attending both to his first-grade schoolteacher, Mrs Murphy, writing the words 'Halley's Comet' in chalk on a blackboard, and to her saying that if the comet strayed off course it might smash into the earth; this memory is juxtaposed with the words of a wild preacher who urged the schoolchildren to repent. Kunitz's poem concludes with the boy stealing in secret on to the roof of his parents' house, 'searching the starry sky, | waiting for the world to end'.[13] Again a wonderful picture is drawn—one can just see it happening, and we are reminded of similar 'preachers' who flourished before recent cometary appearances. The poem's whimsical charm fades into sterner stuff in the last few lines when he addresses his dead father, hoping that the father can see the son on the rooftop. It is interesting that Stanley Kunitz, who must have been in his eighties when he wrote this poem, can recall or maybe even still feels the loss (through suicide) of his father at an early age. On the other hand, if one really did believe the world was about to end, a missing father would be more strongly missed. Mother apparently is no use in these circumstances.

Observing what she poignantly calls the 'only-coming-once' of comet Hale-Bopp and drawing lessons for us all from its coming and its going, the poet Gwyneth Lewis writes of how 'It's no accident that *leave* | fails but still tries to rhyme with *love*'.[14] These words are from her 'Zero Gravity: A Space Requiem', written in 1997 while her sister-in-law was dying of cancer and an astronaut cousin was launching into space. This is the kind of juxtaposition that life sometimes sends us, and she rises to the challenge. The poem melds life and love, death and loss, comets and space flight, with a particularly good interplay between the human and the astronomical. In contrast to some other authors, Lewis is drawing upon the transitory nature of the comet. Entitled 'Zero Gravity', her poem nonetheless possesses a *gravitas*, as indicated by the word 'requiem' in its subtitle. Lighter, more beautifully featherlike, is Michael Longley's 'Halley's Comet'. This poem is subtitled 'Homage to Erik Satie', but perhaps 'Teasing Erik Satie' would be nearer the mark! In a poem whose speaker gets drunk, the lines about how 'inside my left nostril | A hair kept buzzing with signals from Halley's comet' give a surreal feel, and one is far from convinced that nothing similar will happen 'for another seventy-six years'![15]

Longley's is a clever, tantalizing piece of writing, with some of the lovely imagery characteristic of this poet. Its light tone may make it relatively unusual among poems dealing with astronomy. Pascal was speaking for many when he said, 'The eternal silence of these infinite spaces frightens me'.[16] Part of this unhappiness comes from an appreciation of how small and insignificant we humans are. Some are depressed by this thought; others look at how large the universe is and are thrilled. William Empson's 'Letter I' not only quotes part of Pascal's statement—'The eternal silence of the infinite spaces'—but also captures some of Pascal's general discomfort. In part this is through the incompleteness of the truncated Pascal quotation, but it is also through the structure of the poem with its uncomfortable seven-line stanzas, the dangling incompleteness of the Pascal quotation emphasized by a clear rhyme pattern that rhymes 'spaces' with 'pointless places' and sees 'galaxies' as 'void'.[17] A sense of anxiety and discomfort is again present in Leo Aylen's poem 'Orbiting Pluto', which addresses several of the issues around space travel. In 'Orbiting Pluto' we hear the voice of one of the first humans to leave our Solar System for another star and its planet. At the point of writing they have reached Pluto, which represents the edge of the known world. Pluto, in 'this last | Beyond of all beyonds', cannot be described as homely, but compared with the long, black, empty coldness ahead it is.[18] The poet calls on classical imagery of Charon, ferryman of the river Lethe, and of the journey to the underworld to articulate how the space travellers in frozen sleep go over the rim of the known universe into the 'private consciousness' of the beyond. Our fears, our discomfort, our anxieties about the cosmos seem in recent years to have been focused in the poetry about space travel. Iain Crichton Smith's 'The Space-Ship', with its tenor of death and blackness, is another example.[19] Perhaps the focus is thus because with space flight we are now entering into that cosmos (although our penetration is a mere hair's breadth). More scary and more significant, to me, is the future of our planet and the future of our universe. Are we seeing here poetry driven by the personal, the local, and the immediate, rather than engaging with what the scientific subject is telling us? Or is it just that the big picture is too big?

I was putting the finishing touches to this section when news of the 2003 Columbia Space Shuttle accident broke. Have we become too confident, too familiar with space flight? Is the ominous note struck by several of the authors quoted here justified? Rebecca Elson seems to have the right words for this occasion in her poem 'When You Wish upon a Star' with its troubled yet lyrical imagery of stellar lights juxtaposed with space debris, 'a lost screw | Losing height, | Incandescent for an instant'.[20] The setting of such a tiny detail against the hugeness of space is quickening, but also frightening.

One thing we now know better than ever is that the sheer size of the universe is both startling and incomprehensible. That it is expanding, and maybe even accelerating in its expansion, makes it no easier. That we cannot directly see at least 95 per cent of it (the dark matter) leaves us floundering. That we, human beings, are made from the stuff of star death, means we cannot ignore it—in an intimate and ultimate way we too are stars. That its future is hostile to life and will eventually wipe us out, makes us want to ignore it; largeness and largess do not seem to go together. How do poets handle these issues? My impression is that North American authors are more willing to engage than British. This could be for one of several reasons: there are more of them, giving the impression of greater engagement; NASA is conspicuously better at publicity than are the British, so North Americans are more aware of astronomical developments (although it has to be said that NASA publicity crosses the Atlantic); we are less sympathetic, more hostile towards science; and the pragmatic reason—US authors use the World Wide Web more, and hence perhaps more of their poems have come more to my attention!

Who are the main players? The American poet Antler, in 'On learning that on the clearest night only 6000 stars are visible to the naked eye' approaches the big questions in an amusing, almost flippant way, but keeps his feet on the ground and holds the reader well. His concern is entirely with the effect on the individual of the attempt at comprehension of an unpunctuated blur of 'stars galaxies universes | pastpresentfuture'. Though he uses playfully the language of percentage, suggesting that if scientists claim we use only ten percent of our brains' potential, then that ten percent is ignorant of ninety-nine per cent of the universe, his conclusion may be comfortingly, evasively human with its suggestion that perhaps a wine flask under the deep night sky can be 'more powerful | than the largest telescope'.[21]

The universe is so large that light takes an appreciable time to travel across it, and starlight seen tonight may have started its journey tens, hundreds, thousands, or even millions of years previously. Louis MacNeice and Elizabeth Jennings both have poems about this, but the two poems are very different in feel. The latter part of MacNeice's 'Star-gazer' speculates on the long years taken by light to travel to a human perceiver. Light may take longer to travel than even the lifetime of the human species, so that, by the time some light reaches earth there may be no one left alive 'To run from side to side in a late night train | Admiring it and adding noughts in vain.'[22] Elizabeth Jennings's 'Delay' treats of a similar theme with its alignment of love that may be perceived only after 'Its first desire is spent' with the light of a star that shines years back and takes years to arrive, its 'impulse' waiting 'for eyes to claim it beautiful'.[23] When I include Jennings's poem in a public lecture on astronomy, it draws from the audience a gentle, appreciative 'mmmh'—that involuntary note of recognition that is the sound of a poem striking home! It is a much more effective poem than MacNeice's because it is shorter, using fewer, well-chosen words. In MacNeice's poem the profusion of words befuddles the reader—they trip each other up. Elizabeth Jennings has good interplay between the cosmic and the personal, but nonetheless it is the personal element—not least in its last line, 'And love arrived may find us somewhere else'—that is ascendant. Once again the cosmic is used as the vehicle for the personal.

Poetry often articulates personal emotion, but rarely is it able to 'keep up' with modern astrophysics. Astronomy has moved a long way in the past fifty years. There has been the move in the profession away from stargazer to astrophysicist. This is well articulated by Robert Francis in his poem 'Astronomer'. Here the poet situates the figure of his title 'Far far | Beyond the stargazer' in a condition where he 'goes out of his mind' in pursuit of a 'Beyond' which has both scientific and spiritual overtones. Alluding perhaps to 'the peace that passes understanding', yet restating that in a scientific context, Francis's poem takes its astronomer to a zone where, strangely going beyond himself, he exists

> Where no comfort is
>
> And this
> His comfort is
> His irreducible peace.[24]

There are many poems which use astronomical topics as a novel way of illustrating or illuminating human dilemmas but there are few, I feel, that really engage with modern astrophysics. In this respect I am disappointed, for should not poetry engage with the wider world? And does that not include our understanding about the birth and life and death of the universe? The last few poems quoted here are ones that do seem to me to make this engagement; they are in a sense a connoisseur's choice, and may not have much appeal to those unfamiliar with the astrophysics. I appreciate them; it feels good to see one's professional area of work recognized, comprehended, and honoured by being set forth like this.

John Haines in his 'A Little Cosmic Dust Poem' captures beautifully, and with scientific accuracy, how star death and the chemical elements produced thereby become new stars and human life. Writing of the rain of particles produced by the debris of dying stars, he sets out how 'In the radiant field of Orion' new and huge hordes of stars are forming, and finds emerging from 'the cold and fleeing dust' of the cosmos a renewed sense of individual human identity in 'my voice, your face, this love'.[25] Similarly, Pattiann Rogers demonstrates a good technical understanding of the nature of the expansion of the universe and couches it in some lovely images in her 'Life in an Expanding Universe' with its 'cosmic | pinwheels' expelling matter and light as if they were 'fields of dandelions' in a summer wind, 'creating new distances | simply by soaring into them.'[26] John Sokol also contemplates the expanding universe in his 'Thoughts near the Close of Millennium', and handles well the conundrum that the explosion which produced the expansion was 'everywhere' and had 'no centre'. Moving jazzily from Dizzy Gillespie to 'the furthest quasar' the poem punningly mingles loved day-to-day routines with awe, and scientific with colloquial vocabulary as 'We're forever blown away by that first Big Bang'.[27]

Entropy and the heat death of the universe have been written about by several poets. John Updike's 'Ode to entropy' is probably the best known, but, contrasting with Updike's more external approach, Neil Rollinson ('Entropy') has a domestic one as he writes of how, as he watches an ice-cube melting into his glass of wine 'the heat of the Chardonnay passing into the ice | . . . means the universe is dying' and links this to a lover's 'dress that only this morning | was warm to my touch'.[28]

The amount of dark matter in the universe determines its future. It is not yet known what form the dark matter takes (there may be several components) but the quantity fixes the amount of gravity in the universe and hence the nature of the expansion. Rebecca Elson's research was into dark matter. I give her the last word, for she handles the biggest of issues in a wonderful way. How sad she died so young—I would have liked more of her work. Here she is with 'Let there Always be Light (Searching for Dark Matter)'.

For this we go out dark nights, searching
For the dimmest stars,
For signs of unseen things:

To weigh us down.
To stop the universe
From rushing on and on

Into its own beyond
Till it exhausts itself and lies down cold,
Its last star going out.

Whatever they turn out to be,
Let there be swarms of them,
Enough for immortality,
Always a star where we can warm ourselves.

Let there be enough to bring it back
From its own edges,
To bring us all so close that we ignite
The bright spark of resurrection.[29]

# A Fistful of Foraminifera

Sarah Maguire

## With an Introduction

by Norman MacLeod

## Introduction

Though not an avid reader of poetry, I nonetheless consider myself familiar with the poetic experience through my work on foraminiferal systematics. Over the years I've found very few people who can look at the wonderful diversity of shell shapes, colours, textures, and ornaments constructed by these minute creatures and not be moved. Perhaps it was this shared sense of the poetic side of natural history that caused Sarah Maguire and me to establish a rapport almost immediately. Prior to our meeting Sarah had mailed me a copy of her book *The Florist's at Midnight*. Reading through her poems I learned that, aside from writing verse I could relate to, she was familiar with the scientific names of various plant species too. A poet who was comfortable with binomial nomenclature, and had an eye for natural history, even in urban settings. I was impressed.

Our lunchtime discussions ranged widely. Because the subject matter of palaeontology is so vast I brought several objects to show Sarah: a brachiopod shell, a bivalve, a trilobite, and even an arrowhead (representing a human trace fossil). The object that really captured her interest, however, was a small Victorian magnifying bottle into which I'd placed a sample of foraminifera. The bottle's magnification was low. You could just barely recognize the 'sand' as being composed of tiny shells. But that was enough. I don't think Sarah had ever seen shells like these. So small, delicate and perfect, yet so unimaginably old. After lunch in London we strolled down to my workplace, The Natural History Museum, to take a look at other specimens through a proper microscope. There, surrounded by ultra-modern imaging technology, we looked at collections of dust from the bottoms of ancient, far-off oceans lovingly mounted in quaint paper and glass slides by my early-twentieth-century predecessors. There—along with a few current colleagues of indeterminate vintage who happened to be working in the library that afternoon—I introduced Sarah to a thousand or so of my youngest (Pleistocene!) and closest, old foraminiferal friends. She was intrigued.

I think the poem that resulted from these (and a few subsequent) conversations turned out well. Much better than I'd dare hope. The similarities between scientific and artistic creation have been discussed often. Both stem from an innate need to communicate and form groups that is characteristic of our species. But the similarity in our emotional responses to nature is something I have not seen discussed as widely. All scientists—at least, all systematists—respond on an emotional level to their objects of study. Long training in the analytical style of scientific writing squeezes the ability to communicate this emotion, lyricism, and passion out of most of our writing. Contrary to the scientists' public image, however, that doesn't mean we don't feel these things. Indeed, I believe it is precisely those feelings that make us scientists. For me, Sarah's poem really brings this aspect of my science out. The effect is immeasurably heightened by the tidbits of scientific fact she has sprinkled liberally throughout the text. By touching on the aesthetics of foraminiferal shell morphology, their lives, and the way they've become bound up with the lives and history of humans—who are, for the most part, as ignorant of foraminifera as foraminifera are of them—Sarah has captured an important part of palaeontology's appeal. It's as much a glimpse into the palaeontologist's world as a description of its objects. But then, affording such glimpses is what I was always told good poetry was supposed to do.

## A Fistful of Foraminifera

Sand, at first glance—
granular,

a rich grist
of grains and slim seeds,

opening
into a swarm of small homes

painted rose or ochre, saffron, chalk,
some blown steady as glass—

hyaline, diamond,
the pellucid private chamber of a tear.

* * * *

The balanced simplicity of a singlecelled cell,
busy with its business

in absolute silence.
Pseudopodia

float
clear through their apertures,

banners coursing the waters,
furbelows, scarves, ragged skirts;

brief tactful netting,
shy gestures of touch.

Their filigree mansions
are chambered with secrets—

auricular passageways
give onto galleries,

soft arcades,
furrowed with arbours, open

onto balconies, that lean
over doors, propped ajar.

* * * *

Benthic,
their galaxies carpet the depths of the oceans,

a slow chalky ooze
bedded down softly in darkness.

They conjure their houses
from flotsam and jetsam,

tucking grains closely
between alveoli,

secreting a hardy, calcareous mortar;
the shell walls buffed till they shine

or pebbledashed sugary white—
the architectonics of happenstance and grace.

* * * *

Pennies from heaven,
the yellowing bedrock

hewn into slabs
is stuffed full of treasures.

Slipped from their homes
come hundreds of coins,

big stumbling sovereigns,
pocketfuls of pocketmoney,

fit for flipping, fit for hoarding
in chests.

*Nummulites gizahensis,*
the wealth of the pharaohs

is hauled up heavenwards,
a limestone staircase to the stars.

* * * *

Tumbleweeds, spacecraft, seedpearls, squid,
fairylights, pincushions, biodomes, sheaths,

colanders, starfish, thistledown, dhal,
powderpuffs, ammonites, cornichons, teeth,

puffballs, longbones, condoms, bulbs,
thermometers, pomegranates, catapults, hail.

* * * *

Open your fists
and the mortal remains of one million creatures

will spill
through your fingers—

Eocene dust
in the wind.

# The Act of the Mind: Thought Experiments in the Poetry of Jorie Graham and Leslie Scalapino

Adalaide Morris

> The task we now face is not to reject or turn away from complexity but to learn to live with it creatively.
>
> Mark C. Taylor[1]

At moments when change outraces our ability to comprehend it, every system of explanation registers the strain. Oppositions that have long structured thought and guided action slip out of alignment, leaving a culture awash in information it cannot process. If for a while the prefix 'post'—as in post-Newtonian, postindustrial, poststructural, or postmodern—stems confusion by pointing to paradigms we no longer trust, its consolations are temporary and largely negative. The purpose of this essay is to engage moments in contemporary poetry and science that test emerging formations. Its focus is the struggle Wallace Stevens calls 'the mind in the act of finding | What will suffice'.

Stevens's phrase opens the poem 'Of Modern Poetry' by introducing a list of alternatives to nostalgia or rage. When past formations are little more than souvenirs, poetry, Stevens writes, has

> To construct a new stage. It has to be on that stage
> And, like an insatiable actor, slowly and
> With meditation, speak words that in the ear,
> In the delicatest ear of the mind, repeat,
> Exactly, that which it wants to hear, at the sound
> Of which, an invisible audience listens,
> Not to the play, but to itself, expressed
> In an emotion as of two people, as of two
> Emotions becoming one. The actor is
> A metaphysician in the dark . . .

Staged as a brief, internal soliloquy, this poem is an allegory of the mind observing the mind: we, the listeners, are a third invisibility, seeking comfort, like the poet, in 'sudden rightnesses, wholly | Containing the mind'.[2] For Stevens as for many key modernists, the poet's primary responsibility is not personal but speculative, abstract, and theoretical. Poets are not physicians but metaphysicians: they operate, that is, in a theatre of concepts.

The generation of modernists born like Stevens in the 1870s and 1880s entered a world that sorted science and poetry into two distinct realms: the first material, tangible, measurable, and 'real', the second immaterial, intangible, unquantifiable, and 'imaginary'. The job of late-Victorian scientists was to collect and classify facts; the job of late-Victorian poets was to fit these facts into the schema of literary tradition, cultural mythology, religious speculation, and moral law. Poets could write *about* science, as, for example, did Alfred Lord Tennyson, who engaged the geology of Sir Charles Lyell; scientists, in their turn, could wax 'poetic', as, for example, did Charles Darwin, who never hesitated to proclaim the wonder of his findings. No one, however, confused imaginary gardens with real toads.

When scientists began to hypothesize and experimentally verify a range of phenomena beyond the reach of even the most enhanced eye, the borders between the visible and invisible, real and imaginary, scientific and poetic, ceased to be self-evident. Below the threshold of vision, scientists detected smaller and smaller kinds of microentities: electrons, positrons, protons, neutrons, mesons, baryons, leptons, hadrons, numberless 'quarks', in a term snatched from the world of James Joyce, 'for Muster Mark!'[3] These quantum representations, fundamental to twentieth-century science, are hybrid formations that resemble nothing in the visible world but can nonetheless be mathematically verified. They are, in this sense, the inverse of Marianne Moore's sense of the genuine in poetry: imaginary toads, that is, in verifiable gardens.[4]

Poetry and science co-evolve in intricate reciprocities. Just as Newtonian physics developed in tandem with Augustan poetics, relativity and quantum physics accompanied modernist poetry. Before Stevens, Moore, Ezra Pound, H.D., T. S. Eliot, and William Carlos Williams reached maturity, Max Planck had taken the first crucial step towards quantum theory by noting that energy is absorbed and emitted not smoothly, as Newtonian physicists had assumed, but in chunks, packets, or 'quanta'. In 1905, when these poets were finishing their education, Einstein published his theory of special relativity, and in 1916, the year in which several of them published a second or third volume of verse, he completed his greatest work, the theory of general relativity. By 1927, finally, five years after the publication of Joyce's *Ulysses* and Eliot's *The Waste Land*, Niels Bohr and Werner Heisenberg formulated the principles of complementarity and uncertainty that became known as the 'Copenhagen Interpretation' and convinced most scientists of the coherence and correctness of quantum theory.

When strict determinism in the sense that physicists from Newton to Einstein conceived it had to be abandoned, materially verifiable certainties became souvenirs of a simpler past. In this quantum world, the foundations of the universe—from atoms to black holes—became intelligible, and therefore appeared to be real, only through the imaginary pictures scientists composed. Physicists like Bohr and Heisenberg joined Stevens's modern poets as metaphysicians in the dark.

The crucial breakthroughs of relativity and quantum mechanics started not in observations but in a kind of thinking Einstein called *Gedankenexperimenten* or thought experiments: imagine an observer in an elevator in space tugged upwards by someone outside pulling a rope with a constant force; imagine a flash of light between two rockets passing each other in the far reaches of outer space at close to the speed of light; imagine a microscope capable of generating light quanta of such short wavelength that one could use them to measure the positions of electrons in atoms; imagine a cat sealed in a lead box with a small bit of radioactive material and a vial of hydrocyanic acid that may or may not shatter with the release of a decaying atom.[5]

In the sciences of relativity and quantum physics, accurate measurement yields its place to the act of the mind making approximations. In a departure from classical physics that profoundly disturbed Einstein, Heisenberg's uncertainty principle gave mathematical expression to the limits of measurement by formalizing the impossibility of knowing both the position and the momentum of an object. In Heisenberg's thought experiment, the fact that the quantum of light used to ascertain an electron's position inevitably disturbs the electron's momentum means the more sharply we know the electron's position, the more blurred our notion of its momentum must be. 'What we observe [in any physical experiment],' Heisenberg explained in *Physics and Philosophy*, 'is not nature in itself but nature exposed to our method of questioning'. Like the modern poet's meditation, then, the physicist's measurement is a staging or, as Heisenberg puts it, a 'potentia': 'something standing in the middle between the idea of an event and the actual event, a strange kind of physical reality just in the middle between possibility and reality'.[6]

Heisenberg's observation disturbed Einstein because it could not be reconciled with his dream of an ascertainable order, but, interestingly, it was Einstein who provided the crucial clue for Heisenberg's uncertainty principle. In conversation in 1926, Heisenberg recalls, Einstein noted that 'it may be heuristically useful to keep in mind what one has actually observed. But, on principle, it is quite wrong to try founding a theory on observable magnitudes alone. In reality the very opposite happens. It is the theory which decides what we can observe.'[7]

The two poets at the focus of this essay play out in contemporary poetry a dialogue that is similar in its way to the interchange between Einstein and Heisenberg: both use their poems as thought experiments to probe issues germane to postclassical physics and both begin by assuming that our systems of measurement are flawed, but one, like Einstein, attempts to think her way past these flaws toward the dream of a unified field, while the other, like Heisenberg, struggles to capture for thought an indeterminate universe.

The poems this essay juxtaposes are Jorie Graham's 'Event Horizon', a first-person meditative lyric from *Materialism* (1993), Graham's fifth collection of poetry, and Leslie Scalapino's 'bum series', a set of strategic syntactical dislocations from her book-length poem *way* (1988). What interests me in these two poems is the interplay between the *technē* of poetic thought—its forms, its craft, its productive or generative energies—and the contemporary poet's manipulation of issues germane to contemporary science. Although Graham and Scalapino are taken to belong to opposing schools of contemporary poetry—Graham is generally considered mainstream or traditional, Scalapino innovative or avant-garde—my contention here is that both are, in an important and relatively precise sense, experimental poets. In self-reflexively engaging scientific issues, their poems are, in Scalapino's words, ' "scientific experiment": [they aim] to find out what something is, or to find out what's happening'.[8]

Few thinkers would confuse a poem with a series of actions undertaken under controlled circumstances to test a hypothesis or establish or illustrate some known truth. To make sense of Scalapino's claim that writing is 'an experiment of reality',[9] it is helpful to turn to the argument of Daniel Tiffany's brilliant book *Toy Medium: Materialism and Modern Lyric.* Tiffany opens his first chapter, 'Poetics and Materialism', with a clipped statement of the doxa: 'Only a fool', he writes, 'reads poetry for facts.' The assumption that materialism and poetry have not mingled since Sir Francis Bacon first captured fact for science by sequestering fable in the poetic imagination lingers in the popular mind. 'Few ideas are more deeply entrenched in Western society', Tiffany continues, 'than the assumption that poetry and scientific materialism are antithetical modes of knowledge, having produced two disparate—and perhaps incommensurable—cultures.'

To prepare the ground for a reconsideration of poetry's discursive importance in contemporary culture, Tiffany proposes Martin Heidegger's term 'lyric substance' as a join between the discourses of science and poetry. This term, Tiffany suggests, gives body to 'a doctrine of materiality proper to lyric poetry but also congruent with the philosophical problems intrinsic to scientific materialism'.[10] As Tiffany mobilizes the term, lyric substance is a form of modelling used by physicists and poets alike: in its formations, matter cannot be distinguished from the analogies that make it intelligible.

In 'Lyric Substance: On Riddles, Materialism, and Poetic Obscurity', an essay published the year following *Toy Medium,* Tiffany develops and refines this point. 'Philosophical materialism', he writes, 'has been plagued since its inception, starting with the figure of the atom, by its reliance on tropes and imaginary pictures to render the invisible foundation of matter.' Like theory in Einstein's remark to Heisenberg, tropes and imaginary pictures determine the phenomena physicists observe.

Figures of speech and imaginary pictures, however, are fundamental to fiction, drama, and painting as well as poetry. Why *lyric* substance? The factor that throws physicists and poets into close and productive affinity for Tiffany is poetry's heightening of the density, particularity, and opacity of language. 'The innate obscurity of matter in the history of physics, like the inscrutability of things in lyric poetry,' Tiffany writes, 'betrays the inescapable role of language in depicting the nonempirical qualities—the invisible aspect—of material phenomena. The production of verbal or lyric substance in poetry therefore corresponds to an essential aspect of the way science understands the nature of the material world.'[11]

Produced by poets and scientists alike, these approximations of what we cannot see constitute the 'toy medium' of Tiffany's title. Recent developments in the history and philosophy of science amplify the resonance of the term *medium* by drawing attention away from the oppositions of 'imagination' and 'reality' to the figures that mediate between them. In a passage quoted by Tiffany, Bruno Latour provides a succinct summary of these developments: 'The active locus of science,' Latour writes, 'portrayed in the past by stressing its two extremities, the Mind and the World, has shifted to . . . the humble instruments, tools, visualization skills, writing practices, focusing techniques, and what has been called "re-representation". Through all these efforts, the mediation has eaten up the two extremities: the representing Mind and the represented World.'[12] At once empirical and speculative, thought experiments in poetry and science give us our grasp on the real. They are key instruments of the contemporary investigative lyric.

The two poems this essay considers align poetry with rather than against contemporary science by thinking not just *about* but *through* a scientific problem. As Scalapino describes this process in her essay 'How Phenomena Appear to Unfold', each of these poems 'creates or seems to create events, or appears created by them'. The forms of the poems—more traditional, in Graham's case, more innovative in Scalapino's—'are modes of awareness and devices of experimentation, the effect or "function" of which is *not* to be determining order in advance and at the same time to be observing that one is nevertheless doing so'.[13]

Each of these self-reflexive thought experiments emerges in the context of developments in modern and contemporary science. Graham's poem takes its title from one of Einstein's oddest predictions: the hypothesis that if a star contains enough mass in a small enough package, its intense gravitational field will prevent any light or other electromagnetic radiation from escaping. A textbook example of a material phenomenon that cannot, by definition, be observed, a collapsed star pinches itself off from surrounding space-time. The simplest three-dimensional geometry for this phenomenon is a sphere known as a Schwarzschild black hole, the surface of which is termed its 'event horizon' because behind this barrier the inward pull of gravity appears to prevent any information about events in its interior from escaping into the outer universe.

The event horizon, then, is the boundary not between the material and the immaterial but between visible and invisible matter. The title of the collection in which Graham's poem appears—*Materialism*—refers to the theory that physical matter is the only reality and everything, including thought, feeling, mind, and will, can be explained in terms of physical phenomena. In a departure from Graham's four earlier collections, this volume is, like the discourse of science, a collective debate: mixed with her own ruminations on the opacity of things is a series of citations, translations, and adaptations from scientists, philosophers, linguists, naturalists, poets, and cultural critics, each concerned with what Bacon calls 'particulars and their regular series and order'. Opening the roster of poems and scattered throughout is a five-part meditation entitled 'Notes on the Reality of the Self', which is, like its companion poems and excerpts, the lab book of a seeker who wishes, in Bacon's words, 'to form an acquaintance with things'.[14] The initial segment of the poem poses the kind of question that initiates a thought experiment: 'Is there', Graham asks, 'a new way of looking—| valences and little hooks—inevitabilities, proba- | bilities?'[15]

Graham's touchstone in *Materialism* is Bacon's *Novum Organum* (1620), a pivotal document in Bacon's campaign for a theory of scientific knowledge based on observation and experiment. Inductive rather than deductive, Bacon's treatise positions experience as the source of knowledge, but he is not naive about the 'tincture of will and the passions' that inevitably stains human understanding. Scientists must struggle against the tendency to lift their gaze from the object: 'it is better, much better,' Bacon writes, 'to dissect than abstract.'[16]

Among the describers and dissectors who take part in the ensemble speech of *Materialism* are the explorers Columbus and Audubon, whose journals record encounters with trees, birds, and animals they cannot categorize: '*nothing was recognized*,' Graham has Columbus exclaim, 'nothing!'[17] In a parallel recognition of the limits of European metaphysics, Graham cites the linguist Benjamin Whorf's description of a cluster of concepts in the Hopi language as alien to old world thought as the new land's flora and fauna is to its science. 'We dissect nature along lines laid down by our native languages,' Whorf writes in the essay Graham adapts.

The categories and types that we isolate from the world of phenomena we do not find there because they stare every observer in the face; on the contrary, the world is presented in a kaleidoscopic flux of impressions which has to be organized by our minds—and this means largely by the linguistic systems in our minds. We cut nature up, organize it into concepts, and ascribe significances as we do, largely because we are parties to an agreement to organize it this way—an agreement that holds throughout our speech community and is codified in the patterns of our language.[18]

As Graham's choice of speakers in *Materialism* suggests, the codifiers of the patterns of a language are its scientists, philosophers, and poets. The thinkers in the community Graham assembles—among them, in addition to Bacon, Columbus, Audubon, and Whorf, Plato, Dante, Jonathan Edwards, Ralph Waldo Emerson, Walt Whitman, Ludwig Wittgenstein, and Walter Benjamin—are arbiters of the objective: their words, that is, to return to Graham's adaptation of Whorf, contain 'terms that crystallize in themselves the basic postulates of an unformulated philosophy in which is couched the thought of a people'.[19]

The figure in the volume that most decisively collapses the divide between science and art is Leonardo da Vinci, represented in *Materialism* by four observations on movement and weight from his *Notebooks*. 'Gravity and levity', the Renaissance architect, mathematician, engineer, painter, and sculptor writes, 'are accidental powers which are produced by one element being drawn through, or driven into, another.'[20] Movement is not, da Vinci is arguing, part of the essence of a substance but rather the result of a collision with other entities. In addition to its utility as an observation about the interaction of physical bodies, da Vinci's description catches the draw and lift of the cross-cultural and cross-disciplinary encounters in Graham's poems. Columbus's entry into America, Whorf's fieldwork in Native American languages, and the collision that results in the capture of metaphoric or parabolic language for science and the appropriation of scientific concepts for poetry are events that generate our sense of the real. 'In this light', Tiffany writes, 'the forms of meditation and imagination proper to lyric poetry begin to resemble the tools and practices of science—especially, as in physics, when it is a question of depicting unobservable phenomena.'[21] This reciprocal construction of the real gives Heidegger's term 'lyric substance' and Graham's title 'Event Horizon' their explanatory force.

The thought experiment in Leslie Scalapino's 'bum series' also emerges within a context conditioned by the problematics of modern and contemporary science. Scalapino's poem is a serial poem within a larger serial poem itself composed of two long serial poems: 'Later Floating Series', in which 'bum series' is the second of four segments, and the two-part series 'Way'. Published in 1988 under the title *way*, Scalapino's book-length meditation is prefaced by a page of excerpts from quantum theorist David Bohm's *Causality and Chance in Modern Physics*, first published in 1957. Like Bacon's, Bohm's challenge to the science of his contemporaries carries with it a set of keenly apprehended philosophical, ethical, and spiritual implications. Bohm's paragraphs, like the paragraphs of Bacon that open *Materialism*, act as a tuning-fork for the volume as a whole: they strike the pitch, that is, for the poetry that follows.

One of the most distinguished theoretical physicists of his generation, Bohm worked with Einstein during his time at Princeton's Institute for Advanced Studies but was sacked from his post at Princeton for refusing to testify before the House Un-American Activities Committee, and subsequently went into exile, teaching in several countries before taking the post of Professor of Theoretical Physics at the University of London. He augmented the theories of relativity and quantum mechanics with a description of universal interconnection and reciprocity he called implicate—or enfolded—order. 'I tried', Bohm tells an interviewer,

> to get some idea what might be the process implied by the mathematics of the quantum theory, and this process is what I called *enfoldment*. The mathematics itself suggests a movement in which everything, any particular element of space, may have a field which unfolds into the whole and the whole enfolds it in it . . . You could therefore say that everything is enfolded in this whole, or even in each part, and that it then unfolds. I call this an *implicate order*, the enfolded order, and this unfolds into an explicate order. The implicate is the enfolded order. It unfolds into the explicate order, in which everything is separated.[22]

An apt analogy for the implicate order's enfolding and unfolding, Bohm tells his interviewer, is the hologram. Unlike a photograph, which is focused through a lens to produce an image that corresponds point-to-point with the object it represents, a hologram is created without the use of a lens and appears to the naked eye to be an unrecognizable array of stripes and whorls. When pierced by a laser beam or other coherent light source, however, any bit of the hologram unfolds as a three-dimensional representation of the original object. 'In a hologram', Bohm explains, 'the entire object is contained in each region of the hologram, enfolded as a pattern of waves, which can then be unfolded by shining light through it.'[23] The mathematics of quantum theory is, for Bohm, the instrument that captures the dynamic pattern of unfolding and enfolding throughout the whole of space.

The extracts from *Causality and Chance* that Scalapino positions as the epigraph to *way* elaborate three concepts that overlap in the theory of the implicate order: interconnection, reciprocal relationship, and transformation: '[E]very entity', as Bohm explains, 'however fundamental it may seem, is dependent for its existence on the maintenance of appropriate conditions in its infinite background and substructure'. In certain circumstances, this interconnection 'can . . . grow so strong that it brings about qualitative changes in the modes of being of every kind of entity known thus far. This type of interconnection we shall denote by the name of *reciprocal relationship*, to distinguish it from mere interaction' (emphasis in original). 'In this process', Bohm concludes, 'there is no limit to the new kinds of things that can come into being, and no limit to the number of kinds of transformations, both qualitative and quantitative, that can occur.'

The photographs Scalapino selected for the cover of *way* prepare the reader to receive these three concepts. In an interview with Elisabeth A. Frost, Scalapino explains that she encountered these postcard snapshots—captioned 'Couple Dancing in Bar' and 'Men Fighting on Sidewalk'—by chance. Both are public, urban scenes that depict a pair of people clenched together: in each, one person's body, back towards the viewer, curves around the body of the other person whose arms encircle his back. Responding perhaps to the information in the captions rather than to the information in the images, Frost suggests that the point made through this juxtaposition is a point about gender relations—the eroticism between the man and the woman, the violence between the two men—but Scalapino deflects this hypothesis: 'I wanted to counteract the idea of "the Way" as something exalted', she says, 'and to suggest "the way" as something not exalted—it's just what anybody is doing'.[24]

In both scenes, the couple is observed by others, but what the onlookers make of the reciprocal pairings is not available. Although the observers, not the couples, face the viewer, their expressions suspend judgement in anticipation. The scenes Scalapino has chosen for contemplation are not just not exalted: they are, more importantly, not extended into received narratives. The reciprocal relationships the photos depict are interconnections in a now that has not yet resolved into a future: there is no limit to the transformations, both qualitative and quantitative, that could occur. Like Graham's, Scalapino's thought experiment involves 'a new way of looking' at 'inevitabilities, proba- | bilities': to return to the title of Bohm's book, it catches—or attempts to catch—a moment in the interplay of 'causality and chance'.

The information contained in each of the two images is doubled by their juxtaposition on the cover and refracted by their echo in the epigraph, which takes up the spatial position of the photos in a few turns of the page. 'Carrying the analysis further', Bohm writes, concluding the cluster of quotations that forms the epigraph, 'we now note that because all of the infinity of factors determining what any given thing is are always changing with time, *no such a thing can even remain identical with itself as time passes*' (emphasis in original). The point made by the imbrication of the cover, the epigraph, and the poems that follow is not outcome but process: the complexity that exists at the border of order and chaos in the clash of an inexhaustible array of interrelated qualities, 'each', in Bohm's words, 'having a certain degree of relative autonomy'. A third caption within one of the photos—the chance appearance of a store sign above the two men—offers a more productive gloss than the handwritten captions below the photos: 'TIE city', it says, emphasizing not culturally predictable stories of eroticism and violence but the volatile, indeterminate, but verifiable collisions Bohm's quantum physics and Scalapino's experimental poetics struggle to make available for contemplation.

Three contemporary scientific theories—catastrophe, chaos, and complexity theory—situate their inquiries in this borderland between causality and chance, order and chaos, determinacy and indeterminacy. Although the interpretative potential of these theories has yet to be brought into productive tension with contemporary experimental poetics, the thinking of the generation of mathematicians, physicists, biologists, and cultural theorists who formulated these new ways of understanding complexity both shapes and is shaped by the thinking of contemporary artists, humanists, and poets, including, among many others, Susan Howe and Mark Tansey.[25] As N. Katherine Hayles emphasizes in another context, this exchange is bidirectional: 'Culture circulates through science no less than science circulates through culture.'[26] Poems like 'Event Horizon' and 'bum series' do not just cite, translate, or appropriate scientific ideas but actively participate in their interpretation and development. As the chaos theorist Mitchell Feigenbaum remarked to James Gleick,

> In a way, art is a theory about the way the world looks to human beings. It's abundantly obvious that one doesn't know the world around us in detail. What artists have accomplished is realizing that there's only a small amount of stuff that's important, and then seeing what it was. So they can do some of my research for me.[27]

Before reading 'Event Horizon' and 'bum series' in tandem with a problem that emerges most saliently through complexity studies, it is useful to sketch the dynamic models—the toy media or lyric substance—at work in theories of catastrophe, chaos, and complexity. Although they differ in crucial ways, all three theories address discontinuous change in nonlinear dynamic systems. The world they confront is not the orderly, rectilinear world of Euclid, Mozart, or Mondrian but the irregular, looped, and unpredictable universe of Benoit Mandelbrot, John Cage, and Mark Tansey. Beginning as an explanation of such turbulent events as clouds, whirlpools, or population surges and drops, all three of these theories, finally, have proved applicable to such social and cultural phenomena as the epidemiology of AIDS, the rise and fall of commodity markets, or the sudden eruption of mob violence.[28]

In *The Picture in Question*, his study of the painter Mark Tansey, Mark C. Taylor provides a brief but useful account of the differences between catastrophe, chaos, and complexity theories. Starting with the work of the mathematician René Thom in the 1950s and 1960s, catastrophe theory took as its focus the abrupt, qualitative dislocations Thom calls 'singularities': transitions from liquid to gas, for example, the collapse of buildings or bridges, outbreaks of hostilities, or, in the poet Susan Howe's iteration, the 'settling' of the American wilderness invoked in her poem 'Articulation of Sound Forms in Time', published in a volume she titled *Singularities* 'because', she tells an interviewer, 'of Thom'.[29] Although Thom's aim was to understand disruption, however, the upshot of his work was an orderly taxonomy of seven kinds of catastrophe: the fold, cusp, swallowtail, and butterfly, the hyperbolic umbilic, elliptic umbilic, and parabolic umbilic catastrophe. For Tansey, and clearly also for Taylor, then, although Thom's 'morphology of morphogenesis' asks the right questions, it falls short by turning turbulence into structure, stilling the very dynamic it would expose for study.[30]

In the years following Thom's work, Taylor points out, catastrophe theory was taken up into and transformed by chaos theory. The advance in chaos theory lies in its ability to describe dynamic events-in-process: its favoured figures—among them, scaling and iteration, the butterfly effect, the strange attractor, and the Mandelbrot set—trace a system's continuous negotiation of competing options. Like Thom's seven kinds of catastrophe, these models of chaotic dynamics succeed insofar as they make visible processes that Euclidean geometry and Newtonian physics occlude, but, also like catastrophe theory, chaos theory's rage for order runs the risk of reducing apparently haphazard phenomena to law-abiding, docile, and predictable events. 'Just as catastrophe theory discovers permanent structures in changing forms', Taylor summarizes, 'so chaos theory identifies non-random operations at work in apparently random processes. [From this point of view] chaos is, in effect, a state of "deterministic randomness".'[31]

If the undeniable advance in chaos theory is its ability to stress dynamics over structures, complexity theory's advance over chaos theory is its ability to linger at the edge between non-order and order where self-organization occurs.[32] In the emergent order of self-organization, interaction, interconnection, and reciprocal relations are neither structured nor chaotic, neither random nor determined, but exist in a kind of phase space that exceeds these binaries.[33] Like the enfolding and unfolding of Bohm's implicate order, the adaptive systems made visible by complexity theory are systems that hover between organization and collapse.

An early moment in 'Event Horizon' provides an example of the kind of occurrences complexity theory contemplates. As the poem opens, the narrator, who is washing a dress in a basin, pours hot water over soap, producing—unintentionally and by chance—a thin globular sac of water filled with air:

> Sunlight teetered at the edge of the thousand-faced bubble,
> sunlight hovered, pregame, in the chasm of the millisecond,
> played over the ranks,
>
> grazed at the upturned shield-tips, faces and faces, then—pop—went in.[34]

As the poem itself ramifies, collapses, and regroups, its 'swelling instant' unfolds—and enfolds—an array of ecological, historical, political, mythological, and cosmic events. Poised, like the bubble between order and chaos, the poem brings into its system 'the ranks' in battle at Troy, the 'shield-tips, faces and faces' of the police in Tiananmen Square, the refraction of this uprising on the bubble of a TV screen, then, when Beijing cuts off satellite transmission, waves of radio signals, 'hovering, translucent, | inside ... fizzing, clicking golden | frequencies', bringing an audio feed past the still image on the stopped screen. The 'event horizon' of Graham's title marks the edge between invisible but nonetheless material events—the fall of Troy, the rise of Rome, the chaos in Tiananmen Square, the density of a black hole—and their visible, material traces: beyond this margin, the real is available to cognition only through the approximations of lyric substance.

The collapse and reorganization of systems—a bubble, a game, a regime, a civilization, a star—results from the intersection of chance and causality, the aleatory and the necessary, in linked interactions that occur neither inside nor outside structure as such. Here, as calculations of chaos theory emphasize, the non-linearity of systems means occurrences will always be unpredictably disproportionate to their causes. Emerging from the actions and interactions of subsystems distributed throughout a larger system, these occurrences are contingent, dynamic, and non-hierarchical. The challenge of complexity theory is to understand how these systems of systems, networks of networks, function holistically but not totalistically. The thinking of Graham and Scalapino coincides with and contributes to this effort.

Critics have charted the arc of Jorie Graham's development from an early fascination with eloquence, sublimity, and beauty toward a more recent insistence on the flapping and roiling of a world that seems, as the opening poem in *Materialism* puts it, 'all content no meaning. | The force of it and the thingness of it identical'.[35] In an essay written soon after the publication of *Materialism*, Helen Vendler positions these poles—meaningfulness, on the one hand, thingness on the other—as the 'Platonic dualism [that] is both Graham's *donnée* and her demon'. If Graham follows a Platonic paradigm from *Hybrids of Plants and Ghosts*, her first collection of poems, through *The Region of Unlikeness*, her fourth, however, she does so less and less confidently. In my reading of 'Event Horizon', I would like to suggest that Graham is not, as Vendler surmises, following 'the urgent and inescapable need of the modern writer to embody in art a non-teleological universe' but rather working in the trajectory of theorists of chaos and complexity to capture the fine structure in disorderly streams of data and construct toy media or lyric approximations for non-teleological, non-totalizable, unpredictable but always emergent order.[36]

Midway through *Materialism*, between 'Event Horizon' and its companion poem 'The Dream of the Unified Field', Graham inserts three paragraphs of a potentially endless series adapted from Sir Francis Bacon's *Novum Organum*. The first person pronoun that anchors Bacon's paragraphs is the collective voice of scientific experimentation. 'We took a metal bell', the opening paragraph reads,

> of a light and thin sort, such as is used for saltcellars, and immersed it in a basin of water so as to carry the air contained in its interior down with it to the bottom of the basin. We had first, however, placed a small globe at the bottom of the basin, over which we placed the bell. The result was, that if the globe were small compared with the interior of the bell, the air would contract itself, and be compressed without being forced out, but if it were too large for the air readily to yield to it, the latter became impatient of the pressure, raised the bell partly up, and ascended in bubbles.[37]

The speaker of this paragraph begins not with abstractions but with things. Like Columbus and Audubon, he describes and dissects; like Whorf, he is aware—and wary—of the skew of language. His aim is neither to impose idealized, top-down, Platonic form nor to expose a postmodern aleatory universe but to use the constrained observations of an experiment to catch the bubble of order in the act of emerging.

The matter-of-fact record that opens 'Event Horizon'—'Then I took the red dress out, put it in a basin. Soap. | Brought the kettle out, poured till full'—has the prosaic drive of an observer determined to pass from notions to things. Its discipline is the effort to scrub away the contamination Bacon calls the 'tincture of will and the passions'. The speaker aims 'to get the dumb stain out', and, indeed, the poem comes to its conclusion with a clean and empty dress hung on a line to dry—'the flapping thrumming dress', as Graham describes it, 'all sleeves of wind'.[38]

As the poem moves forward, the poet-experimenter's gaze travels upwards, as we have seen, from the basin's spherical film of reflecting liquid—'the thousand-faced | bubble'—through a series of homologous forms at increasingly higher levels of organization, all the way to the distant event horizon of the title. At an intermediate level, midway between the basin and the cosmos, the poet describes colliding currents that gash the surface of a nearby river:

> There on a spot in the middle of its back,
> where the sun hits first and most directly,
> where a person can hardly look,
> a little gash on the waterfilm,
> an indentation, almost a cut—a foothold—
> where the dizziness seems to be rushing towards form,
> pressing down hard where the river flows, down on that skin,
> . . .
> everything at the edges of everything else now rubbing—[39]

Like the forms Tiffany calls 'toy media' or 'lyric substance', this pattern is not Platonic: it is neither pure form nor pure matter, neither thought nor thing, but a spot of self-organization that forms at the border where complexity dwells.

It is hard not to note that this description no longer has the spare, lab notation matter-of-factness of the poem's opening but forms, as it were, a rhetorical beauty spot, an eruption of eloquence and elegance, in Graham's thought experiment. Throughout her career, a number of Graham's critics have cast a suspicious eye on such outbursts of will and passion: to Charles Altieri, for example, Graham's 'poetics of eloquence' relies on 'lyric ecstasies [that] seem to come virtually on demand'; to Bonnie Costello, although such ecstasies represent 'an inevitable, laudable shift away from the timid appetite of the much-spurned "workshop poem" ', they frequently seem not just forced but callow; to James Longenbach, finally, however strenuously Graham's poems may attempt to elude 'the ethical or political repercussions of aesthetic closure', spots like these function to 'click [them] shut'.[40]

Although it might be argued—perhaps with justice—that this poem offers yet another display of forced eloquence, a cross-disciplinary reading would point out that these lines are not decorative but substantial: they aim, that is, to formulate the kind of investigative figure characteristic of post-Newtonian science and poetry:

> a blueprint somewhere down there on a scrap of paper
> an idea down there somewhere in the mind
> of the one looking up, squinting, figuring . . .[41]

The blueprint—the pattern of information intuited by scientist and poet alike—inhabits Latour's middle ground between the perceiver and the perceived: it is the lyric substance that makes invisible matter available for cognition.

'You don't see something until you have the right metaphor to let you perceive it', chaologist Robert Shaw observed of the strange attractor, the blueprint of chaos theory that once perceived became visible everywhere, not just in the phase space of computer screen modelling but in the snapping flags, rattling fenders, and dripping faucets of daily life. Graham's 'flapping thrumming red dress' drying on the line is an instance of an irregular regularity in the turbulence of dynamic processes, part of the hitherto imperceptible chaotic events James Gleick calls 'the flapping, shaking, beating, swaying phenomena of . . . everyday lives'.[42]

Leslie Scalapino's 'bum series' could not be accused of eloquence. Emerging not out of the tradition of Milton, Keats, Yeats, T. S. Eliot, and Wallace Stevens, but from a line that runs jaggedly through Gertrude Stein, George Oppen, Jack Spicer, Robert Creeley, and Philip Whalen, Scalapino puts into play a different set of visualization skills, writing practices, and focusing techniques to think through—or with—contemporary theories of non-hierarchical order. Like Graham's thought experiments, Scalapino's investigative poems are driven by the desire to find 'a new way of looking' at 'inevitabilities, proba- | bilities', but, unlike 'Event Horizon', which looks towards Einstein's dream of the unified field, 'bum series' hews to Heisenberg's uncertainty principle.

An analogy for the difference between Graham's first-person narrative and Scalapino's serial poem within a serial poem within a serial poem is the contrast between a photograph and a hologram that Bohm used to illustrate the difference between classical particle physics and the quantum physics of the implicate order. In Graham's meditative lyric, the 'I' of the speaker acts as a lens that brings all elements of the picture into focus. In Scalapino's serial poem, by contrast, the speaker's 'I' is a detail that disappears into details, each of which yields equal access to a whole that is embedded or enfolded in every part.

In the first-person meditative lyric, however strenuously the poet may struggle against it, the 'I' tends to absorb into itself the interconnections, reciprocities, and transformations that belong not to it but to the whole. As Jack Spicer explains this phenomenon in *After Lorca*, a serial poem that appeared in the same year as Bohm's *Causality and Chance*:

> The seagulls, the greenness of the ocean, the fish—they become things to be traded for a smile or the sound of conversation—counters rather than objects. Nothing matters except the big lie of the personal—the lie in which these objects do not believe.[43]

The pivot of 'Event Horizon' is the capacious mind of the woman washing the stain from her red dress: in this mind, and only in this mind, do the soap bubble, the massed shields at Troy, the face of Helen, the figure of Aeneas carrying his father, Anchises, the events in Tiananmen Square, the interrupted TV transmission from Beijing, the exiled poet Bei Dao, the gash in the river's surface, and the event horizon of a black hole come together in a drive towards closure. Whether or not it sets out to do so, the virtuoso performance of the focusing mind draws the reader's attention to its own acuity as much as—or perhaps more than—to the unfolding of parts in the emergent vision of the whole.

In Scalapino's 'bum series', by contrast, the poem's paratactic construction and syntactical spin pull a reader's attention away from the 'I' towards the recombinatory elements in the scene, any one of which is likely, at any moment, to emerge into the foreground or recede from view. Here are the poem's first two stanzas:

> the men—when I'd
> been out in the cold weather—were
> found lying on the street, having
> died—from the weather; though
> usually being there when it's warmer
>
> the men
> on the street who'd
> died—in the weather—who're bums
> observing it, that instance
> of where they are—not my
> seeing that[44]

The startling final phrase of this sequence—'not my | seeing that'—deflects attention towards the materiality that comes before and endures beyond the passage of this speaker's particular point of view. Like the rest of Scalapino's insistently awkward poem, this locution—blending 'my' into 'not my' and 'seeing' into 'seeing that'—binds the subjective and objective in a complexity Spicer's friend the poet Robin Blaser defines as 'an act or event of the real, rather than a discourse true only to itself'.[45]

The subtitle to 'Delay series', the final section of the 'Later Floating Series' that includes as one of its elements 'bum series', recycles a phrase from the volume's epigraph to link Bohm's theory of the implicate order with Spicer's postmodern serial poem: it reads, in its entirety, '[*The series as | qualitative infinity*]'.[46] In contrast to the 'quantitative infinity' of classical or mechanistic physics, the 'qualitative infinity' of quantum theory emphasizes not separate and therefore countable particles but fields of force capable of generating infinite levels of depth and complexity.[47] The risky thought experiment of 'bum series'—the experiment that makes the poem also, in its way, a 'Bohm series'—is to jettison the apparatus of the late romantic personal meditative lyric in order to fully immerse the reader in the process through which—as Bohm's epigraph puts it—'all *things eventually undergo qualitative transformations*'.

Scalapino's capture of this process is both thematic and formal. Thematically, in the American sense, a 'bum' is, by definition, one who has no relation—a tramp, a vagrant—but, like a Zen wayfarer, the bum is also one who is attached to nothing and is, therefore, paradoxically, related to everyone and everything: a citizen, to return to one of the volume's cover photographs, of 'TIE city'. Always on the way, in the way, of the way, the figure of the bum passes like a wave through all the poem's personages: the men who 'died—from | the weather', 'the | man with the dyed blonde hair' in 'new wave baggy pants', 'the man—who's | accustomed to | working in the garage—| as having | that relation to | their whole setting', a public figure, perhaps 'our present | president', and, last as well as least, the poem's sporatic 'I'.[48] The shifting recombinations of these figures render any fixed or quantitative definition impossible: in the experiment of the poem, they are described not as isolate or separate particles but as a propagating wave passing through a particular landscape at a specific moment in time.

This thematic emphasis is everywhere doubled by the stutters and delays through which Scalapino's reader must make her way: syntactically skewed repetitions and reiterations, the aural overlaps and permutations through which *died* shifts to *dyed*, *present* to *president*, or *wave* to *wait* to *way*, and adverbial nodes—*as*, *so*, *by*, *or*—that jut out at the end of lines to derail narrative and syntax alike. If the dynamic pattern of Graham's poem seems to be 'dizziness ... rushing toward form', the pattern of Scalapino's poem is not its opposite—form dissolving into dizziness—but the unresolvable, determined yet unpredictable unfolding and enfolding of the implicate order.[49]

The final stanza of 'bum series' is, therefore, neither an ending nor a beginning but an iteration of spatial, temporal, causal, and chance interactions through which, in Bohm's words, 'no . . . thing can even remain identical with itself as time passes':

> the bums—
> found later—in the whole setting

—though when the car
hadn't been repaired—and so
their grinding and
movement in relation to it[50]

If we take Bohm's hypothesis seriously, as Scalapino clearly does, it is counterproductive to build a 'whole setting' using the blueprints that constructed the poems of Milton, Keats, or Yeats. The vehicle, in this sense, can't be repaired. The act of the mind in Scalapino's poem—its processual bravery—is to try to think the whole without regularizing its 'grinding and | movement', 'movement in relation', or 'relation to it': the act of the mind thinking *with* or *through* Bohm's notion of the implicate order of quantum physics.

In 'Event Horizon' and 'bum series', contemporary science is thought through the modes and procedures of two kinds of contemporary poetry. Although the so-called poetry wars of the past decades pit the meditative lyric and the serial poem against one another, my intent in this essay is not to argue the case for one over the other but to try, in my turn, to view a whole setting in which these parts represent overlapping interpretative strategies at work in the larger culture. Through poems like these, contemporary readers learn to think not against but with the paradigms of science, paradigms that, in their turn, come into sight through the lyric substance or toy medium of poetry.

# Once I Looked into Your Eyes

Paul Muldoon

## With an Introduction

by Warren S. Warren

## Introduction

I won't pretend I can write like Paul Muldoon. But I might be able to make more interesting pictures.

Many of the spectacular achievements of twentieth-century science followed a simple paradigm. As new directions in basic atomic or molecular physics matured, they were adopted by chemists and applied physicists. This work in turn enabled applications in biological, clinical, and environmental science. The centres I direct at Princeton (including POEM, the centre for Photonics and Electronic Materials) support this process by bridging the gaps between innovation, technology, and application.

Imaging technologies provide many of the best-known illustrations of this evolution. Fifty years ago, measurements of the magnetism created when atomic nuclei 'spin' were at the forefront of esoteric physics research, with no conceivable application. Gradually the applications became clear, and by the 1960s every modern chemistry department had 'nuclear magnetic resonance' spectrometers. By the 1980s most hospitals had 'magnetic resonance imagers' ('nuclear' was dropped to avoid scaring patients) which give beautifully detailed images of soft tissue.

Imaging *function*, not just structure, is the modern research frontier, and new methods are unravelling the workings of the brain. Part of my project with Paul Muldoon involved black and white images from a conventional MRI of a volunteer, similar to what you would get in a hospital. A special image produced in the project shows coloured dots at points that differed when the patient read

Muldoon's poem as distinct from a non-emotive text. The obvious activation in the prefrontal cortex came as no surprise: it is the most evolved part of the brain, and a centre of both critical and emotional response.

More extensive studies (with multiple subjects and multiple tasks) can give better spatial resolution. In recent papers, scientists have imaged differences in the brain activation between viewing a lover and viewing an opposite-sex friend; between male and female perceptions; and between moral reasoning and simple decision-making.

Some would say that the mind-imaging revolution threatens to convert the field of psychology into a quantitative science over the next few decades. For this to happen, new technological advances must improve both spatial and temporal resolution. One promising advance involves lasers. Starting with a very short lump of light (in time), we can sculpt pulses that quickly change amplitude and colour in complex patterns. So, for instance, the 'gremlin pulse' is a very simple pulse used in my laboratories to test shaping capabilities (we can actually programme hundreds of features simultaneously). One application of shaped pulses is 'making molecules dance', or producing just the right colour and time distribution to excite specific compounds. A related application is imaging. The human body is almost transparent at specific near-infrared wavelengths, just slightly outside of the visible region (but easily detected by modern instruments), and subtle brain changes can change the amount of transmitted light. Unfortunately, light scattering currently makes high-resolution pictures impossible. Pulse shaping may provide an attractive solution, allowing low-power lasers to see through scattering and find hidden chemical signals.

We are not yet able to probe truly deep questions (brain sensors will not replace literary critics for some time). Still, the evolving ability to image the mind has enormous consequences that range far beyond neuroscience. The world needs more poets who follow science, and more scientists who learn to appreciate beauty in words.

## Once I Looked into Your Eyes

Once I looked into your eyes
and the only tissue I saw through
was the tissue of lies
behind everything you do.

Once I looked into your heart
and imagined I could trace
the history of the art
of deception in your face.

Now there's something more than a chance
of making molecules dance
I'm somewhat gratified to find

that by laser-enhanced
magnetic resonance,
if nothing else, I may read your mind.

# The Art of Wit and the Cambridge Science Park

Drew Milne

C. P. Snow's *The Two Cultures* suggests that 'Cambridge is a university where scientists and non-scientists meet every night at dinner.'[1] Dining at 'High Table' provides a forlorn example of the shared life-world in which natural scientists and literary intellectuals resist dialogue. Cambridge is also a town in England, and many poets who live and work there, such as Tom Raworth, John James, and Peter Riley, do so without reference to Cambridge University as much more than a local irritation. For Snow, the clash of 'cultures' ought to produce 'creative chances' but he observes instead a vacuum: 'Now and then one used to find poets conscientiously using scientific expressions, and getting them wrong.'[2] Potential for mystification is evident, although Snow does not show *how* poems get things wrong, or how this differs from scientific trial and error. Friction between poetry and science has nevertheless been constitutive for the seriousness of poetic practice in Cambridge from I. A. Richards and William Empson right up to the institutional gulf evident in the contrast between the Cambridge Science Park and residual poetry spaces such as the Cambridge Conference of Contemporary Poetry.[3] At the centre of such developments is the status of poetic knowledge, from modernist assimilations of scientific vocabulary in 'metaphysical wit' to cognitive claims made on behalf of the poems of J. H. Prynne, a highly influential Cambridge poet who until recently taught in the English Faculty:

Liberal humanist literary criticism, in the Arnoldian and Leavisite traditions, has tended to position poetry as a humanizing cultural sphere, in opposition to science, technology and other forms of specialist and utilitarian expertise. This division has been reproduced in the split between arts and sciences which has structured educational institutions, particularly in

England. Prynne's strategies can be read as resistance to this cultural structure, and the limitations of the space it reserves for poetry.[4]

Poets continue to resist the demarcated reservations known as literature departments, seeking less enclosed poetry parks. N. H. Reeve and Richard Kerridge (whose study of Prynne I have just quoted) underplay the way resistances to poetry's cognitive marginalization are constitutive of modern poetry itself. Since the 1960s there have been conflictual and collaborative clusters of poets working through a shared awareness of connections made through Cambridge, with shared resistances to science and prevailing divisions of intellectual labour. These clusters involve poets too numerous to list.[5] As Peter Riley puts it:

For many decades Cambridge has been a focus in English poetry of a kind of metaphysical modernism . . . a serious and total commitment to poetry as the supreme record of the transaction between self and the world. . . . Cambridge has been a centre for a view of poetry as precisely *advanced* rather than experimental or merely up to date. And it's advanced because it spreads over human experience like a sky and comprehends or covers all other forms of knowledge, but levered on the one person, the poet.[6]

Poetic technique and formal reflexivity become mediating means of leverage, with varying emphases on personhood. Cambridge's relative isolation from experiences of industrialized urban life—elsewhere so important for modernist literature—generates a different pressure to transcend the local through more socially abstracted models of communication and discourse. Resulting projections often bespeak an anti-humanist orientation towards language as 'world-disclosure',[7] or utopian demands for radical reorientations of social being. 'Seriousness', accordingly, carries with it a burden of proof at odds with the socialized pleasures of literary recognition.

Recognition of science within poetry gives rise, then, to different poetics of resistance,[8] poetics working at the limits of wit. Pressures to locate 'wit' within pre-existing communities of interpretation conflict with the ideology of university wit and with post-modern paradigms of knowledge, notably the antagonisms of different language-games and what Jean-François Lyotard terms 'differends'.[9] 'Wit' provides one description of how conflicting language-games are negotiated through playful argument rather than being grounded in propositional truth-claims or what I. A. Richards theorized as 'pseudo-statements'.[10] Understood speculatively, wit is the recognition of knowledge made sociable.[11] Wit mediates between cognitive seriousness and satirical critiques of science's unacknowledged presumptions and unintended 'life-world'[12] consequences. The difficulty is the extent to which the sociality of wit can be developed as an art which transcends the conversational context of language-games. Poetics of 'wit' struggle less with scientific knowledge than with the social art of language. One line of development goes through T. S. Eliot's 'metaphysical wit' paradigm.[13] William Empson's account of wit in Pope's *Essay on Criticism* remains exemplary.[14] Conservative, anti-metaphysical, and anti-modernist conceptions of poetic wit emerge with Movement poets and the reworking of Augustan wit, notably through Donald Davie. This anti-metaphysical conception of wit feeds the debased coffee-table wit and gimmickry of much contemporary poetry. Alternative genealogies reconfigure poetic wit through romanticism, symbolism, and Wallace Stevens, or through Poundian traditions associated with William Carlos Williams and Charles Olson.

Emergent intellectual formations in Cambridge develop what might be called 'postmetaphysical wit', critical of precedents in the poetics of metaphysical wit and philosophically postmetaphysical in ways comparable to philosophical critiques of science.[15] Such philosophical critiques implicate Cambridge's development as a strategic sector for the 'knowledge-based' economy of post-industrial capitalism, a model of the university town or provincial campus providing a flexible, non-metropolitan environment for inter-disciplinary research and development clusters. The relative autonomy of the Cambridge Science Park from the University has some geographical specificity, but the essential models of collaboration and knowledge are understood to be universal and reproducible, as if geographical location were merely a social accident or economic convenience. In principle, the truth content of a science park could be translated anywhere. Poetry's models of collaboration and knowledge, by contrast, more often highlight site-specific resistances to information processing, and to geographical or linguistic translation. Print and information technology's globalization create new architectures of writing and 'text', despite conservative desires to reduce poetry to singular, speaking voices. Demands that poems transcend 'situation' are met by demands that they are nevertheless produced by someone writing somewhere. The social disaggregation of the metropolitan city becomes thematic in modernist poetry, from Baudelaire's Paris to Frank O'Hara's New York: the city somehow embodies the vortex of capitalist communication.[16] Recent instances of urban poetics might include Roy Fisher's Birmingham, Iain Sinclair's London, and Doug Oliver's New York, but Cambridge remains curiously unrepresented in poetic forms, perhaps because so evidently unrepresentative. Despite residual dreams about organic communities, the life-world of Cambridge dramatizes the socially disaggregated situation of the deracinated intellectual, haunted by power and privilege. Veronica Forrest-Thomson, a Scottish poet who completed a Cambridge Ph.D. on poetry and science, provides notable illustrations of the difficulties. Allusion to everyday experience in Cambridge may aspire to cool bathos, reflexive self-portraiture in the manner, say, of François Truffaut or Jean-Luc Godard:

> Spring surprised us, running through the market square
> And we stopped in Prynne's rooms in a shower of pain
> And went on in sunlight into the University Library
> And ate yogurt and talked for an hour.[17]

Or as another of Forrest-Thomson's poems 'Le Signe (Cygne)' has it: 'Godard, the anthropological swan | floats on the Cam when day is done.'[18] Post-structuralist semiotic wit aside, there is a risk of appearing to endorse salad days complacency, intellectual pastorale in the manner, say, of *Brideshead Revisited* meets Alan Bennett.

The democratic resonances of café life in New York or Paris somehow do not extend to evocations of the university library tea-room. 'Michaelmas', the opening poem of Forrest-Thomson's *Language-Games*, for example, explores estrangements provoked by this example of a Cambridge-specific idiom. The poem uses definitions and historical citations of 'Michaelmas' from the Oxford English Dictionary (*OED*), to develop a collage of quotations. The poem's artifice develops a witty conflict between Wittgenstein's questions about contexts of language-use and what it means to use the *OED* in poetry or literary criticism. An authorial note to *Language-Games* acknowledges that: 'Most of these poems are obviously about the experience of being engaged in a certain activity, in a certain place, at a certain time: the activity, research in English Literature, the place,

Cambridge, the time, 1968–9.' These poems nevertheless 'express' an underlying theme: 'the impossibility of expressing some non-linguistic reality, or even of experiencing such a reality.' Wittgenstein, a Cambridge phenomenon, is cited accordingly, but through a second, main pre-occupation: 'the relationship between "pure" intellectual activity, in fields such as philosophy and theoretical science, and their appearance in an "applied" context, as one element among others in one's attempt to make sense of concrete experience.'[19] Play across different levels of knowledge becomes a question of poetic technique, rather than an invitation to infer biographical content or self-expression, but there is a curious imbalance between the non-referential claims of poetic artifice and the privileging of local features of Cambridge experience.

Subsequent poems by Forrest-Thomson, such as 'Cordelia: or, "A Poem Should not Mean, but Be" ', are more loosely concerned with Wittgenstein, moving more freely through differentials of experience and inter-textuality. Without an explicit 'language-games' framework, the ruse of dramatizing 'applied' Wittgenstein opens the possibility that her poems will be mistaken for insular exercises in university wit:

> Di pensier in pensier
> from impasse to impasse, from Christmas tree
> to jelly-fish, stranded on the sandy bed
> of the semiotic sea, his network in the dust;
> his vehicle for macroscopic structures,
> dismembered by bicycle handlebars
> as we crossed King's Parade[20]

These lines can be motivated in relation to the poem's title, but inevitably suggest image constructions dependent on Cambridge-specific recognitions, even if contrasts between science and life-world have a more general referentiality. Uncertainty as to the poem's seriousness reflects the way its wit resists being read too quickly against social horizons, posing questions as to the interpretative communities in which the poem might be re-cognized. Poetic wit's fragility reflects its vulnerability to recontextualization within specific idioms and contexts, as opposed to being recognizable as a poetic collation of language-games. As with metaphor, the quality of recognition achieved in wit abstracts from use, suggesting how rule-bound language-games can be reimagined and rethought. This abstraction from use generates a relative poetic autonomy which can nevertheless undermine confidence in the seriousness with which 'wit' is to be entertained. It is often unclear whether poetic wit is to be understood as its own specialized or obscure language-game, a metalanguage of poetic association, or as a more referential commentary on language as social being.

Constructive motivation of the poem also threatens to fall into what Forrest-Thomson calls bad 'naturalization', the reduction of poetic artifice to statements about the non-verbal external world.[21] Whereas Empson's poems assimilate scientific vocabulary through a high degree of closure within conventional forms, Forrest-Thomson seeks to open out formal conventions in ways that provide less evident frameworks through which thematic relevance can be construed. The weight of Cambridge experience makes it hard to specify the extent to which Forrest-Thomson's poems are playful or 'serious' metaphysical inquiries. This indeterminacy becomes characteristic of conflicts in Cambridge poems between poetically autonomous technique and cognitively motivated research, with 'wit' as the precarious middle term.

Campus poetry remains, thankfully, an obscure and marginal genre. It is a feature of Cambridge poems that they are located anywhere but in the university, often exploring worlds and experiences through a domestic locus for which the university workplace is marginal. University referentiality is implicitly taboo, not least out of a desire to escape the loop in which poetry is immediately ploughed back into classrooms. The way poems address 'world-disclosure' works through knowledge frameworks which are only accidentally Cambridge-specific. Implied address to possible interpretative communities and poetic application is comparable to the socially abstracted research and development model of a science park. Ivory tower ideology works to disguise the issues of work and lived experience, not least the local forces of land ownership and property rights so important in Cambridge's development. Daily contrasts between feudal monuments, industrial cottages, and entrepreneurial science parks make it hard for any but tourists or pre-programmed students to dream of gleaming spires. Lines of global information relay increasingly suspend poetry in a virtual, electronic geography. Qualitative mediation continues to depend on local interfaces, but the meaning of experience in Cambridge is as much transnational as local, a situation reinforced by the university population's transience. A cluster of scientific researchers might assume unintelligibility to lay persons, working against a presumed horizon of universalizable rationality reproducible by the international scientific community. A comparable cluster of poets working with shared paradigms of poetry are more likely to be viewed sceptically if not immediately intelligible to general readers. Confidence in the universalizable rationality of poetry sounds nakedly ideological. Poetry is called upon to be readable, even by scientists, against presumed horizons of domestic interest and linguistic transparency, as if poetry's task were to represent the vanity of minor differences in the human spirit. 'Applied' science also generates economic opportunities, such as science parks, very different from the spin-offs of 'applied' poetry and its virtual knowledge parks.

A traditional defence of poetry's role might hint at cultural critique: Lavinia Greenlaw has written that 'Poetic freedoms can be used to express scientific ideas in a more broadly comprehensible manner and can locate them within the cultural, historical and ultimately human context by which science itself is driven and defined.'[22] Such freedoms look like false borrowings in Cambridge: intellectual cohabitation dramatizes the instability of what passes for human contexts, and assigns cultural relativism to popular science journalism and intellectual history. Poetry written in the shadow of the Cambridge Science Park resists the unscientific circumscription of poetry within popular humanism and the reduction of expression to comprehensible subjectivity. Given conflicts generated around poetic and scientific obscurity, it is surprising to find proponents of science conceding the validity of poetic and literary values. Graham Farmelo argues for the beauty of scientific equations by analogy with poems, claiming that: '$E = mc^2$ is in many ways similar to a great poem.'[23] This claim modulates into the bizarre proposition that the 'seminal equations of modern science . . . through their concision, power and fundamental simplicity can be regarded as some of the most beautiful poetry of the twentieth century'.[24] The imprecise 'power' of poetry provides an unlikely model for cognitive value. What might Farmelo make of the symbolic equation which serves as an epigraph to J. H. Prynne's pamphlet *Triodes*? Farmelo's book nevertheless provides striking indications that ideals of beauty have been important in the formation of scientific thought, notably in Paul Dirac's intuitions that mathematical beauty is a valid criterion for the quality of fundamental theories. Such unholy alliances of science and poetics reveal the extent to which science may owe more to idealizations of meaning than criticism would concede to poetry.

Recourse to abstract ideals of beauty—with implicit codes determined by economies of symmetry, harmony, simplicity, and ordered elegance—marks a crisis in the social legitimation of science and poetry. Whereas science and poetry conceived as vocational orientations might be thought of as ends in their own right, the claim of beauty shifts the value of activity from process to product, from pure science or pure poetry to applied arts. Just as the hermeneutics of suspicion directed towards pure science situates science within the cultural relativism of human contexts, so the literary critical suspicion of poetry as an end in its own right situates poetry within the cultural play of localized interests, with sociology claiming a third culture between science and literature.[25] There is then a curious affinity between demands that poetry and science be made accountable to local economies of production such as those of the Cambridge Science Park. The cognitive claims of poetry and science nevertheless resist such contextualization. Strategies of research, inquiry, and experiment may share a sociological context, but the impact on scientific legitimation is very different from the pressure on poetry to be an art resistant to academic assimilation.

A measure of such problems in Cambridge is the preference for models of independent cognitive research over avant-garde propaganda strategies. This reflects the difficulty of making academic alliances and a deep-rooted sense that avant-gardism is merely a metropolitan publicity strategy.[26] Contemporary poetics are now more often constituted through cognitive research paradigms, part of the general assimilation of intellectual life within scientific models. The delimitation of rationality according to models of scientificity has entered cultural cognition more deeply than C. P. Snow imagined possible. Scientific cognition has also become more awkwardly relativist, not least through the suggestive poetics of modern physics, evolutionary biology, genetic coding, chaos theory, and the surprisingly Platonic cosmologies of space-time and the 'big bang'. Heisenberg concedes that 'one of the most important features of the development and the analysis of modern physics [is] the experience that the concepts of natural language, vaguely defined as they are, seem to be more stable in the expansion of knowledge than the precise terms of scientific language, derived as an idealization from only limited groups of phenomena.'[27] The division between 'natural' and 'scientific' language merits the rebuke to the expression '*natural* gas' offered by J. H. Prynne: 'Whoever in some sheltered | domain called that vapour "natural" deserves | to laugh right into the desert.'[28] As Habermas suggests, 'even in physics, theory (as Mary Hesse has shown) is not free of metaphors, which are necessary if new models, new ways of seeing things and new problematics are to be made plausible (with intuitive recourse to the preunderstanding established in ordinary language). No innovative break with tried-and-true cognitive forms and scientific habits is possible without linguistic innovation.'[29] Despite problematic associations with the capitalist culture of innovation, the claim to be 'linguistically innovative' has become a key slogan in poetry propaganda. The awkward language of scientific legitimation motivates hermeneutic reorientations suggested by poetry, not least regarding language's historicity as a horizon of preunderstanding. Consider Stefan Collini's account of shifts since Snow's 'two cultures' model:

> The role of imagination, of metaphor and analogy, of category-transforming speculation and off-beat intuitions has come to the fore much more (some would argue that these had always had their place in the actual processes of scientific discovery, whatever the prevailing account of 'scientific method'). As a result, more now tends to be heard about the similarity rather than the difference of mental operations across the science/humanities divide, even if some of the similarities, it must be said, seem to be of a rather strained or at best analogical kind.[30]

Such strains are thematic in attempts to redefine the limits of poetic cognition, and in rethinking the legacy of romantic idealism evident in terms such as imagination, speculation, and intuition.[31]

The art of poetic wit can be understood, accordingly, as offering speculative and sceptical challenges to science, exploring shared processes and techniques, not least regarding linguistic embodiments of cognitive experience. Even if poetic analogies are constitutive of scientific processes, however, poetic embodiments remain resistant to scientific objectification. Indeed, poetic appropriations of science are more akin to a negative theology of science, a negative relation to the spirit of science that could be traced back through neo-Platonist poetry into the Greek origins of scientific thought. Insofar as modern poems play with scientific motifs, neither affirming nor denying the validity of science *per se*, they take up with science as one among the available parameters of experience. What becomes known as metaphysical poetry situates appropriations of science between parodic pastiche and more affirmative or speculative fellow-travelling. 'Metaphysical' claims can be read as witty but strained analogy-mongering, Dr Johnson's yoking of heterogeneous ideas, or as speculations with more serious ontological entailments. Whether John Donne merely toyed with science or developed unorthodox metaphysical claims provides an important test case.[32] Critical 'proof' struggles to provide more than loose frameworks through which metaphysical poetry can be contextualized: what resists naturalization is the autonomy of poetic wit as a cognitive paradigm. The way 'metaphysical' is used both pejoratively and approvingly points to the indeterminacy of claims for poetic wit as a science in its own right.

An alternative strategy, more favoured by literary critics than by poets, claims that poetry is itself a scientific practice. Steven Meyer claims of Gertrude Stein that, 'It is not just that her ideas about writing were influenced by science; she reconfigured science *as* writing and performed scientific experiments *in* writing.'[33] As with psychoanalysis, such claims generate scepticism regarding verifiability and objectivity: scientific processes in poetic production are only meaningful as 'results' through interpretative reconstruction. Literary criticism becomes the public sphere of scientific recognition. Curiously, the term 'experimental' survives as a pseudo-category used to describe modernist poetic practices analogous with scientific method. What emerges is a literary critical idealization in which poems somehow constitute an alternative universe of scientific cognition. Such utopian conceptions confuse claims for poetry as anti-science with more suggestive claims for poetry as a call for fundamental shifts in the organization of knowledge. Monumental and remarkable modernist follies have been developed out of such idealizations, from Heidegger's reinterpretation of Hölderlin to the cognitive claims embodied, via Alfred North Whitehead, in Charles Olson's poetry.

J. H. Prynne's poetry is informed by a critical reception of

Heidegger and Olson, but specification of the resulting postmetaphysical thematics proves difficult to sustain, in part because Prynne has spared readers the embarrassment of explanatory authorial statements. Birgitta Johansson, for example, struggles to gauge differences between satirical citations of scientific vocabulary and subtended ontological inquiries in Prynne's poems: '*Wound Response* alludes to biodynamics in poems that illustrate, as well as challenge and mock, aspects of the research carried out in medicine and biology. "The *Plant Time Manifold* Transcripts", for instance, satirises an academic discussion about higher versus lower organisms.'[34] Differences between satirical mockery and ontological challenges frame the indeterminacy of post-metaphysical wit. 'The *Plant Time Manifold* Transcripts' contains moments of undergraduate knockabout, but also concatenates different registers. The cosmological strain of immanent horizons of meaning is evident in the concluding lines: 'But this again was before the more sane label, the negative flower of the Cosmos, itself after the recognition of polynucleotides streaming out from the epoch such as shyne in our speech like the glorious stars in Firmament. There is a set of loops somewhere in this great & forcible floud like the aurora and in this total purge of the horizon both ways I stop before I do.'[35] The 'wit' of 'The *Plant Time Manifold* Transcripts' strains readerly patience by being mischievously frivolous while also implying a more 'serious' or radical challenge to scientific thought.

Prynne's more convincing poems offer less naked contrasts between scientific jargon and poetic experience, working outwards from the more explicitly argued inquiries of *Kitchen Poems* and *The White Stones* to the dense intertextuality of language and lyric edge which is at its most rebarbative in recent sequences such as *Red D Gypsum* (1998), *Unanswering Rational Shore* (2001), and *Acrylic Tips* (2002):

> avulsed by slung jollops in fear of hardship overshot
> cascade soral membrane, xylem star retes up in flames
> licked under, crepitate the knock racket fumigant spar.[36]

The yoking together of seemingly heterogeneous forms of language in Prynne's poems can be read as a radicalization of the scientific indeterminacy evident in Donne's reception. Moving through domestic puns to the historicity of human settlement in language, Prynne's poems engage with the limits of worldliness and cosmology. Readers learn to value invitations to speculative reading, engaging in thought experiments and counter-factual inquiries which extend the limits of what poems can be or become. At the limits of poetic form, however, it remains difficult to distinguish moments of local wit—what might be called the differends of conflicting language-games—from the claims of postmetaphysical thought.

Forrest-Thomson, akin in this regard to Empson, was happy to provide explanatory authorial statements. Her poems can also be read back through her critical writings. The self-sufficiency of poetic knowledge nevertheless depends on a willingness to recognize the poem's autonomy from such supporting frameworks. Her Ph.D. thesis construes such problems as the 'use' of science by poets, understood through Wittgenstein's talismanic injunction: 'Do not forget that a poem, even though it is composed in the language of information, is not used in the language-game of giving information.'[37] Forrest-Thomson is sceptical of the uses of science in the work of Pound, Williams, and Hugh MacDiarmid. The problem is not what poems say about science, but the juxtaposition of different language-contexts effected by poetic structure. Poems such as MacDiarmid's 'On a Raised Beach', with its scientific inaccuracies,[38] exemplify the failure to develop metaphorical transformation within poetic form: 'MacDiarmid's real business is with using the natural world as a "metaphor for poetry" . . .'.[39] Accordingly, 'when a poet's interest is deflected from a preoccupation with the formal arrangements of scientific concepts to some kind of attempt to appropriate the objects of science themselves—the reality behind the concepts—he is apt to leave science behind altogether'.[40] Forrest-Thomson distinguishes the way Pound mythologizes not only his material, but also the way his poetic techniques become part of the subject-material: 'Knowledge and experience have become a matter of the collation of texts; metaphysics is absorbed by poetic construction.'[41] For Forrest-Thomson, Empson develops the mathematics of poetic form such that 'Technique itself becomes an image of modes of discourse as determining and defining the status of objects of knowledge. The poet can now see his claim to knowledge as having equal validity with that of the scientist, but at the cost of the implication that both are equally subjective and relativistic.'[42] Her account generates fascinating readings of Empson's poetry, but leaves unresolved the extent to which poetic artifice can be recognized as having a validity and rationality 'equal' to scientific thought. Her own poems work through arguments between Wittgenstein and Empson towards a post-structuralist conception of the autonomy of poetic artifice, with a stress on non-meaningful aspects of poetic language that eschews science.

Despite her early death, Forrest-Thomson's work makes an important contribution to the understanding of poetic artifice by dramatizing the limits of cognition possible through poetic technique. Her work prefigures subsequent lines of development. In *Poetic Artifice* she foregrounds John Ashbery's poetry as an example of 'everything in Artifice which is productive, innovatory'.[43] After Ashbery, what has become known as 'language' poetry develops witty collations of language-games which can be read through Forrest-Thomson's explorations in Wittgenstein, Empson, and post-structuralist semiotics, though her stress on the lessons of Empson has been less widely recognized. Lines of influence and affinity are explicit in Charles Bernstein's *Artifice of Absorption* (1987), while Tom Raworth's poems offer perhaps the most sustained articulation of a poetics of language-games in recent poetry.[44] These developments explore a variety of techniques which could be described as exercises in postmetaphysical wit, but with a less evidently serious interest in postmetaphysical inquiry.

Within Cambridge, the latter emphasis is more evident in the example and influence of J. H. Prynne's poems, though usually at the cost of neglecting poetic artifice in favour of an emphasis on poetry as a mode of cognition and research. In *Poetic Artifice*, Forrest-Thomson attempts to analyse how Prynne's poem 'Of Sanguine Fire' 'restores both the resources of lyric and the resources of thinking in poetry . . . to make poetry again capable of powerful order and powerful thought'.[45] Her critical reading sits uncomfortably, however, with her own emphasis on the autonomy of poetic artifice, perhaps because for Prynne relations between poetry and language are less evidently mediated by poetic 'technique'. Forrest-Thomson suggests that in 'Of Sanguine Fire' 'irrational obscurity is a cover for a deeper and more profound rationality which, while discontinuous with the world of ordinary language, is continuous with a world which is an imagined alternative.'[46] Prynne's radicalization of post-Olsonian poetics is more sceptical of such oppositions between rationality and irrationality, or between poetic and ordinary language, offering something more akin to a post-phenomenological inquiry into knowledge and language. As the opening lines of 'Die A Millionaire' suggest:

> The first essential is to take knowledge
> back to the springs, because despite
> everything and especially the recent
> events carried under that flag, there is
> specific power in the *idea* of it[47]

'Wit' seems, accordingly, like the wrong term through which to understand Prynne's poetics of language: the underlying questions come closer to a radical empiricism confronting the limits of existing historical horizons and metaphysical commitments. Simon Jarvis points to a refusal in Prynne's work 'to take up the sheltered but displaced ground of a relative aesthetic autonomy whence whatever is written need not be taken literally'.[48] In this sense, postmetaphysical inquiry questions the modernist organization of knowledge and art, posing the problem of the grounds from which knowledge in any form of radicalized poetic wit might be recognized. A poem such as 'Thanks for the Memory'[49] contrasts its idiomatic title with an assimilation of scientific jargon, implying either a satirical citation of found texts, or more critical inquiries into the chemistry of recollection. The seriousness of the wit depends on the seriousness with which it is interpreted. Readers can engage Prynne's poems philologically within poetic research paradigms, or read them as more speculative assertions of a poetics of postmetaphysical wit. Critical legitimation of Prynne's poems as forms of scholarly knowledge obscures the challenge to academic and scientific paradigms posed by postmetaphysical poetic wit. Put differently, these poems can be read as examples of applied poetic thinking, a virtual Cambridge science park, or as critical recognitions of the limits and amnesia of existing paradigms of knowledge, a living refutation of the science 'park'. However such alternatives are finessed as false binaries delimiting poetry's conditions of possibility, a conflict emerges between models of pure, poetic cognition and models of poetic art engaged in language as a mediated site of socialized recognitions.

John Wilkinson develops a poetics of postmetaphysical wit in ways that can be situated between Forrest-Thomson and J. H. Prynne. His poems are suffused with metaphorical transformations that go beyond neat divisions of intellectual labour, but the stakes are less those of artifice, science, or knowledge than of a somatic, poetic intelligence in full flight from the parks and enclosures of meaning. As with Prynne, 'wit' at first seems an unhelpful critical optic, but Wilkinson's work come close to achieving qualities suggested by T. S. Eliot's conception of metaphysical poetry: 'a quality of sensuous thought, or of thinking through the senses, or of the senses thinking, of which the exact formula remains to be defined.'[50] An early poem, 'The Reason', exemplifies metaphysical wit as love lyric.[51] Wilkinson did not include this poem in *Oort's Cloud*, perhaps retrospectively distrustful of the programmatic structure of the conceit. 'Sweetness & Light' offers a more characteristic play of scientific metaphoricity in a longer sequence that breaks the boundaries enabling thematic naturalization:

> /stars stabilized temporarily to make charts
> /carved up periodically in the space-race
> /far bourn for the aimless positivist
> /where I've been known to have it so good, one
> pampering space
> protruding, copped in the neck in the fast tunnel, it
> ends in an imploded
> now-now[52]

Fluidity of register works through recognizable idiom clusters without spelling out connections or pseudo-propositional inquiries. In this and subsequent works there is a free-moving dynamism—sometimes Bacchanalian, sometimes bleakly sceptical—which is levered around the poet's person. Rather than expressing worlds which are somehow privately or intimately treasured, however, this dynamism works through experiences of personhood thrown upon the violence of worlds disclosed by and in language. Whereas the reception of Prynne's poems suggests a continuing anxiety about the ontological or cognitive claims his poems might articulate, Wilkinson's poems are more evidently concerned with somatic pleasures and pains attendant upon poetry as a lived orientation to language and society. The wit of these poems is postmetaphysical to the extent that it extends the assimilative tendencies of metaphysical poetry into projective identifications with different idioms and life-worlds. Insofar as the consequences are structured around the interests, desires, and needs of the life-world, the pressures of science are recognized and registered, but without the pathos of poetry as an unacknowledged legislative or cognitive power. Poetic perception is more evidently ungrounded, fleeting, and postmetaphysical, as if affirming a wounded sublimity of struggles for recognition within experiential pragmatism. The opening lines from 'Laboratory Test Report' serve to illustrate the characteristic fluidity of collated conceits:

> For incubator one now dreams not one since
> Who knows when I
> Bluely struggling in my bubble belfry,
> basking in my pellucid tent—
> now when secularised
> butts of tissue like Phrygian cloth!
> drape the frontage of shingle beach,
> billow out or in beautiful detail *grafted*
> coats of many colours, gathering up
> for comfort, or to imitate
> raw linen, spiked toque—It's natural
> now designed genetics pride their new
> basic shape for autumn, & a catwalk
> of self-correcting lathes & jigs,
> technology with a
> human edge *intends* these slight variants.[53]

Wilkinson offers a tentative exploration of poetic techniques animating such textures in a talk entitled 'The Metastases of Poetry'. He describes how late modernist writing, such as his, inducts readers 'into the language, or as I would prefer, the gestural repertoire of the sequential work'.[54] With reference to 'Facing Port Talbot',[55] he describes the play of rhythmic insistence and impure diction:

> These constructions are provisional as a shanty, they never result in anything I can continue to occupy as a satisfactory place. I'm not willing, and I'm unable, to try to explain such a poem, but what I can do is point out a principle of organisation which I call metastatic. I tend to work across a number of poems simultaneously, and in a long poem like this, across its

various parts simultaneously. What gives the poems such coherence as they exhibit is not a metaphorical development, but a set of linked and transforming entities, which can be syntactical gestures, vowel and consonant patterning, imagistic or discursive modes. 'Metastatic' is a term in rhetoric, but my use derives from a brief experience of nursing in a cancer hospice, the metastatic tumours echo about the body and these nodes define the shape of the body subjectively, through pain.[56]

This provides a helpful summary of relations between poetic artifice and imagistic nodes constitutive of postmetaphysical wit. Wilkinson points to the torus in 'Facing Port Talbot' as a figure morphing across 'the life-saving ring, the lobster-pot, the body, and the starry envelope echoed by the bedcovers'.[57] The poem moves accordingly between domestic perception and competing cosmological models, including literary associations with Henry Vaughan's poem 'I saw eternity the other night'. The recognitions made possible are described by Wilkinson as 'a good example of the uncertainty principle—the particles arrange themselves according to the quality of attention brought to bear, and their specificity is indeed called into being through attention'.[58] This implies a critical model through which to read the poetics of postmetaphysical wit: a play of uncertain dividends, animated by qualities of attention and recognition rather than objective interpretation.

Recognition of poetic wit involves both the suspension of authorial personality as a key to what poems are and a willingness to supply dialogues of linguistic and textual context without naturalizing poetry's differential relation to such contexts. If the context of poetic wit is naturalized as university wit, for example, or even as a more fluid type or style of 'social' wit, then the seriousness of poetic wit is naturalized as a reflection of pre-existing communities of recognition. Poetic wit invites possible naturalizations, but also holds open new qualities of recognition, not least recognition of the social prescription of the limits of wit. Poetic wit asks not to be socialized or cashed out as one among an array of possible meanings, but to be or become poetically embodied structures of recognition. The importance of construing such structures as 'wit' lies in the mediated conditions of poetry as an art of recognition, of recognitions articulated in and through language, and not as a pure or unmediated cognitive relation to being, experience, or language as such. In this sense, poetry is not a scientific or cognitive orientation to world-disclosure embodied in language, but a negotiation of the differences between poetry and language, notably the difference between the cognitive contents embodied in poetic technique and the extent to which poetic technique can make language 'use' recognizable as the circumscribed content of different contexts of meaning. Modernist interest in metaphysical wit is motivated by recognition of poetic techniques for assimilating new kinds of scientific knowledge within existing poetic conventions. Such techniques do not embody scientific thought, or even a sensuous thinking through of science, so much as reveal historical dissociations in the resources of poetry as compared with those of science. The means provided by poetic technique emerge as decidedly limited instruments for any cognitive inquiry with comparable ambitions to science, becoming recognizable in the pejorative sense as instruments which are merely 'witty'. Postmetaphysical poetry recognizes the historical limits of existing poetic techniques, radicalizing such techniques through experiential constraints. The art of wit attempts, then, to reckon with the consequences of the linguistic turn evident in the challenges posed to philosophy by modern science. Poetic wit remains merely witty in the pejorative sense insofar as it fails to radicalize its techniques to allow poetry to become an autonomous recognition of language as a cognitive medium. The radicalization of poetic wit situates poetry accordingly as a critique of wit's social and historical fate, and as something more than an unacknowledged science park.

# The Organ Bath

David Kinloch

## With an Introduction

by Alison Gurney

Having failed to think of an appropriate object that could safely be taken from my laboratory to lunch, I took along a sheet of images of blood vessel preparations labelled with fluorescent markers when I met with David Kinloch. The images were representative of my main research interest, which is the mechanisms controlling the diameter of blood vessels in the lung and thereby regulating pulmonary blood pressure. David had read my web page in advance of the meeting and had a number of questions about its content. In conjunction with the images, these questions led the initial discussion, mainly about the nature of my research. After lunch I gave David a brief tour of my laboratories, where he saw a range of technologies used to investigate various aspects of blood vessel function. It is interesting that he chose to write about the organ bath, which is a double-walled, glass chamber through which warm water circulates to maintain isolated, intact organs (e.g., blood vessels) in an environment close to that found in the body. The organ bath does not represent the mainstream of my research, which is on individual cells removed from vessels, but it has an important use in establishing the physiological significance to the intact vessels of our findings at the single cell level. Moreover, the organ bath is the classical tool of the pharmacologist and has been instrumental in the discovery of many widely used therapeutic drugs.

Before our meeting I had little interest in poetry and had not read any since school, but I was curious to see what a poet would make of what we do. Although I was unable to read David's poetry before our meeting, I could see from his web page that science is not among his usual choices of subject matter and he later confirmed that his participation in science also ended with school. Nevertheless, the meeting was productive, resulting initially in a lighthearted poem 237 lines long. We discussed the use of language in science. Although this discussion covered specialized scientific terminology, David also pointed out common words used in a scientific context where the meaning was not obvious. This interest in language is evident in his previous poetry and in his poem about the organ bath, where words and concepts associated with different aspects of my research are connected in unusual ways and the word 'organ' is explored in different contexts. It is interesting how these connections are made. Although the first lines deal with scientific concepts, the poem then diverges into a musical theme, returning to science again at the end. Such freedom to change direction is not afforded to the scientist, who works in an increasingly focused way. I perhaps gained most insight into the process of creating poetry from the initial, much longer version of David's poem, where the flow between ideas was more gradual and detailed than it is in the shortened, revised version published here. My feeling is that scientists and poets both make use of lateral thinking in formulating ideas, but otherwise they work in quite different ways.

## The Organ Bath

*for Alison Gurney*

Just as you record the ions flowing
Through lung membrane strung
Between the test tubes of an 'organ bath',
So I encourage electron transport
Across the gap junction of connected words
And amplify the current linking them:
Imagine flooding 'organ' with 'Lucifer
Yellow', a fluorescent dye that illuminates
The evanescent footprint of warm air
Among the pathways of the body;
The word lights up and all its associations
Sing as Ion did to Socrates: 'reed organ'
Conducts you to the 'organ-pipe cactus',
'Organ-pipe coral', but some organs

Are just more loveable than others,
Above them all the Steam Calliope,
Named for 'the fair voiced' muse of epic poetry,
Whose tiny knurled wheels inked rollers up
With sound and kept the Mississippi riverboats
In fine, full-throated voice. Implements,
Musical instruments, organs of the body
Leviathan the flood which pours down
From the Indo-European *worg
And gave Greek 'ergon', meaning 'work'.
This is our work, our 'organ bath':
'Work immersed in water, in mud',
The world, the body, the poem
Breathed through the lungs of language,
Steaming out its Calliope songs.

# Contemporary Psychology and Contemporary Poetry: Perspectives on Mood Disorders

Kay Redfield Jamison

It is not always obvious when listening to scientists or talking with poets that their intellectual and emotional worlds overlie. But of course they do. Poetry and science have common roots in observation and they take their cues from the rhythms and patterns of the natural world. Scientists and poets alike must put words to what they see and think and both require rigorous intellectual discipline in order to do so. Scientists and poets share a keen response to the beauty of nature and take delight in the act of discovery or creating. Both must communicate their ideas to others and so appreciate the use of language and a clarity of image. Psychological science, in particular, has in common with poetry a profound interest in human nature and emotion.

From my perspective, as someone trained as a scientist and clinical psychologist but who has read and loved poetry from the time I was a young child, there is a tension between literature and the neurosciences (those research disciplines which deal with behaviour and the brain; for example, psychology, psychiatry, neurochemistry, neuropharmacology, neurogenetics, and neurology), but the tension is not so great as often imagined. The methods of science are not those of the arts and the ways of communicating are different, yet there is much that poets can learn from psychology and psychologists can learn from poets. The divide between psychological science and the arts is real and not to be minimized but it makes no sense to emphasize differences in methods to such an extent that shared elements are underreckoned.

In general, I think, scientists tend to be better versed in the arts than artists are in the sciences. Some of this is due to the nature of the educational process: schools and universities require a more extensive background in the humanities than in the sciences. It is also much easier to educate oneself in the arts than in the sciences, which are no longer as comprehensible as they were in Sir Humphrey Davy's nineteenth-century world of vapours and gases, or Charles Darwin's of finches and evolutionary theory. Modern chemistry and molecular biology are far more complex and daunting, requiring a level of scientific and mathematical knowledge unimaginable to Byron, Coleridge, and Shelley who, with other Romantic poets, were fascinated by the science of their times. Contemporary science is less accessible, faster-paced, and often more threatening to those who do not professionally read or study it.

This is true as well for modern psychological science. While most contemporary poets are broadly familiar with the principles of psychoanalysis, and many literary critics have incorporated psychoanalytic theories into their teaching and writings, the science of psychology has moved far past this body of work. Indeed, academic psychology was almost always ambivalent in its attitude toward psychoanalysis and, for the most part, perceived it as speculative and extreme. Many psychologists and psychiatrists believe that the literary excesses of psychoanalytic interpretation have made it difficult for more scientific studies of writers to be taken with the seriousness they warrant. Case-histories, the description and psychological interpretation of individual lives, are no longer central to scientific psychology. Contemporary psychology is based more upon the results of experimental studies of normal behaviour, psychopathology, and research findings from genetics, cognitive science, brain-imaging techniques, neurochemistry, pharmacology, and investigations of gene–environment interactions.

What happens to the dialogue between poetry and psychology in such times of exceedingly rapid and sophisticated neuroscience research, research which is radically changing our fundamental understanding of how we feel, think, learn, and behave? What can psychologists learn from poets and what, in turn, can poets learn from modern psychology? I believe, in fact, that both can learn a great deal from one another and that nowhere is this more apparent than in our attempts to understand the nature and meaning of normal and pathological moods and the role that moods play in the creative process. I will focus on this area of intellectual overlap, in part because mood disorders are my academic and clinical speciality and, in part, because moods are such an essential part of what it means to be human.

Poets contribute uniquely to our psychological understanding of moods. They are able to conjure moods in their work that are among the most subtle, yet profound expressions of human emotions that exist. Poets articulate in their descriptions of their own experiences of depression and mania, as well as in their poetry, what the extremes of moods—despair and exultation—feel like, and they give unsurpassed accounts of the toll mental illness can take. They give words to the inexpressible and make palpable the unimaginable and harrowing. On occasion, they also articulate the role that these extremes in moods, as well as the suffering caused by them, play in their creative work. While it is bad literary criticism and even worse science to argue psychiatric diagnosis from the poetry itself, there has been, as we shall see, a great deal of scientific study of depressive illness in the lives of poets. Before turning to those psychological investigations of mood disorders in poets, however, it is important to take note of the essential perspective on moods, and disorders of mood, that modern poets bring to psychologists. Because it is inappropriate to analyse the mental state of living poets, the poets I will discuss are from a slightly earlier time.

Robert Lowell (1917–77), like many poets of his era, wrote with brutal honesty about his own mania and depressions; he was not, he made clear, alone in experiencing this kind of suffering: 'I feel the jagged gash with which my contemporaries died,' he said. There was 'personal anguish everywhere. We can't dodge it, and shouldn't worry that we are uniquely marked and fretted and must somehow keep even-tempered, amused, and in control. John B[erryman] in his mad way keeps talking about something evil stalking us poets. That's a bad way to talk, but there's some truth in it.'[1] Indeed, among his American contemporaries, John Berryman, Theodore Roethke, Elizabeth Bishop, Louise Bogan, Delmore Schwartz, Randall Jarrell, Anne Sexton, and Sylvia Plath were only a few of the many poets who had the same or related illnesses (as did, in the generation slightly before them, Hart Crane, Vachel Lindsay, Edna St Vincent Millay, and Sara Teasdale). Berryman, Crane, Lindsay, Plath, Sexton, Teasdale, and quite probably Jarrell as well, committed suicide. Most also drank to excess, which is characteristic of those with depressive illnesses, especially manic-depression.

Scottish poet Douglas Dunn has observed that Lowell dissolved the line between person and persona and, in so doing, expanded the territory of poetry; his poetic advances, he believes, were paralleled by his private terrors. This is certainly true. Lowell described his private terrors in poetry that was, to his dismay, labelled 'confessional'. As Frank Bidart has rightfully pointed out, 'confessional' was a misnomer: Lowell's 'audacity, his resourcefulness and boldness lie not in his candor but his art'.[2] Whatever the label, Lowell's power was such that he put his madness into both the public and the psychological domain. He wrote about mania particularly, as well as about its lingering, devastating impact on his life. His words give a psychological understanding only possible through poetry, or through prose written by a poet. I frequently use Lowell's writings about his illness when teaching medical students and residents about mania because there is simply no better description available. Here, for example, he describes the grandiosity and paranoia of one of his manic attacks:

> Seven years ago I had an attack of pathological enthusiasm. The night before I was locked up I ran about the streets of Bloomington Indiana crying out against devils and homosexuals. I believed I could stop cars and paralyze their forces by merely standing in the middle of the highway with my arms outspread . . . Bloomington stood for Joyce's hero and Christian regeneration. Indiana stood for the evil, unexorcised, aboriginal Indians. I suspected I was a reincarnation of the Holy Ghost, and had become homicidally hallucinated. To have known the glory, violence and banality of such an experience is corrupting.[3]

'Pathological enthusiasm' is one of the best descriptions for mania I know. A medical recitation of manic symptoms—grandiosity, irritability, restless energy, paranoia, euphoria, lack of need for sleep, poor judgement, hallucinations, delusions—cannot begin to capture the complexity of the madness that Lowell portrays so brilliantly. Elsewhere, in an essay 'Near the Unbalanced Aquarium', he writes, 'I began to feel tireless, madly sanguine, menaced, and menacing. I entered the Payne-Whitney Clinic for all those afflicted in mind . . . the old menacing hilarity was growing in me.'[4] It is hard to imagine a more powerful or concise portrayal of mania: 'tireless, madly sanguine, menaced, and menacing.' It says in a few words what paragraphs of clinical description in a medical textbook cannot begin to. But Lowell is perhaps most powerful when writing about the effects of treatment, which, in his time, was more deadening and less effective than it is now. (In fact, Lowell responded well to lithium when he was prescribed it in the late 1960s. He relapsed only when his lithium level was lowered precipitously.) Consider his description of being admitted to a psychiatric ward, the day-to-day indignities of living with the realities of madness, and the stifling effects of Thorazine, one of first drugs used to treat psychosis:

> I was then transferred to a new floor, where the patients were deprived of their belts, pajama cords, and shoestrings. We were not allowed to carry matches, and had to request the attendants to light our cigarettes. For holding up my trousers, I invented an inefficient, stringless method which I considered picturesque and called Malayan. Each morning before breakfast, I lay naked to the waist in my knotted Malayan pajamas and received the first of my round-the-clock injections of chloropromazene [sic]: left shoulder, right shoulder, right buttock, left buttock. My blood became like melted lead. I could hardly swallow my breakfast, because I so dreaded the weighted bending down that would be necessary for making my bed. And the rational exigencies of bedmaking were more upsetting than the physical. I wallowed through badminton doubles, as though I were a diver in the full billowings of his equipment on the bottom of the sea. I sat gaping through Scrabble games, unable to form the simplest word; I had to be prompted by a nurse, and even then couldn't make any sense of the words the nurse had formed for me.[5]

Then, too, is his immensely poignant description of the grim territory between mad and normal, the period of recuperating, the long, dreary time to recovery. In 'Home After Three Months Away' Lowell writes of this and his psychological fragility:

> Recuperating, I neither spin nor toil.
> Three stories down below,
> a choreman tends our coffin's length of soil,
> and seven horizontal tulips blow.
> Just twelve months ago,
> these flowers were pedigreed
> imported Dutchmen, now no one need
> distinguish them from weed.
> Bushed by the late spring snow,
> they cannot meet
> another year's snowballing enervation.

I keep no rank nor station.

Cured, I am frizzled, stale and small.[6]

The damage from mania was not to Lowell alone. In letters to T. S. Eliot he apologized for his behaviour when he was manic—'When the "enthusiasm" is coming on me it is accompanied by a feverish reaching out to my friends,' he wrote. 'After it's over I wince and wither'—and spoke of the acute embarrassment he felt: 'The whole business has been very bruising, and it is fierce facing the pain I have caused, and humiliating [to] think that it has all happened before and that control and self-knowledge come so slowly, if at all.'[7]

Many other poets of Lowell's era provide formidable insights into mania and depression as well, but here I will give example from just three: Velimir Khlebnikov on manic thinking, Sylvia Plath on her murderous rages, and John Berryman on living in the shadows of suicide. Khlebnikov, who was at times institutionalized for his illness, imagined in his manic delusions that he possessed equations which would explain everything: the stars, life, and even death. He gives an unparalleled example of the expansive, not to say cosmic thought patterns so typical of mania:

> The surface of Planet Earth is 510,051,300 square kilometres; the surface of a red corpuscle—that citizen and star of man's Milky Way—0.000, 128 square millimetres. These citizens of the sky and the body have concluded a treaty, whose provision is this: the surface of the star Earth divided by the surface of the tiny corpuscular star equals 365 times 10 to the tenth power ($365 \times 10^{10}$). A beautiful concordance of two worlds, one that establishes man's right to first place on Earth. This is the first article of the treaty between the government of blood cells and the government of heavenly bodies. A living walking Milky Way and his tiny star have concluded a 365-point agreement with the Milky Way in the sky and its great Earth Star. The dead Milky Way and the living one have affixed their signatures to it as two equal and legal entities.[8]

Sylvia Plath, in a journal entry, addressed the more savage moods that can underlie both suicide and violence toward others:

> I have a violence in me that is hot as death-blood. I can kill myself or—I know it now—even kill another. I could kill a woman, or wound a man. I think I could. I gritted to control my hands, but had a flash of bloody stars in my head as I stared that sassy girl down, and a blood-longing to [rush] at her and tear her to bloody beating bits.[9]

John Berryman took on suicide itself, speaking as one whose father and aunt had committed suicide, as well as someone who would eventually do the same himself. In his poem 'Of Suicide' he wrote: 'Reflexions on suicide, and on my father possess me | . . . Of suicide I continually think;'[10] in another, he wrote yet again of the painful legacy left by his father's suicide:

> The marker slants, flowerless, day's almost done,
> I stand above my father's grave with rage,
> often, often before
> I've made this awful pilgrimage to one
> who cannot visit me, who tore his page
> out: I come back for more,
>
> I spit upon this dreadful banker's grave
>
> Who shot his heart out in a Florida dawn[11]

Poets can inform the work of both clinicians and researchers by articulating the subtle and extreme changes which occur in pathological mood states. In order to understand and intelligently treat mania or depression it is not enough simply to establish the presence or absence of a clinical syndrome; it is necessary to have a genuine feel for the phenomenology of the symptoms that make up the syndrome, a visceral awareness of the devastating consequences of having depression or mania, and some sense of what it is like to live with the often difficult side-effects of the medications used to treat depressive illnesses. Personal accounts by writers are irreplaceable sources in helping to do this.

Just as I would argue that psychologists and psychiatrists cannot fully understand depression and mania without reading first-person accounts of illness, I would also argue that writers, biographers, and literary critics profit immensely by having a grounding in psychological science. Moods and temperament, as we know from a large number and wide variety of types of studies, are enormously important not only in understanding the lives and work of poets, but also in understanding the nature of the creative process itself. There is a large body of scientific research that shows a consistent and powerful link between actual disorders of mood—depression and manic-depression—and imaginative work. More than thirty studies have found that artists, writers, and other creative individuals are far more likely than the general public to suffer from depressive illnesses.[12] Clearly, most people who are creative do not have mood disorders and most people who have mood disorders are not unusually creative. But the evidence is strong that creative individuals have a *disproportionately* high rate of depression and manic-depression; they are also more likely to die by suicide.

Along with other psychologists and psychiatrists, I have studied the close relationship between intense moods, psychopathology, and imaginative thought. In a recent book, *Exuberance*,[13] I discuss the possible underlying explanations for the relationship between manic thinking and behaviour and creative work and in an earlier book, *Touched With Fire: Manic-Depressive Illness and the Artistic Temperament*,[14] I looked at the role not only of mania but of depression as well. I draw on my experience in writing these books before turning to a discussion of the implications of such findings for poets and their poetry.

Many theories have evolved to explain the disproportionately high rates of mood disorders in poets and other writers—high levels of energy and enthusiasm, a tendency to take risks, an underlying restlessness and discontent, more sensitively tuned senses, and a wide range and intensity of emotional experiences shared in common by the artistic and manic-depressive temperaments—but the most commonly and scientifically tested are the overlapping changes in mood and thinking which take place in manic and creative thought.

Both creative and manic thinking are distinguished by fluidity and by the capacity to combine ideas in ways that form new and original connections.[15] Thinking in both tends to be dendritic in nature: less bound to specific goals, more divergent. Diversity and scattering of ideas were first noted thousands of years ago as one of the hallmarks of manic thought and are now incorporated into the formal diagnostic criteria for mania. The expansiveness of manic thought can open up a wider range of cognitive options and broaden the field of observation.

Manic patients and writers, when evaluated with a variety of neuropsychological tests, tend to combine ideas or images in a way that 'blurs, broadens, or shifts conceptual boundaries', a type of thinking that is called conceptual overinclusiveness.[16] They vary in this from normal subjects and patients with schizophrenia. Researchers at the University of Iowa, for example, have shown that 'both writers and manics tend to sort in large groups, change dimensions while in the process of sorting, arbitrarily change starting points, or use vague distantly related concepts as categorizing principles.' The writers were better able than the manics to maintain control over their patterns of thinking, however, and used 'controlled flights of fancy' rather than the more bizarre sorting systems used by the patients.[17]

Manic thought is quick and often imaginatively combinatory; especially in its milder forms, it contributes significantly to performance on tests measuring creativity. Nineteenth-century physicians who tested their patients for fluency of word associations during mania found that it increased dramatically. Later, in the 1940s, researchers at the Payne Whitney Clinic in New York showed that their manic-depressive patients when elated also showed greatly increased verbal and associative ability.[18] They found that normal subjects, when given a mild dose of the stimulant dexedrine sulphate, improved on tests of associative fluency. The performance of the normal subjects while on dexedrine remained significantly lower than that of the manics, however.

Rhyming, punning, and a wide variety of sound associations also increase during mania, and recent studies find that the number of unusual responses to word-association tasks increases threefold. The number of statistically common responses drops dramatically.[19] The increase in word associations is generally proportionate to the severity of manic symptoms. Patients when manic often spontaneously write poetry and speak in rhyme, even though when they are well they have no particular interest in poetry.

Psychologists have also shown that by artificially inducing elevated moods in some individuals and not in others, those who have had their moods elevated show striking changes in originality and fluency of thinking.[20] They give a larger number of total responses, as well as more original ones, to words presented during a word-association task, a psychological measure that is associated with creativity. They are also more likely to classify concepts in a broader rather than a more narrow way. Depressive mood has the opposite effect, namely, it inhibits spontaneous and creative thought.

Mood and thinking changes during mania are of course far more intense than those induced by psychologists during experimental studies. This suggests several things. The relationship between elated mood and fluency of thinking is probably, up to a point, a direct one: the more elevated the mood, the more fluent and diverse the thinking. Too much elevation, however, results in fragmented thinking and even psychosis. Likewise, the level of enthusiasm with which an idea is held has an impact on the likelihood that an idea will be put into action. (People who have manic-depressive illness are, when manic, utterly certain of their convictions and therefore more likely to act without the brakes or judgement provided by rational thought.) In other words, mood affects not only thought but action. Mood has a direct impact on the uses to which thought is put.

Several years ago I conducted a study of eminent writers and artists and found, like most researchers before and after me, that they were far more likely than the general population to have been treated for mania or depression.[21] One of my major interests was to look not just at psychopathology, however, but to better understand the role of moods in the creative process itself. Virtually all of the writers and artists had experienced extended periods of intense creative activity characterized by striking increases in enthusiasm, energy, rapid and fluent thought, and self-confidence. Most of the writers and artists reported that a sharp rise in their mood usually *preceded* the onset of their creative work. Ruth Richards and Dennis Kinney, in a Harvard study of manic-depression and creativity, found that the overwhelming majority of their subjects experienced mildly to very elevated moods during the periods when they were most creative. When moods were highest, so too was the expansiveness of their thinking and the quickness of their mental associations.[22]

Clearly, the act of creating often creates elation. But studies of mania and creativity, along with the results from literally scores of studies of experimentally induced positive mood, suggest that the opposite may be as or more important: that is, elevated or expansive moods come first; creative thinking follows. Creativity may then elevate mood, which can, in turn, lead to extended periods of reverberating moods, energies, and imagination. High mood and energy may lead to decreased sleep as well, which often further elevates mood.

Characteristics of a non-cognitive nature also link mania with the artistic temperament. Many of these are related to the tempestuous side of the manic temperament which, when coupled with pre-existing creativity and discipline, can radically change the nature of a writer's life and work. Normal judgement, when replaced by reckless disinhibition, is usually destructive but, in some circumstances, it can be put to good creative use.

Depression, when severe, is almost always antithetical to creative work. But in its milder forms and, in its aftermath as an influence on a writer's beliefs and emotions, depression can be a positive if painful force. Anne Sexton spoke of the centrality of pain in her poetry: 'I, myself,' she wrote, 'alternate between hiding behind my own hands, protecting myself anyway possible, and this other, this seeing, touching other. I guess I mean that creative people must not avoid the pain that they get dealt . . . Hurt must be examined like a plague.'[23]

Robert Lowell, who was generally sceptical about depression as an asset to his imaginative life—'I don't think it is a visitation of the angels but a weaking of the blood,'[24] he once said—qualified his scepticism elsewhere. 'Depression's no gift from the Muse,' he wrote. 'At worst, I do nothing. But often I've written, and wrote one whole book—*For the Union Dead*—about witheredness . . . Most of the best poems, the most personal, are gathered crumbs from the lost cake. I had better moods, but the book is lemony, soured, and dry, the drought I had touched with my own hands. That, too, may be poetry—on sufferance.'[25]

Depression forces not only reflection, it forces a slower, more ruminative pace. It also brings to many a new sensitivity and compassion for the suffering of others, gives a capacity to feel that may not have been there before (Lowell, for example, wrote of 'seeing too much and feeling it | with one skin-layer missing.')[26] and makes death more immediate and less deniable. Depression and mania can change a writer's life, often for the worse; sometimes, however, it is for the better. Extreme mood states, which are brought about by changes in the brain, in turn also change the brain, and it is both the causal and secondary changes that are of particular interest to neuroscientists. The repeated demonstration of higher rates of depression and mania in writers (rates that are even higher in poets) raises several important questions, and concerns, for both poets and scientists.

Neuroimaging techniques, which allow scientists to study activation patterns in the brain while subjects are looking, imagining, listening, or computing, are giving us a new understanding of the complex geography of moods and thought. Although still very much a developing technology, brain imaging has begun to pinpoint the biology and functions of moods. It has also opened the possibility of mapping the brains of poets or scientists as they create, and visualizing those areas of the brain which are activated, or 'light up', as an individual writes when manic, depressed, or normal.

In a recent hint of the possibilities to come, Warren Warren, professor of chemistry at Princeton, showed that, at least in the one subject tested, the prefrontal cortex (a highly evolved part of the brain which is implicated in both reasoning and emotion) was far more activated when the person was reading a poem than when reading bureaucratic, unemotional prose.[27] The poem, 'Once I Looked Into Your Eyes,' was written by Paul Muldoon after a visit to Warren's laboratory as part of the project of this present book. Muldoon imagined what would happen if brain-imaging techniques were able to trace a lover's lies and deceits:

> Once I looked into your eyes
> and the only tissue I saw through
> was the tissue of lies
> behind everything you do.
>
> Once I looked into your heart
> and imagined I could trace
> the history of the art
> of deception in your face.
>
> Now there's something more than a chance
> of making molecules dance
> I'm somewhat gratified to find
> that by laser—enhanced
> magnetic resonance
> if nothing else, I may read your mind.[28]

Muldoon's poem is an imaginative rendering of the unforeseeable possibilities of neuroscience. There are many such unforeseeable possibilities, including questions that bear directly on the role of intense moods in the creation of poetry. What, for example, are the effects of current psychiatric treatments such as lithium, psychotherapy, the anticonvulsants, antidepressants, and antipsychotics on creativity? Once the genes for the highly hereditable manic-depression are identified, what are the potential uses and abuses of that information by parents, doctors, insurance companies, universities, and society at large? What will happen when pharmacological enhancements of mood are developed, as they inevitably will be? What will it mean to the arts, and to society, when some combination of genetic testing, diagnostic brain imaging, and pre-symptomatic treatment make extremes in mood optional or non-existent? Do we risk 'normalizing' society to such an extent that we lose diversity and boldness of temperament? Are teachers in the arts and humanities responsible for knowing enough about depression and its treatments to help their students who are at high risk for depression and suicide? If so, is there an obligation to be familiar with what is known scientifically, rather than persisting to hold beliefs about mental illness and treatments that may be decades out of date? How much should biographers learn about psychology, temperament, and psychopathology (in addition to the history, culture, and languages they more usually are taught)? Can a writer's life and work really be understood without at least a rudimentary scientific understanding of emotions, temperament, cognitive psychology, and genetics? Can neuroscientists, in turn, truly understand mood and emotion without understanding them from an individual, humanistic perspective? Can a neuroscientist meaningfully study mental associations and cognitive processing without appreciating the extraordinary capacities for verbal fluency, rhythm, and emotional memory that mark the work of a poet?

Psychological science is going to become far more complex over the coming decades, not less so. We need poets who can comprehend the human implications of these complexities, and neuroscientists who are aware of this.

# Afterword

Gillian Beer

How do we avoid collapsing the differences between science and poetry in our eagerness to explore their interactions? Questions of the diversity between such forms of experience, of the distance between them in approach, scope, and truth-telling, are mooted in the present collection; sometimes these questions are set aside, sometimes sides are taken. But the questions continue to come back, to be answered anew. Even the anxiety about kinship shows that all the contributors have moved a long way from the common assumption that science and poetry have little to say to each other, because their uses of language are inimical. That is a position that continues to be sustained even among the most radical thinkers about science. Witness the opening sentence to *Keywords in Evolutionary Biology*:

> Unlike poets, and even unlike most speakers of ordinary prose, scientists expect and indeed generally assume that their language is (or at least ought to be) both precise and clear.[1]

Thus Evelyn Fox Keller and Elisabeth A. Lloyd open their challenging introduction to the collection of essays by scientists that draws inspiration for its method from Raymond Williams's *Keywords* (1983, revised edition). Of course, they do not let the matter rest there: implicit already is their later contention that the language of scientists is freighted with ambiguity and that technical terms 'carry, along with their ties to the natural world of inanimate and animate objects, indissoluble ties to the social world of ordinary language speakers'. Still, their prime example of the figure whose language is not 'precise and clear', and who feels no need for it to be so, is the poet. Gathered in that example are a great many assumptions about the language of poetry. It is implicitly understood as vague, obscure, transcendent, concerned to raise rather than to describe—or perhaps, more positively, to open out rather than focus sharply. As they describe the purpose of scientific terms the contrast intended with poetry becomes more specific:

> Scientific terms are intended to mean neither more nor less than what they say, and to say neither more nor less than what they mean.

Keller and Lloyd know how hard it is to achieve and sustain such stabilization.

Implicit in their description of scientific terms as meaning 'neither more nor less than what they say' is a set of co-workers who can judge the exact equivalence of meaning to performance within their joint project, and students who can learn that accepted equivalence. Certainly, scientific terms once taken from the context of the original joint project have a way of merging again with the loose talk of common life and acquiring a nimbus of possible significations not vouched for by their progenitors (witness: selection, chaos theory, even DNA). Moreover, as Hugh Aldersey-Williams has recently pointed out:

> Scientific writing does not produce—or usually wish to produce—a lasting bond with the reader. Its purpose is to persuade, and it is the peculiarity of scientific literature that if it succeeds in this task it ceases to be read.[2]

Most of what is being invoked in this collection is 'science', not 'scientific writing': that is, the concerns here are with ecology, physics, astronomy, psychiatry, and other forms of gathered and shifting knowledge, rather than with specific scientific papers or books. The poets feel great pleasure in scientific terms as 'strange dialects' ('From *zymogens* to *Avogadro's Number*' as Robert Crawford puts it in his poem 'Biology').[3] They also invoke the help of such knowledge in 'navigating the world', in John Burnside's phrase, but as he declares:

> this is a writer's way of looking at things, a concern with language and concepts, rather than an appreciation of method or mathematics. Yet I think of my own work as a discipline as much akin to *scientia* as it is to rhapsody.

In the present collection Miroslav Holub argues that a scientist writing poetry must remain a scientist because that guarantees a 'scientific hard-centred approach in the essential idea or theme of the poem' and in his conclusion he asserts that science in poetry is 'not the function of scientific terms, expressions, results, and technical ideas' but rather that the scientist as a member of an assured intellectual community is relieved of 'abysmal feelings' and can express hard-centred 'immanent optimism'. The strength of the scientist poet, it seems, derives from *being elsewhere* as well as in the usual vocabulary of the poet. Ethical assurance is what counts in Holub's self-definition.

Yet, language does count too: earlier in the essay, Holub seeks to extend the range of poetic allusion to include terms 'from pulsars to leptons, from prokaryotic organisms to our lymphocytes and interferons'. He adds the rather limp proviso, 'provided they can be used in a comprehensible way' but then jettisons or goes beyond that to accept their value as 'dark images or sounds in an otherwise clear development of the poem'. So, change the context of reading and scientific terms become 'dark images or sounds' rather than being 'precise and clear'. They are the mysteries, the sonorities, within the 'clear development' of the poem's reasoning. Holub here recognizes, if a little uneasily, that terms can shed their professional stability and re-emerge as dark matter, not to be described, simply present.

Holub's emphasis on the scientist as poet, in the sense of the scientist writing verse, is unusual among the contributors here, many of whom are poets responding to scientific possibilities without claiming extensive professional expertise. The scientist who writes verse is a well-established figure and, in verse, the most creative of them can present warnings, alternatives, and satires of science. Take, for example, the great Scottish scientist James Clerk Maxwell's poem 'Molecular Evolution', written for the Red Lion Club at Belfast in 1874, a roistering intellectual club within the British Association for the Advancement of Science. The prime audience thus knows the limits of the satire as well as feeling its shafts. Maxwell in the poem broods on chance, eroticism, and nonsense as aspects of the material world and of scientific insight. The poem opens:

At quite uncertain times and places,
  The atoms left their heavenly path,
And by fortuitous embraces,
  Engendered all that being hath.
And though they seem to cling together,
  And form 'associations' here,
Yet, soon or late, they burst their tether,
  And through the depths of space career.

The poem's last two high spirited verses run:

Hail, Nonsense! dry nurse of Red Lions,
  From thee the wise their wisdom learn,
From thee they cull those truths of science,
  Which into thee again they turn.
What combination of ideas,
  Nonsense alone can wisely form!
What sage has half the power that she has,
  To take the towers of Truth by storm?

Yield, then, ye rules of rigid reason!
  Dissolve, thou too, too solid sense!
Melt into nonsense for a season,
  Then in some nobler form condense.
Soon, all too soon, the chilly morning,
  This flow of soul will crystallize,
Then those who Nonsense now are scorning,
  May learn, too late, where wisdom lies.[4]

Maxwell understands how sudden 'combination of ideas' and dissolving the rigid rules of reason' may 'take the towers of Truth by storm'. 'The flow of soul' melting the boundaries of solid sense leads to nonsense and also to wisdom: the two, he suggests, may be—for a time at least—the same. Clerk Maxwell certainly did not eschew carefully controlled experiment or the hard graft of repeated observation and calculation. But he recognizes how leaps and condensations are part of the scientific imagination and of the scientist's work: to *express* that, and to keep the recognition within bounds, he requires the permissive form of satirical poetry. So there is a backlash within the enterprise. The Red Lion Club is respectable because its members are distinguished scientists; that distinction allows them, in semi-private, to scoff a little at the solemnities of science.

In another poem from the same occasion, 'Song of the Cub', a novice scientist is shocked by their activities:

My life's undivided devotion
  To Science I solemnly vowed,
I'd dredge up the bed of the ocean,
  I'd draw down the spark from the cloud.
To follow my thoughts as they go on,
  Electrodes I'd place in my brain;

Nay, I'd swallow a live entozoon,
New feelings of life to obtain.

O where are those high feasts of Science?
O where are the words of the wise?
I hear but the roar of Red Lions,
I eat what their Jackal supplies.[5]

The frolics of the elders trouble the young. Maxwell, though, knows that their freedom has been earned by their scientific labour. As Edwin Morgan writes, in the guise of the astronomer Giordano Bruno, 'It is reason sets imagination free.' Nonsense relies on prior sense even while it generates fresh meaning.

There is assured intellectual community here, certainly, as Holub claims, but there is also willingness to test the claims of scientific method and to acknowledge processes that lie beyond the peripheries of measured reason. Scientists, Clerk Maxwell proposes, here and in other of his writings, must acknowledge the degree to which unconscious accords carry conscious investigation forward. Here, it may seem, is where poets come back in to the argument. But it is worth noticing first that Maxwell is an extraordinarily adept maker of pastiche, able to operate the Pindaric Ode, complex Latin metres, and every kind of prosodic trick. That is, he is very much alongside the *conscious* skills of the poet and uses those skills to drive his praise of unknown processes.

That emphasis on multiple systems active in synchrony and syncopation must be one of the meeting points of poetry and mathematics. The poet works with line-ending, with cursive syntax that often overflows line-ending and shifts the meaning of the precedent line (which yet retains its prior autonomy). These overlapping motions run alongside delayed structures of sense in which verbs are withheld, and the recoil of rhyme that forestalls the usual processes of auditory forgetting, elongating and sustaining connections that cannot be rationalized. In rhyme the ear is often in contention with the eye, challenging hierarchies of sense. All these systems play across each other; none dominates; none perishes. Here, even the least mathematical of us can glimpse parallels to the ways in which mathematicians condense multiple skeins of thinking into theorems that can express simultaneity as much as sequence.

But as Simon Armitage warns, the word 'poet' in relation to scientific knowledge can imply simply 'the inability to engage with the subject at the approved and accepted level'—as in the offered course he cites, 'Astronomy for Poets'. Most of the poets who write here, however, have no intention of pretending to be scientists. Rather, they are not content to curtail their vocabulary or their concerns; yet they recognize that their contact with current scientific theories may—often, must—be fugitive and partial. Other people, scientific workers, have spent their lives gathering particular specialized knowledge on the base of many other lives spent gathering such knowledge. The language of the scientific paper is intricate, precise, and occluded, its information available immediately and securely to a participating group of co-workers, and hardly available at all to those beyond that group. Take for example a typical description of method:

Hepatotoxicity was assessed by liver histopathology and by measuring plasma alanine amino transferase (ALT) levels as previously described (Fariss et al, 1993). Briefly, liver sections were fixed in 10% neutral buffered formalin and stained with either Periodic acid-Schiff reagent or Harris hematoxylin and cosin reagents.[6]

The spell-check on my computer went wild among these unknown forms claiming to be words. The experiment described involved feeding poison to rats. The project was to discover which compound gave greater protection against that poison.

There is no need to apologize for not being able to live several lives to the full at once. Instead, encounter may be the way through. This is where the volume undertakes something quite fresh. The encounters between working scientists and poets chart the exploration each undertakes and that they undertake together, registering sometimes bafflement, sometimes enthusiasm, a sense of things opening and stirring. Out of that encounter the poet produces a poem and the scientist reads it, with pleasure or puzzlement, or both. The poems are there now for us all to read: made work, experiments in time.

Did any of the scientists feel that they understood their own work differently as a result of the encounter? Kevin Warwick, who works on implants to the nervous system, describes with subtlety and honesty his reading of Michael Donaghy's poem 'Grimoire'. For the first time he had to work at the task of reader, he says. And he understood his research from the outside, for the first time, as 'frightening', though from inside he does not feel it so. His last paragraph movingly registers the disturbance and the expansion he experienced through his encounter with the poet's words: 'Through Michael's words I was able to look at myself in a ten-dimensional space.'

The poet's words count. They multiply encounters. They do not redirect research but place it and the person working to produce it in manifold positions simultaneously. The scientist Kevin Warwick here offers a compelling description of the way poetry works, for readers of many sorts.

# NOTES

## INTRODUCTION

1. Alice Crawford, *Paradise Pursued: The Novels of Rose Macaulay* (Madison, Wis.: Fairleigh Dickinson University Press, 1995), 64; Rose Macaulay, *Potterism* (London: Collins, 1920), 231.
2. Hugh MacDiarmid, *Collected Poems* (New York: Macmillan, 1962), 50.
3. Ian F. A. Bell, *Critic as Scientist* (London: Methuen, 1981); see also Alan J. Friedman and Carol C. Donley, *Einstein as Myth and Muse* (Cambridge: Cambridge University Press, 1985).
4. Hugh MacDiarmid, *The Complete Poems*, ed. Michael Grieve and W. R. Aitken (London: Martin, Brian and O'Keeffe, 1978), 2 vols., ii. 802.
5. Adalaide Morris, 'Science and the Mythopoeic Mind: The Case of H. D.', in N. Katherine Hayles (ed.), *Chaos and Order: Complex Dynamics in Literature and Science* (Chicago: University of Chicago Press, 1991), 195–220; Adalaide Morris (ed.), *Sound States: Innovative Poetics and Acoustical Technologies* (Chapel Hill, NC: University of North Carolina Press, 1997), 32–55.
6. Robert Crawford, *The Modern Poet: Poetry, Academia, and Knowledge since the 1750s* (Oxford: Oxford University Press, 2001), ch. 4.
7. See C. P. Snow, *The Two Cultures*, with an introduction by Stefan Collini (Cambridge: Cambridge University Press, 1998).
8. Philip Cornford (ed.), *The Personal World: John Macmurray on Self and Society* (Edinburgh: Floris Books, 1996), 120–1.
9. Paul Muldoon, *The Annals of Chile* (London: Faber and Faber, 1994), 115.

## RAMPAGE, OR SCIENCE IN POETRY

1. See also my essay 'Poetry and Science', in Miroslav Holub, *The Dimension of the Present Moment*, ed. David Young (London: Faber and Faber, 1990), 122–46.
2. Miroslav Holub, *The Rampage*, trans. David Young with Dana Hábová, Rebekah Bloyd, and the author (London: Faber and Faber, 1997), 49.
3. Miroslav Holub, *Shedding Life: Diseases, Politics, and Other Human Conditions*, trans. David Young (Minneapolis: Milkweed Editions, 1997), 1.
4. Holub, *The Rampage*, 71–2.
5. Aldous Huxley, *The Collected Poems*, ed. Donald Watt (London: Chatto and Windus, 1971), 106.

6. Miroslav Holub, *Vanishing Lung Syndrome*, trans. David Young and Dana Hábová (London: Faber and Faber, 1990), 64.
7. Edgar Allan Poe, *Poetical Works* (London: Ward Lock, n.d.), 146.
8. See Miroslav Holub, *Poems Before and After: Collected English Translations*, trans. Ian and Jarmila Milner, Ewald Osers, George Theiner (Newcastle: Bloodaxe Books, 1990), 28.
9. Ibid. 35.
10. Holub, *The Rampage*, 71.
11. Holub, *Vanishing Lung Syndrome*, 45.
12. William Carlos Williams, *Collected Poems*, ed. Christopher MacGowan (Manchester: Carcanet, 1987–8), 2 vols., ii. 419.

### POETRY AND VIRTUAL REALITIES

1. Lucretius, *De Rerum Natura*, ed. Martin Ferguson Smith (Cambridge, Mass.: Harvard University Press, 1992), 82 (i. 999).
2. Ibid. 80 (i. 965–7).
3. T. J. Hogg, *The Life of Percy Bysshe Shelley* (London: Dent, 1933), 56.
4. P. B. Shelley, *Poetical Works*, ed. Thomas Hutchinson, rev. G. M. Matthews (London: Oxford University Press, 1970), 264 (*Prometheus Unbound*, iv. 418–23).
5. John Davidson, *The Poems*, ed. A. Turnbull (Edinburgh: Scottish Academic Press, 1973), 2 vols., ii. 374.
6. Ibid. 444–5.
7. Hugh MacDiarmid, in John Davidson, *A Selection of his Poems*, ed. Maurice Lindsay (London: Hutchinson, 1961), 47–8.
8. Hugh MacDiarmid, *Complete Poems, 1920–1976*, ed. M. Grieve and W. R. Aitken (London: Martin, Brian and O'Keeffe, 1978), 2 vols., ii. 1028–9.
9. Ibid. 1015.
10. Ibid. 782.
11. Ibid. 1057–8.
12. Ibid. 1054.
13. Edwin Morgan, *Collected Poems* (Manchester: Carcanet, 1990), 115.
14. Ibid. 115–16.
15. Ibid. 191.
16. Edwin Morgan, *Sweeping Out the Dark* (Manchester: Carcanet, 1994), 84.
17. Morgan, *Collected Poems*, 486.

18. Philip Larkin, *Required Writing: Miscellaneous Pieces 1955–1982* (London: Faber and Faber, 1983), 53.
19. Edwin Morgan, *Demon* (Glasgow: Mariscat Press, 1999), 7.
20. M. C. Vaz, *Industrial Light & Magic* (London: Virgin, 1996), 231.
21. William Shakespeare, *The Complete Works*, ed. Peter Alexander (London and Glasgow: Collins, 1951), 1151 (V.ii.146–9).
22. Robert Burns, *Poems and Songs*, ed. James Kinsley (Oxford: Oxford University Press, 1969), 251.
23. Edwin Morgan, *Virtual and Other Realities* (Manchester: Carcanet, 1997), 47.
24. Ibid. 54.
25. Ibid. 68.
26. Ibid. 76.
27. Ibid. 91.

#### SPIRIT MACHINES: THE HUMAN AND THE COMPUTATIONAL

1. *Jonathan Swift, A Tale of a Tub and other Works*, ed. Angus Ross and David Woolley (Oxford: Oxford University Press, 1986), 70.
2. See the entry for 'computer' in original, unsupplemented *OED*.
3. See Neil Rhodes and Jonathan Sawday (eds.), *The Renaissance Computer* (London and New York: Routledge, 2000).
4. Robert Crawford, 'Nelson', in Kathleen Jamie and Donny O'Rourke (eds.), *The Glory Signs (New Writing Scotland 16)* (Glasgow: Association for Scottish Literary Studies, 1998), 31.
5. T. S. Eliot, *The Use of Poetry and the Use of Criticism*, 2nd edn. (London: Faber and Faber, 1964), 148.
6. See e.g. Robert Crawford, *Devolving English Literature*, 2nd edn. (Edinburgh: Edinburgh University Press, 2000) and *The Modern Poet* (Oxford: Oxford University Press, 2001), as well as Robert Crawford and Hamish Whyte (eds.), *About Edwin Morgan* (Edinburgh: Edinburgh University Press, 1990).
7. See both W. N. Herbert's chapter in the present book, and Robert Crawford, 'Contemporary Poetry and Academia: The Instance of Informationism', in Andrew Michael Roberts and Jonathan Allison (eds.), *Poetry and Contemporary Culture* (Edinburgh: Edinburgh University Press, 2002), 85–100.
8. Robert Crawford, *A Scottish Assembly* (London: Chatto and Windus, 1990), 10.
9. See Christopher Whyte's meticulous edition of Somhairle MacGill-Eain/Sorley MacLean, *Dain do Eimhir/Poems to Eimhir* (Glasgow: Association for Scottish Literary Studies, 2002).
10. *A Scottish Assembly*, 17.

11. Robert Crawford, 'Cosmopolibackofbeyondism', in W. N. Herbert and Matthew Hollis (eds.), *Strong Words: Modern Poets on Modern Poetry* (Tarset: Bloodaxe Books, 2000), 262–4.
12. *A Scottish Assembly*, 42.
13. See the first three essays in Alice Fulton, *Feeling as a Foreign Language* (St. Paul, Minn.: Graywolf Press, 1999).
14. Robert Fergusson, 'Elegy, On the Death of Mr David Gregory', in *The Poems*, ed. Matthew P. McDiarmid, 2 vols. (Edinburgh: Blackwood for the Scottish Text Society, 1954 and 1956), ii. 1; Hugh MacDiarmid, 'To a Friend and Fellow Poet', in *Collected Poems*, ed. Michael Grieve and W. R. Aitken (London: Martin, Brian and O'Keeffe, 1978), ii. 1057.
15. David Rintoul and J. B. Skinner (eds.), *Poet's Quair* (Edinburgh: Oliver and Boyd, 1966), 430.
16. William Wordsworth, 'Preface' to *Lyrical Ballads* (1805), in *Lyrical Ballads*, ed. Derek Roper, 2nd edn. (London: MacDonald and Evans, 1976), 35–6.
17. Robert Crawford, *Masculinity* (London: Jonathan Cape, 1996), 60.
18. T. S. Eliot, *Collected Poems 1909–1962* (London: Faber and Faber, 1974), 115.
19. Wordsworth, 'Preface', 41.
20. *A Scottish Assembly*, 54.
21. Robert Crawford, *Spirit Machines* (London: Cape, 1999), 65.
22. Fiona Macleod, *The Silence of Amor* (London: Heinemann, 1910), 9.
23. Dante, *Inferno*, Temple Classics edn. (London: Dent, 1900), 2.
24. *Spirit Machines*, 66–7.
25. Robert Crawford, *The Tip of My Tongue* (London: Cape, 2003), 7.

## TESTAMENT AND CONFESSIONS OF AN INFORMATIONIST

1. William Wordsworth, *Selected Poems*, ed. John O. Hayden (Harmondsworth: Penguin, 1999), 445.
2. Stephen Prickett, *Words and the Word* (Cambridge: Cambridge University Press, 1989), 24.
3. See W. N. Herbert, 'God's Astronomer: The Peculiar Universe of the Reverend Thomas Dick', in *Duende: A Dundee Anthology*, *Gairfish*, 2.4 (1991), 49–61.
4. Prickett, *Words and the Word*, 24.
5. Wordsworth, *Selected Poems*, 443.
6. S. T. Coleridge, *Biographia Literaria*, ed. George Watson (London: Dent, 1977), 91.

7. W. B. Yeats, ' "Noetry" and Poetry', *The Bookman*, September 1892, 182.
8. Ezra Pound, *The ABC of Reading* (1934; repr. London: Faber and Faber, 1951), 29.
9. John Davidson, 'The Wasp', in *The Poems*, ed. Andrew Turnbull (2 vols.; Edinburgh: Scottish Academic Press, 1973), i. 179.
10. Hugh MacDiarmid, *Complete Poems* (2 vols; London: Martin, Brian and O'Keeffe, 1978), ii. 885.
11. Edwin Morgan, *Collected Poems* (Manchester: Carcanet, 1990), 275, 462, 415, 283, 559.
12. Thomas Mann, *The Genesis of a Novel* (London: Secker and Warburg, 1961), 115–16.
13. Quoted in Prickett, *Words and the Word*, 40.
14. See Robert Crawford, *Devolving English Literature*, 2nd edn. (Edinburgh: Edinburgh University Press, 2000) and Robert Crawford (ed.), *The Scottish Invention of English Literature* (Cambridge: Cambridge University Press, 1997).
15. Blair, quoted in Prickett, *Words and the Word*, 43; Wordsworth, *Selected Poems*, 434.
16. Coleridge, *Biographia Literaria*, 172, 174.
17. Seamus Heaney, *Preoccupations: Selected Prose, 1968–1978* (London: Faber and Faber, 1984), 217.
18. Coleridge, *Biographia Literaria*, 188–200.
19. Seamus Heaney, *Preoccupations: Selected Prose 1968–1978* (London: Faber and Faber, 1980), 195–6.
20. George Davie, *The Democratic Intellect* (Edinburgh: Edinburgh University Press, 1961), 13.
21. George Davie, *The Crisis of the Democratic Intellect* (Edinburgh: Polygon, 1986), 154.
22. MacDiarmid, '*In Memoriam James Joyce*', in *Selected Poetry*, ed. Alan Riach and Michael Grieve (Manchester: Carcanet, 1992), 246.
23. Davie, *The Democratic Intellect*, 176.
24. MacDiarmid, 'The Kind of Poetry I Want', *Selected Poetry*, 217.
25. Tristan Tzara, 'Dada Manifesto on Feeble Love and Bitter Love', *Seven Dada Manifestos and Lampisteries*, trans. Barbara Wright (London: John Calder, 1981), 42.

### A SCIENCE OF BELONGING: POETRY AS ECOLOGY

1. Ludwig Wittgenstein, *Tractatus Logico-Philosophicus*, trans. D. F. Pears and B. F. McGuinness (London: Routledge and Kegan Paul, 1974), 73.

2. Paul Shepard, *The Only World We've Got: A Paul Shepard Reader* (San Francisco: Sierra Club Books, 1996), 156.
3. Don DeLillo, *Underworld* (New York: Scribner, 1997), 65.
4. Mark Doty, *Still Life with Oysters and Lemon* (Boston: Beacon Press, 2001), 6.
5. Ibid. 67.
6. See Jonathan Bate, *The Song of the Earth* (London: Picador, 2000).
7. C. McEwen and M. Statman (eds.), *The Alphabet of Trees: A Guide to Nature Writing* (New York: Teachers and Writers Collaborative, 2000), 220.
8. Nelson Mandela, *The Long Walk to Freedom* (London: Abacus, 1994), 672.
9. S. T. Coleridge, *Poetical Works*, ed. E. H. Coleridge (London: Oxford University Press, 1967), 366–7.
10. Harald Gaski, *Introduction to Sami Culture in a New Era: The Norwegian Sami Experience* (Karasjohka: Davvi Girji, 1997), 24.
11. Wordsworth and Coleridge, *Lyrical Ballads*, ed. Derek Roper, 2nd edn. (London: MacDonald and Evans, 1976), 428 ('Advertisement' to *Lyrical Ballads* (1798) ).
12. Frederico Garcia Lorca, *Canciones y Primeras Canciones*, ed. Piero Menarini (Madrid: Espasa-Calpe, 1986), 188, translation by John Burnside.
13. Shepard, *The Only World We've Got*, 156.
14. John Burnside, *The Good Neighbour* (London: Cape, 2005), 41–3.
15. See Boris Pasternak, *Doctor Zhivago*, trans. Max Hayward and Manya Harari (London: Fontana, 1961), 509.
16. Gary Snyder, *Earth House Hold: Technical Notes & Queries to Fellow Dharma Revolutionaries* (New York: New Directions, 1969).

## MODELLING THE UNIVERSE: POETRY, SCIENCE, AND THE ART OF BETAPHOR

1. Simon Armitage doesn't do footnotes, though readers may like to know that they can find the Housman poem used as this essay's epigraph in *The Poems of A. E. Housman*, ed. Archie Burnett (Oxford: Clarendon Press, 1997), 151, while the Simon Armitage poems can be found in Simon Armitage's books as follows: 'The Tyre' in *Selected Poems* (London: Faber and Faber, 2001), 118–19; 'The Shout' in *The Universal Home Doctor* (London: Faber and Faber, 2002), 3; 'Newton's Third Law' in *Zoom!* (Newcastle upon Tyne: Bloodaxe, 1989), 15; 'The Whole of the Sky' in *CloudCuckooLand* (London: Faber and Faber, 1997), 25–112.

## ASTRONOMY AND POETRY

1. Frederick Seidel, 'The New Cosmology', in K. Brown (ed.), *Verse and Universe* (Minneapolis: Milkweed Editions, 1998), 23.
2. Diane Ackerman, *Jaguar of Sweet Laughter: New and Selected Poems* (New York: Random House, 1991), 7.
3. Diane Ackerman, *The Planets: A Cosmic Pastoral* (New York: Morrow, 1976).
4. Miroslav Holub, *Selected Poems*, trans. Ian Milner and George Theiner (Harmondsworth: Penguin, 1967), 47.
5. Job 38.4 (Revised English Bible).
6. Patric Dickinson, 'Jodrell Bank', in N. Albery (ed.), *Poem for the Day* (London: Chatto and Windus, 2001), 377.
7. Alfred (Lord) Tennyson, *Tennyson Poems and Plays*, ed. T. Herbert Warren (Oxford: Oxford University Press, 1975), 810.
8. Adrienne Rich, *Collected Early Poems 1950–1970* (New York: Norton, 1993), 361.
9. Jennifer Clement, 'William Herchel's Sister, Caroline, Discovers Eight Comets', in K. Brown (ed.), *Verse and Universe* (Minneapolis: Milkweed Editions, 1998), 301.
10. Simon Armitage, *CloudCuckooLand* (London: Faber and Faber, 1997), 113.
11. Sheenagh Pugh, *Stonelight* (Bridgend: Seren Books, 1999), 57.
12. Kenneth Rexroth, *The Collected Shorter Poems of Kenneth Rexroth* (New York: New Directions, 1966), 237.
13. Stanley Kunitz, *The Collected Poems of Stanley Kunitz* (New York: Norton, 1966), 256.
14. Gwyneth Lewis, *Zero Gravity* (Newcastle: Bloodaxe, 1998), 23.
15. Michael Longley, 'Halley's Comet', in A. Motion (ed.), *Here to Eternity* (London: Faber and Faber, 2002), 364.
16. Blaise Pascal, *Pensées sur la Religion*, trans. W. F. Trotter (New York: Collier, 1909–14), part 3, 206.
17. William Empson, *Collected Poems* (London: Chatto and Windus, 1962), 19.
18. Leo Aylen, *Dancing the Impossible: New and Selected Poems* (Salzburg: University of Salzburg Press, 1997), 142.
19. Iain Crichton Smith, *Love Poems and Elegies* (London: Gollancz, 1972), 17.
20. Rebecca Elson, *A Responsibility to Awe* (Manchester: Carcanet, 2001), 11.
21. Antler, 'A second before it bursts', in K. Brown (ed.), *Verse and Universe* (Minneapolis: Milkweed Editions, 1998), 42.
22. Louis MacNeice, *Selected Poems* (London: Faber and Faber, 1988), 158.
23. Elizabeth Jennings, *New Collected Poems* (Manchester: Carcanet, 2002), 1.

24. Robert Francis, 'Astronomer', in K. Brown (ed.), *Verse and Universe* (Minneapolis: Milkweed Editions, 1998), 26.
25. John Haines, in Timothy Ferris (ed.), *The World Treasury of Physics, Astronomy and Mathematics* (Boston: Little, Brown, 1991), 770.
26. Pattiann Rogers, in K. Brown (ed.), *Verse and Universe* (Minneapolis: Milkweed Editions, 1998), 49.
27. John Sokol, in K. Brown (ed.), *Verse and Universe* (Minneapolis: Milkweed Editions, 1998), 258.
28. Neil Rollinson, in M. Riordan and J. Turney (eds.), *A Quark for Mister Mark* (London: Faber and Faber, 2000), 41; see also John Updike, *Facing Nature: Poems* (London: Andre Deutsch, 1986), 86.
29. Elson, *A Responsibility to Awe*, 14.

## THE ACT OF THE MIND: THOUGHT EXPERIMENTS IN THE POETRY OF JORIE GRAHAM AND LESLIE SCALAPINO

1. Mark C. Taylor, *The Moment of Complexity: Emerging Network Culture* (Chicago: University of Chicago Press, 2001), 4.
2. Wallace Stevens, *Collected Poetry and Prose* (New York: Library of America, 1997), 219.
3. On the naming of quarks, the building blocks of the atomic nucleus, see Murray Gell-Mann, *The Quark and the Jaguar: Adventures in the Simple and the Complex* (New York: W. H. Freeman, 1994), 11, 180.
4. Marianne Moore, 'Poetry', in Richard Ellmann and Robert O'Clair (eds.), *The Norton Anthology of Modern Poetry*, Second Edition (New York: Norton, 1961), 457.
5. See Jeremy Bernstein, *Einstein* (New York: Penguin, 1973), 121, 212; also Robert H. March, *Physics for Poets* (New York: McGraw-Hill, 1970), 109.
6. Werner Heisenberg, *Physics and Philosophy: Encounters and Conversations* (New York: Harper and Row, 1971), 58, 41.
7. Ibid. 63.
8. Leslie Scalapino, *The Public World / Syntactically Impermanence* (Hanover, NH: Wesleyan University Press, 1999), 25.
9. Ibid. 8.
10. Daniel Tiffany, *Toy Medium: Materialism and Modern Lyric* (Berkeley: University of California Press, 2000), 11, 12, 6–7.
11. Daniel Tiffany, 'Lyric Substance: On Riddles, Materialism, and Poetic Obscurity', *Critical Inquiry* 28.1 (2001), 76, 75.
12. Bruno Latour, quoted in Tiffany, *Toy Medium*, 4.

13. Leslie Scalapino, 'How Phenomena Appear to Unfold', in *How Phenomena Appear to Unfold* (Elmwood, Conn.: Potes and Poets Press, 1989), 103.
14. Francis Bacon, quoted in Jorie Graham, *Materialism* (Hopewell, NJ: Ecco Press, 1993), p. ix.
15. Graham, *Materialism*, 3.
16. Bacon, quoted in Graham, *Materialism*, p. ix.
17. Graham, *Materialism*, 19 (Graham's emphasis).
18. Benjamin Whorf, *Language, Thought and Reality: Selected Writings* (Cambridge, Mass.: MIT Press, 1956), 213.
19. Whorf, quoted in Graham, *Materialism*, 79.
20. da Vinci, quoted in Graham, *Materialism*, 130.
21. Tiffany, *Toy Medium*, 5.
22. David Bohm, 'Art, Dialogue, and the Implicate Order: David Bohm interviewed by Louwrien Wijers', in Lee Nichol (ed.), *On Creativity* (New York: Routledge, 1998), 106 (Bohm's emphasis).
23. Ibid. 105.
24. 'An Interview with Leslie Scalapino, Conducted by Elisabeth A. Frost', *Contemporary Literature* 37.1 (1996), 18–19.
25. See Susan Howe, *Singularities* (Hanover, NH: Wesleyan University Press, 1990) and Mark C. Taylor, *The Picture in Question: Mark Tansey and the Ends of Representation* (Chicago: University of Chicago Press, 1999), ch. 5.
26. N. Katherine Hayles, *How We Became Posthuman: Virtual Bodies in Cybernetics, Literature, and Informatics* (Chicago: University of Chicago Press, 1999), 21.
27. Mitchell Feigenbaum, quoted in James Gleick, *Chaos: Making a New Science* (New York: Viking, 1987), 186; compare Mark Taylor on Mark Tansey's paintings in *The Picture in Question.*
28. See especially Gleick, *Chaos*, 301–17.
29. Susan Howe, *Singularities* (Hanover, NH: Wesleyan University Press, 1990); Susan Howe, *The Birth-mark: Unsettling the Wilderness in American Literary History* (Hanover, NH: Wesleyan University Press, 1993), 173.
30. Taylor, *The Picture in Question*, 116.
31. Ibid.
32. Ibid. 118–19.
33. A term from physics that also plays a key role in chaos theory, 'phase space' is a multi-dimensional field in which each axis corresponds to one of the coordinates required to specify the state of a physical system. In the phase space of, say, a strange attractor, all the coordinates of a system are represented so that a point in phase space corresponds to a state of the system.

34. Graham, *Materialism*, 50.
35. Ibid. 3.
36. Helen Vendler, *The Given and the Made: Strategies of Poetic Redefinition* (Cambridge, Mass.: Harvard University Press, 1995), 92.
37. Graham, *Materialism*, 78.
38. Ibid. 50, ix, 54.
39. Ibid. 53.
40. Charles Altieri, 'Jorie Graham and Ann Lauterbach: Towards a Contemporary Poetics of Eloquence', *Cream City Review* 12 (1988), 47; Bonnie Costello, 'The Big Hunger', *The New Republic* (1992), 36–9; James Longenbach, *Modern Poetry after Modernism* (New York: Oxford University Press, 1997), 165.
41. Graham, *Materialism*, 51 (ellipsis in original).
42. Graham, *Materialism*, 54; Gleick, *Chaos*, 262.
43. Jack Spicer, *The Collected Books of Jack Spicer*, ed. Robin Blaser (Santa Rosa, Calif.: Black Sparrow Press, 1989), 48.
44. Leslie Scalapino, *way* (San Francisco: North Point Press, 1988), 51.
45. Robin Blaser, 'The Practice of Outside', in Spicer, *Collected Books*, 271.
46. Scalapino, *way*, 99 (emphasis in original). For a generative analysis of Scalapino's 'Delay series' and a larger discussion of postmodern serial and procedural poetics, see Joseph M. Conte, *Unending Design: The Forms of Postmodern Poetry* (Ithaca, NY: Cornell University Press, 1991), especially 47–163 and 267–82.
47. For a more extensive description of 'qualitative infinity' see Bohm, *Causality and Chance*, ch. 5.
48. Scalapino, *way*, 53, 57, 55.
49. Graham, *Materialism*, 53.
50. Scalapino, *way*, 61.

### THE ART OF WIT AND THE CAMBRIDGE SCIENCE PARK

1. C. P. Snow, *The Two Cultures*, introduction by Stefan Collini (Cambridge: Cambridge University Press, 1998), 15.
2. Ibid. 16.
3. Compare <http://www.cambridgesciencepark.co.uk/home.htm> with <http://www.cccp-online.org/index.html>.
4. N. H. Reeve and Richard Kerridge, *Nearly Too Much: The Poetry of J. H. Prynne* (Liverpool: Liverpool University Press, 1995), 4.
5. For samplings of Cambridge poets see Andrew Crozier and Tim Longville

(eds.), *A Various Art* (London: Paladin, 1990); Denise Riley (ed.), *Poets on Writing* (Basingstoke: Macmillan, 1992); and Iain Sinclair (ed.), *Conductors of Chaos* (London: Picador, 1996).

6. Peter Riley, in Kelvin Corcoran, 'Spitewinter Provocations: An Interview on the Condition of Poetry with Peter Riley', *Reality Studios*, 8 (1986), 4.
7. For the term 'world-disclosure', see e.g. Cristina Lafont, *Heidegger, Language, and World Disclosure* (Cambridge: Cambridge University Press, 2000).
8. See J. H. Prynne, 'Resistance and Difficulty', *Prospect*, 5 (1961); and D. S. Marriott, 'Contemporary British Poetry and Resistance: Reading J. H. Prynne', *Parataxis: modernism and modern writing*, 8/9 (1996), 159–74.
9. Jean-François Lyotard, *The Postmodern Condition: A Report on Knowledge*, trans. Geoff Bennington and Brian Massumi (Minnesota: University of Minnesota Press, 1984); and *The Differend: Phrases in Dispute*, trans. George Van Den Abbeele (Minnesota: University of Minnesota Press, 1988).
10. I. A. Richards, *Science and Poetry* (London: Kegan Paul, 1926).
11. See, for example, Drew Milne, 'Wit', in Julian Wolfreys (ed.), *Glossolalia: An Alaphabet of Critical Keywords* (Edinburgh: Edinburgh University Press, 2003), 325–38.
12. The term 'life-world' loosely translates Edmund Husserl's conception of *Lebenswelt*, but is used here more in the sense developed by Jürgen Habermas, *Theory of Communicative Action*, 2 vols., trans. T. McCarthy (Cambridge: Polity, 1984–7).
13. Cf. T. S. Eliot, *The Varieties of Metaphysical Poetry*, ed. Ronald Schuchard (London: Faber, 1993).
14. William Empson, 'Wit in the Essay on Criticism', *The Structure of Complex Words* (1951; repr., London: Hogarth, 1985), 84–100.
15. See, Jürgen Habermas, 'Themes in Postmetaphysical Thinking', *Postmetaphysical Thinking*, trans. William Mark Hohengarten (Cambridge: Polity, 1992), 28–53. Habermas builds on Edmund Husserl, *The Crisis of European Sciences and Transcendental Philosophy*, trans. David Carr (Evanston, Ill.: Northwestern University Press, 1970); Martin Heidegger, *The Question Concern Technology and Other Essays*, trans. William Lovitt (New York: Harper and Row, 1977); and Max Horkheimer and Theodor Adorno, *Dialectic of Enlightenment*, trans. John Cumming (London: Verso, 1979).
16. Compare Monroe K. Spears, *Dionysus and the City: Modernism in Twentieth-Century Poetry* (New York: Oxford University Press, 1970) with Marshall Berman, *All That Is Solid Melts Into Air: The Experience of Modernity* (London: Penguin, 1988).
17. Veronica Forrest-Thomson, 'Cordelia: or, 'A Poem Should not Mean, but Be', *Collected Poems and Translations* (London and Lewes: Allardyce, Barnett, 1990), 109.

18. Forrest-Thomson, 'Le Signe (Cygne)', *Collected Poems and Translations*, 74.
19. Forrest-Thomson, 'Note', *Collected Poems and Translations*, 261–2.
20. Forrest-Thomson, 'The Dying Gladiator', *Collected Poems and Translations*, 63.
21. Veronica Forrest-Thomson, *Poetic Artifice* (Manchester: Manchester University Press, 1978).
22. Lavinia Greenlaw, 'Unstable Regions: Poetry and Science', in Francis Spufford and Jenny Uglow (eds.), *Cultural Babbage: Technology, Time and Invention* (London: Faber and Faber, 1996), 217.
23. Graham Farmelo, 'Foreword: It Must Be Beautiful', in Graham Farmelo (ed.), *It Must be Beautiful: Great Equations of Modern Science* (London and New York: Granta, 2002), p. x.
24. Ibid., p. xvi.
25. Wolf Lepenies, *Between Literature and Science: The Rise of Sociology*, trans. R. J. Hollingdale (Cambridge: Cambridge University Press, 1988). (Originally published in German as *Die Drei Kulturen* (1985).)
26. See, for example, Drew Milne, 'Agoraphobia, and the Embarrassment of Manifestos: Notes towards a Community of Risk', *Parataxis: modernism and modern writing*, 3 (1993), 25–39.
27. Werner Heisenberg, *Physics and Philosophy: The Revolution in Modern Science* (1958), trans. anon. (London: Penguin, 1989), 139.
28. J. H. Prynne, 'Numbers in Time of Trouble', *Poems*, 18.
29. Jürgen Habermas, 'Philosophy and Science as Literature?', *Postmetaphysical Thinking*, 205.
30. Collini, 'Introduction', C. P. Snow, *The Two Cultures*, p. xlviii. Cf. David Locke, *Science as Writing* (New Haven: Yale University Press, 1992).
31. See, for example, Drew Milne, 'Speculative Assertions: Reading J. H. Prynne's *Poems*', *Parataxis: modernism and modern writing*, 10 (2001), 67–86.
32. See John Haffenden's exceptionally helpful introduction to William Empson, *Essays on Renaissance Literature: Donne and the New Philosophy* (Cambridge: Cambridge University Press, 1993), 1–61.
33. Steven Meyer, *Irresistible Dictation: Gertrude Stein and the Correlations of Writing and Science* (Stanford, Calif.: Stanford University Press, 2001), p. xxi.
34. Birgitta Johansson, *The Engineering of Being: An Ontological Approach to J. H. Prynne* (Umeå: Umeå University, 1997), 90.
35. J. H. Prynne, 'The *Plant Time Manifold* Transcripts', *Poems* (Newcastle upon Tyne: Bloodaxe, 1999), 237 and 242.
36. J. H. Prynne, *Red D Gypsum* (Cambridge: Barque, 1998), 12.
37. Ludwig Wittgenstein, *Zettel*, 2nd edn., ed. G. E. M. Anscombe and G. H. von Wright, trans. G. E. M. Anscombe (Oxford: Blackwell, 1981), §160, p. 27.

38. Edwin Morgan, 'Poetry and Knowledge in MacDiarmid's Later Work', in K. D. Duval and Sydney Goodsir Smith (eds.), *Hugh MacDiarmid, a Festschrift* (Edinburgh: K. D. Duval 1962), 129–39.
39. Veronica Forrest-Thomson, 'Poetry as Knowledge; The Use of Science by Twentieth-Century Poets', Cambridge, unpublished doctoral dissertation, 1971, 141.
40. Ibid. 143.
41. Ibid. 183.
42. Ibid. 250.
43. Forrest-Thomson, *Poetic Artifice*, 146.
44. Tom Raworth, *Collected Poems* (Manchester: Carcanet, 2003).
45. Forrest-Thomson, *Poetic Artifice*, 146.
46. Ibid. 51.
47. J. H. Prynne, 'Die A Millionaire', *Poems*, 13.
48. Simon Jarvis, 'Quality and the Non-Identical in J. H. Prynne's "Aristeas, in seven years" ', *Parataxis: modernism and modern writing*, 1 (1991), 78.
49. Prynne, *Poems*, 220.
50. T. S. Eliot, *The Sacred Wood* (1920; repr. London: Methuen, 1960), 23.
51. John Wilkinson, 'The Reason', *Useful Reforms* (Richmond: Arnica Press, 1976).
52. John Wilkinson, 'Sweetness & Light', *Oort's Cloud: Earlier Poems* (Cambridge and Honolulu: Barque and Subpress, 1999), 151–63.
53. John Wilkinson, 'Laboratory Test Report', *The Interior Planets* (1986–90), in *Flung Clear: Poems in Six Books* (Brighton: Parataxis Editions, 1994), 89.
54. John Wilkinson, 'The Metastases of Poetry', *Parataxis*, 8/9 (1996), 49.
55. John Wilkinson, 'Facing Port Talbot', *Effigies Against the Light* (Cambridge: Salt, 2001), 113–26.
56. Wilkinson, 'The Metastases of Poetry', 54.
57. Ibid. 54.
58. Ibid. 55.

## CONTEMPORARY PSYCHOLOGY AND CONTEMPORARY POETRY: PERSPECTIVES ON MOOD DISORDERS

1. Robert Lowell, 'For John Berryman, 1914–1972', *Collected Prose*, ed. Robert Giroux (New York: Farrar, Straus and Giroux, 1987), 114–15; letter from Robert Lowell to Philip Booth, 10 October 1966, cited in Ian Hamilton, *Robert Lowell: A Biography* (New York: Random House, 1982), 351.

2. Frank Bidart 'Introduction: You Didn't Write, You *Rewrote*', in *Robert Lowell: Collected Poems*, ed. Frank Bidart and David Gewanter (New York: Farrar, Straus and Giroux, 2003), p. vii.
3. Lowell, quoted in Hamilton, *Robert Lowell*, 157.
4. Lowell, 'Near the Unbalanced Aquarium', in *Robert Lowell: Collected Prose*, 350–1.
5. Ibid. 353.
6. Lowell, 'Home After Three Months Away', *Collected Poems*, 185–6.
7. Hamilton, *Robert Lowell*, 286 and 307.
8. Velimir Khlebnikov, *The Longer Poems of Velimir Khlebnikov* (Westport, Conn.: Greenwood Press, 1975), 362–3.
9. Sylvia Plath, *The Journals of Sylvia Plath 1950–1962*, ed. Karen V. Kukil (London: Faber and Faber, 2000), 395.
10. John Berryman, 'Of Suicide', in *John Berryman: Collected Poems: 1937–1971*, ed. C. Thornbury, (New York: Noonday Press, 1989), 206.
11. John Berryman, '235', *The Dream Songs* (New York: Farrar, Straus and Giroux, 1969), 254.
12. See e.g.: C. Martindale, 'Father's Absence, Psychopathology, and Poetic Eminence', *Psychological Reports*, 31 (1972), 843–7; A. Storr, *The Dynamics of Creation* (London: Secker and Warburg, 1972); W. H. Trethowan, 'Music and Mental Disorder', in M. Critchley and R. Henson (eds.), *Music and the Brain* (London: Heinemann, 1977), 398–442; R. Richards, 'Relationships between Creativity and Psychopathology: An Evaluation and Interpretation of the Evidence', *Genetic Psychology Monographs*, 103 (1981), 261–324; N. C. Andreasen, 'Creativity and Mental Illness: Prevalence Rates in Writers and Their First-Degree Relatives', *American Journal of Psychiatry*, 144 (1987), 1288–92; R. L. Richards, D. K. Kinney, I. Lunde, and M. Benet, 'Creativity in Manic-Depressives, Cyclothymes, and Their Normal First-Degree Relatives: A Preliminary Report', *Journal of Abnormal Psychology*, 97 (1988), 281–8; K. R. Jamison, 'Mood Disorders and Patterns of Creativity in British Writers and Artists,' *Psychiatry*, 52 (1989), 125–34; K. R. Jamison, *Touched with Fire: Manic-Depressive Illness and the Artistic Temperament* (New York: Free Press, 1993); F. Post, 'Creativity and Psychopathology: A Study of 291 World-Famous Men,' *British Journal of Psychiatry*, 165 (1994), 22–34; J. J. Schildkraut, A. J. Hirshfeld, and J. M. Murphy, 'Mind and Mood in Modern Art: II. Depressive Disorders, Spirituality, and Early Deaths in the Abstract Expressionist Artists of the New York School', *American Journal of Psychiatry*, 151 (1994), 482–8; A. M. Ludwig, *The Price of Greatness: Resolving the Creativity and Madness Controversy* (New York: Guilford Press, 1995); F. Post, 'Verbal Creativity, Depression, and Alcoholism: An Investigation of One Hundred American and British Writers', *British Journal of Psychiatry*, 168 (1996), 545–55.

13. The discussion of mania and creativity is based upon work in K. R. Jamison, *Exuberance* (New York: Alfred A. Knopf, 2004).
14. K. R. Jamison *Touched With Fire: Manic-Depressive Illness and the Artistic Temperament* (New York: Free Press, 1993).
15. F. K. Goodwin and K. R. Jamison, *Manic-Depressive Illness* (New York: Oxford University Press, 1990).
16. Ibid.; D. Schuldberg, 'Schizotypal and Hypomanic Traits, Creativity, and Psychological Health', *Creativity Research Journal*, 3 (1990), 218–30.
17. N. Andreasen and A. Canter, 'The Creative Writer: Psychiatric Symptoms and Family History', *Comprehensive Psychiatry*, 15 (1974), 123–31; N. Andreasen, and P. Powers, 'Creativity and Psychosis: An Examination of Conceptual Style', *Archives of General Psychiatry*, 32 (1975), 70–3.
18. L. Welch, O. Diethelm, and L. Long, 'Measurement of Hyper-Associative Activity during Elation', *Journal of Psychology*, 21 (1946), 113–26.
19. L. Pons, J. I. Nurnberger, and D. L. Murphy, 'Mood-Independent Aberrancies in Associative Processes in Bipolar Affective Disorders,' *Psychiatry Research*, 14 (1985), 315–22.
20. See e.g.: M. Natale, 'Effects of Induced Elation-Depression on Speech in the Initial Interview', *Journal of Consulting and Clinical Psychology*, 45 (1977), 45–52; J. D. Teasdale and S. J. Fogarty, 'Differential Effects of Induced Mood on Retrieval of Pleasant and Unpleasant Events from Episodic Memory', *Journal of Abnormal Psychology*, 88 (1979), 248–57; A. M. Isen and K. A. Daubman, 'The Influence of Affect on Categorization', *Journal of Personality and Social Psychology*, 47 (1984), 1206–17; A. M. Isen, M. M. S. Johnson, E. Mertz, and G. F. Robinson, 'The Influence of Positive Affect on the Unusualness of Word Associations', *Journal of Personality and Social Psychology*, 48 (1985), 1413–26; T. R. Greene and H. Noice, 'Influence of Positive Affect upon Creative Thinking and Problem Solving in Children', *Psychological Reports*, 63 (1988), 895–8; S. C. Baker, C. D. Frith, and R. J. Dolan, 'The Interaction between Mood and Cognitive Function Studied with PET', *Psychological Medicine*, 27 (1997), 565–78; L. Clark, S. D. Iverson, and G. M.Goodwin, 'The Influence of Positive and Negative Mood States on Risk Taking, Verbal Fluency, and Salivary Cortisol', *Journal of Affective Disorders*, 63 (2001), 179–87.
21. K. R. Jamison, 'Mood Disorders and Patterns of Creativity in British Writers and Artists', *Psychiatry*, 52 (1989), 125–34.
22. R. Richards and D. K. Kinney, 'Mood Swings and Creativity', *Creativity Research Journal*, 3 (1990), 202–17.
23. L. G. Sexton and L. Ames (eds.), *Anne Sexton: A Self-Portrait in Letters* (Boston: Houghton Mifflin, 1977), 105.
24. Robert Lowell, 'A Conversation with Ian Hamilton', *Collected Prose*, 286.
25. Ibid. 287.

26. Lowell, 'Home', *Collected Poems*, 285.
27. L. O'Brien, 'A Poem in the Science Lab', *Princeton Alumni Weekly*, 10 September 2003, 30–1.
28. Ibid. 31.

## AFTERWORD

1. Evelyn Fox Keller and Elisabeth A. Lloyd (eds.), *Keywords in Evolutionary Biology* (Cambridge, Mass.: Harvard University Press, 1992), 1.
2. Hugh Aldersey-Williams, *Findings: Hidden Stories in First-Hand Accounts of Scientific Discovery* (Norwich: Lulox Books, 2005), 2.
3. Unless otherwise stated, passages quoted in this Afterword are drawn from the earlier sections of the present book.
4. Lewis Campbell and William Garnett, *The Life of James Clerk Maxwell* (London: Macmillan, 1882), 637–8.
5. Ibid. 638.
6. Mark A. Tirmenstein, Tammy L. Leraas, and Marc W. Fariss, *Toxicology Letters*, 92 (1997), 67–77.

# INDEX

*Note*: Contributors only appear in the index if they refer to their own poetry or if they are mentioned by fellow contributors.


Ackerman, Diane 126
  'We Are Listening' 130–1
*ahimsa* 93
Albright, Daniel, *Quantum Poetics* 1
Aldersey-Williams, Hugh 205
aleatory connections 7, 155–7, 159, 161
Altieri, Charles 162
American Association of Physicians-Poets 12
analogy 155, 176, 178–9
animation 43
Antler, 'On learning that on the clearest night only 6000 stars are visible to the naked eye' 137
archaeology 36
Aristotle 119
Armitage, Simon 3, 4, 7, 8, 208–9
  'Eclipse' 133
  'Newton's Third Law' 116
  'The Shout' 114
  'The Tyre' 112–13
Ashbery, John 182
astronomy 36, 40, 84, 110–11, 116–17, 123–4, 125–40, 151–2
Auden, W. H. 66
Audubon, John James 152, 153, 161
aureate diction 54
authenticity 81–2, 85, 94
authority 81–2, 85
avant-gardism 177
Aylen, Leo, 'Orbiting Pluto' 135–6

Bachelard, Gaston 96
Bacon, Sir Francis 150, 152, 153, 154, 160, 161
Baird, Logie 56
Baudelaire, Charles 173
beauty 176–7
Bede, Venerable 76
Beer, Gillian 1
belief 73–4, 88
Bell, Ian F. A. 1
Benjamin, Walter 153
bereavement 35–6, 62–4, 65, 134
Bergson, Henri 101
Bernstein, Charles 182
Berryman, John 193, 196, 197
Bible 73, 79–80, 82, 131
Bidart, Frank 194
Big Bang 129, 139
biochemistry 36
bipolar psychosis, *see* manic-depression
Bishop, Elizabeth 193
black holes 151–2, 159, 163
Blair, Hugh 79
Blaser, Robin 164
Bogan, Louise 193
Bohm, David 154–5, 159, 163, 164–6
Bohr, Niels 148
Bold, Alan 33
Bradbury, Ray 40
Bragg, Melvyn 70
brain scans 9–10, 168–9, 201–2
Brewster, Sir David 52–3
Browne, Sir Thomas 52
Burnell, Jocelyn Bell 4, 8
Burns, Robert 80
Burnside, John 10, 205
  'By Kautokeino' 103–4
  'Steinar Undir Steinahlithum' 107–9
Byron, Lord 192

Cambridge Science Park 170–87
Cambridge University 170, 173–5
campus poetry 173–5
Camus, Albert 24

Cassady, Neal 41
catastrophe theory 157, 158
causality 155–7, 159
Celtic Twilight 62–3, 64
chaos theory 7, 157, 158, 159, 160, 162, 177, 205
childbirth 60
chromosomes 70
cinema 43, 75
Clare, John 100
Clement, Jennifer, 'William Herschel's Sister, Caroline, Discovers Eight Comets' 133
Clerk Maxwell, James, 'Molecular Evolution' 206–8
Clydesdale, Matthew 45
Cocteau, Jean 37
Coleridge, Samuel Taylor 74, 79, 80, 81, 100, 192
  'Dejection: An Ode' 98–9
Collini, Stefan 178
Collom, Jack 97
colour-blindness 41
Columbus, Christopher 152, 153, 161
comets 133–5
complexity theory 7, 157, 158–60
composition 86, 101, 116–17
computers 2, 9, 37–8, 42–3, 52–3, 62–4, 65, 121
concrete poetry 38–9
consumerism 102, 104–5
'Copenhagen Interpretation' 148
corporations 92, 93, 94, 97, 100, 105
cosmology 27–8, 45–7, 100, 119, 128, 129, 136–40
Costello, Bonnie 162
Crane, Hart 193
Crawford, Robert
  'Alford' 66–8
  'Biology' 69–71, 205
  'Deincartion' 63–4
  on English Literature 79
  'Exchange' 64
  'The Handshakes' 60
  'Photonics' 57
  'The Saltcoats Structuralists' 56
  'Scotland' 57–8
  'Semiconductor country' 56
  *Spirit Machines* 63–8
  *The Tip of My Tongue* 68
creativity 127, 199–200
Creeley, Robert 163
cryptography 37, 38, 65
cultural theory 56, 57, 75–6
cybernetics 2, 37, 38, 48, 49, 95

da Vinci, Leonardo 36, 153
Dante Alighieri 27, 28, 66, 100, 153
Dao, Bei 163
dark matter 136, 139–40
Darwin, Charles 192
Darwin, Erasmus 29
Darwinism 5
Davidson, John 30, 55
  'Fleet Street' 31
  Informationism 76, 83
  MacDiarmid on death of 31–2
  'The Wasp' 76–7
Davidsz de Heem, Jan 96
Davie, Donald 172
Davie, George 6, 55, 76, 82–3, 84
Davy, Sir Humphry 29, 192
death 45, 52, 62, 68, 100
  suicide 193, 196–7
Deguy, Michel 55, 58–9
DeLillo, Don, *Underworld* 95–6
dematerialization 64
*The Democratic Intellect* (Davie) 55, 82–3, 84
Democritus 119
Dennis, John 79
depression 193, 194, 197–8, 199, 200, 201, 202
Dick, Reverend Thomas 73
Dickinson, Patric, 'Jodrell Bank' 131–2, 134
digitalization 43, 65
Dirac, Paul 177
DNA 68, 70, 205
*Doctor Faustus* (Marlowe) 43
Donaghy, Michael 48–51
  'Grimoire' 49–51, 209–10

Donne, John 179
Doolittle, Hilda (H.D.) 2, 129, 147
Doty, Mark, *Still Life with Oysters and Lemon* 96
Dunbar, William 54
Dunn, Douglas 194

eclecticism 55
ecology 10, 68, 91–7
education 13, 15, 82–3
Edwards, Jonathan 153
Einstein, Albert 1, 3, 5, 148, 149, 151, 154
electricity 29–30, 45, 59, 115, 119
Eliot, T. S. 1, 75, 119, 147
  Lowell's letters to 196
  'Marina' 61
  metaphysical wit 172
  on pre-logical mentality 53
  *The Waste Land* 2, 5, 148
Elson, Rebecca 129
  'Let there Always be Light' 139–40
  'When You Wish upon a Star' 136
Emerson, Ralph Waldo 153
Empson, William 170, 172, 181, 182
  'Letter I' 135
encyclopaedism 55, 65
enfoldment 154–5, 159
English Literature 79, 173
entropy 139
eroticism 155–6
Euclidean geometry 157, 158
Euripides 102
evolutionary biology 177
existentialism 14
experimentation 151, 152, 160, 179

fairy tales 100
familiarity and strangeness 54
Farmelo, Graham 176
farmers 107–9
fascism 93
fax machines 44
Feigenbaum, Mitchell 157
Fergusson, Robert 58
Ferrier, J. F. 76
Feyerabend, Paul 22
Fisher, Roy 173
foraminifera 141–5
Forrest-Thomson, Veronica 173–5, 181–2
fractal poetry 58
Francis, Robert, 'Astronomer' 138
Frazer, J. G. 76
Freud, Sigmund 21
Frost, Elizabeth A. 155–6
Frost, Robert 126, 128
Fukuyama, Francis 92
Fulton, Alice 58
Fulton, Hamish 97
fusion 33–4

Gaelic poetry 7, 57, 62
Galileo 28–9
galvanisation 45
Gaski, Harald 99, 100
Geddes, Patrick 76
gender relationships 155–6
generalism 55, 83, 84
Genesis 73, 79
genetic code 25–6, 68, 70–1, 177
geology 34–5
Gibson, William 46
Giordano, Bruno 46–7
Gleick, James 6, 157, 162
Glenday, John 8
  'Circadian' 123–4
GM foods 94
Godard, Jean-Luc 173
Goethe, Johann Wolfgang von 5, 27, 29
governments, and science 94
Grabo, Carl 29
Graham, Jorie, 'Event Horizon' 7, 149, 151–4, 159–62, 163, 165, 166
Greenlaw, Lavinia 176
Guinea worms 33–4
Gurney, Alison 9

Habermas, Jürgen 178
Haines, John, 'A Little Cosmic Dust Poem' 138
Hardy, Thomas 128
  'The Comet at Yell'ham' 134
Hayles, Professor N. Katherine 3, 157

H.D. (Hilda Doolittle) 2, 129, 147
healing process 127
Heaney, Seamus 80, 81
Heidegger, Martin 93, 150, 154, 179, 180
Heisenberg, Werner 148–9, 163, 177
Herbert, W. N. 4, 8, 88
  'The Working Self' 89–90
Herschel, Caroline 132, 133
Herschel, William 29
Hesiod 5, 55
Hesse, Mary 178
heterojunctive 53–4
history 92, 94
Hogg, Thomas Jefferson 29
Hölderlin, Friedrich 179
holograms 155
Holub, Miroslav 4, 6, 7, 10, 55, 61, 208
  'Because' 20
  'The Corporal who killed Archimedes' 22–3
  'In the Microscope' 21–2
  'Kuru, or the Smiling Death Syndrome' 23–4
  'Literary Bash' 12–13
  'Night at the Observatory' 131
  'The Rampage' 13, 16–18, 21, 22
  on science in poetry 205–6
  'Spacetime' 19
Houseman, A. E. 110, 119
Howe, Susan 157, 158
Hughes, Ted 117, 118
Hume, David 76
humour 20, *see also* wit
hunter-gatherers 102
Huxley, Aldous 10
  'Fifth Philosopher's Song' 18–19

Icelandic language 112
Ignatieff, Michael 13
imagination 7, 79, 126–7, 150, 178, 198
imaging technology 167–8, 210–12
immunology 7, 10
implicate order theory 154–5, 159, 163, 164, 165–6
indigenous peoples 99–100, 152–3
Informationism 55, 63, 73, 75–87
intellectuals 13–14
interconnection 120–1, 127, 154–6, 158
Internet 66–8, 137
investigative science 113–15
Ishihara test 41

James, John 170
Jamison, Kay Redfield 4, 7, 8, 10
jargon 76, 81
Jarrell, Randall 193
Jarvis, Simon 182
Jeffers, Robinson 128–9
Jeffrey, Francis 84
Jennings, Elizabeth, 'Delay' 125, 126, 137–8, 164
Johansson, Birgitta 180
Johnson, Dr 179
Joyce, James 1, 5, 147, 148
*Jurassic Park* (1993) 43

Kaluza's theory 19–20
Keller, Evelyn Fox and Lloyd, Elisabeth A. 204, 205
Kerridge, Richard 171
Khayyàm, Omar 27
Khlebnikov, Velimir 196
Kinloch, David 75
  'The Organ Bath' 188–90
knowledge 12, 13, 15, 28
  academe 60
  demolishing myth 129, 132, 134
  experience and 152, 181
  materialism 150
  specialization 36
  'two cultures' model of 6, 55, 170, 177, 178
  unity of 32
  wit and 172
Kuhn, Thomas S. 13
Kunitz, Stanley, 'Halley's comet' 134

landscape 57–8
language 52–4, 57, 61, 161
  authenticity and 80–1
  natural and scientific 177–8, 204–5
  patterns of 152–3

language-games 171, 173–5, 181–2
'language' poetry 182
Larkin, Philip 42
Latour, Bruno 151, 162
*The Lawnmower Man* (1992) 43
Leopardi, Giacomo 27, 29
Lewis, Gwyneth, 'Zero Gravity' 129, 135
Lewis, Wyndham 75
Lightman, Alan 13
Lindsay, Vachel 193
listening 130–1
lists 32–3, 66
literary criticism 179
logic 69
Long, Richard 97
Longenbach, James 162
Longinus 79
Longley, Michael, 'Halley's Comet' 133, 135
Lorca, Frederico Garcia, 'Despedida' 100–1
love poetry 56–7, 60, 70–1
Lowell, Percival 129
Lowell, Robert 193–6, 201
Lucretius 2, 5, 36, 55
  *De Rerum Natura* 27–8
Lyell, Sir Charles 147
Lyotard, Jean-François 171
lyric poetry 100, 150–1, 154, 161–2, 163, 165
*Lyrical Ballads* (Wordsworth)
  Preface to 59–60, 73, 74
  'real' language of 81–2

Macaulay, Rose 1
McCarey, Peter 75
MacDiarmid, Hugh 1, 2, 30–7, 40, 55, 57, 59, 76
  'The Bonnie Broukit Bairn' 61
  'Crystals Like Blood' 34–5
  'Fleet Street' 31
  *In Memoriam James Joyce* 83–4
  'The Innumerable Christ' 61
  'The Kind of Poetry I Want' 32–3, 85
  *Mature Art* 77
  'On a Raised Beach' 181
  'To a Friend and Fellow-Poet' 33–4
  use of Scots 83
  use of vocabulary 58, 80–1, 83–4
Machado, Antonio 100
MacLean, Sorley 57
Macleod, Fiona, 'Nocturne' 64
MacLeod, Norman 9
MacNeice, Louis, 'Star-gazer' 137, 138
Maguire, Sarah, ' A Fistful of Foraminifera' 141–5
Mair, John 76
Mandela, Nelson 97–8
Mandelstam, Osip 80, 100
mania 194–203
manic-depression 7, 15, 194, 197, 199, 200, 202
Mann, Thomas 79
March, Robert H. 3
Marlowe, Christopher 43
Marxism 22
materialism 150–4
materialization 64
mathematics 83, 112
  beauty 177
  quantum theory 154–5
  rhyme 208
  uncertainty principle 148–9, 163
Maxwell, Clerk 3, 56
Mayakovsky, Vladimir 1
measurement 148–9
Medawar, Peter 12
media 72, 75, 85
memory 52, 65, 86, 88–90
metaphor 1, 6, 16, 54, 61, 115, 162, 174, 178
  extended 79
  Fred Trueman on 115
  refinement of 119–20
  technological 62–5
  transformations 181
metaphysical poetry 184–5 187
metaphysics 152, 179, 181
Meyer, Steven 179
Midgley, Mary 3
Millay, Edna St Vincent 193
Miller, Hugh 76

Milne, Drew 4
Milton, John, *Paradise Lost* 27, 28–9
mimetics 119
modernism 1, 2, 75, 146–7, 171
modernity 60
mood disorders 193–203
Moore, Marianne 147
Morgan, Edwin 2–3, 4, 6, 7, 55, 57, 61, 76, 83
  'Early Days' 45–6
  'From the Video Box' 41
  'Golden Apples' 40
  Informationism 76, 77–8
  'March' 44–5
  'The Moons of Jupiter, The' 40
  Preface to *Lyrical Ballads* 59
  'Submarine Demon' 42
  'Trilobites' 78
  'Unscrambling the Waves at Goonhilly' 40
  *Virtual and Other Realities* 44–7
  'The Whittrick' 37–8
Morris, Adalaide 2, 7, 8
Morris, Chris 75
MRI (magnetic resonance imaging) scanners 167–8, 201–2
Muldoon, Paul 5, 7, 9–10
  'Once I Looked Into Your Eyes' 167–9, 202
Murray, Les 6
mythology 92, 100, 102, 129, 132, 134

NASA 137
natural history 91, 92
nature 42, 99–100, 117
Nazism 93
news 75–6
Newton, Sir Isaac 53
Newtonian physics 55, 147, 158, 163
Nilsson, Lennard 18
'noetry' 74, 76, 79
Norse settlements 107

observation 84, 149, 152, 153, 156
observatories 131
oceanography 42
O'Hara, Frank 173
Oliver, Doug 173
Olsen, Charles 172, 179, 180
oncology 36
Oppen, George 163
Ossian 62–3
*Othello* (Shakespeare) 43–4
ownership 102

palaeontology 141–5
Palestine 98
pararhymes 26
parasitology 36
Pascal, Blaise 135
Pasternak, Boris, 'Hamlet' 105
Paterson, Don, 'As Above' 25–6
Patocka, Jan 14
permutational poetry 40
Pessoa, Fernando 2
philosophy 14, 27, 57, 82, 95, 96, 150
photography 65, 155–6
physicians 12
physics 138
  atomic 2–3
  language and 177–8
  Newtonian 55, 147, 158, 163
  quantum physics 5, 147–9, 154, 163, 166
  theoretical 19–20
Pitter, Ruth 33
placenames 57
Planck, Max 147
Plath, Sylvia 193, 196
Plato 42, 153
plenitude 62, 68
Poe, Edgar Allan 20–1
politics 93, 94, 97–8, 105
popular culture 75
postmetaphysical poetry 181–7
postmodernism 6, 55, 57, 81
poststructuralism 56
Pound, Ezra 1, 11, 75, 147, 181
prediction 113, 115
Price, Richard 75
Prickett, Stephen 73–4, 79
Priest, Eric 8, 9

Prynne, J. H. 170–1, 176, 178, 179–81, 182–3
psychoanalysis 192
psychology 7, 13, 15, 168, 191–203
Pugh, Sheenagh, 'The Comet-Watcher's Perspective' 134
pulmonary blood pressure 188–90
pulsars 132
puns 199
'Pylon poets' 59

quantum physics 5, 147–9, 154, 163, 166

radio astronomy 127–32
rationality 14–15, 177
Raworth, Tom 170, 182
reality 91–2
  virtual 42–7, 63, 66–7
reciprocal relationships 154–6, 158
Reeve, N. H. 171
Reid, Thomas 76
relationships 56–7, 154–6, 158
relativity theories 1, 148, 154
religion 79–80, 85, 129
remembrance 65
Rexroth, Kenneth 134
rhymes 7, 21, 25, 26, 199, 208
Riach, Alan 75
Rich, Adrienne. 'Plantetarium' 132
Richards, I. A. 2, 170
Richards, Ruth and Kinney, Dennis 200
Riley, Peter 170, 171
Rilke, Rainer Maria 131
ritualism 101, 117
robotics 37
rocketry 127–8
Roethke, Theodore 193
Rogers, Pattiann, 'Life in an Expanding Universe' 139
Rollinson, Neil, 'Entropy' 139
Romanticism 5, 74, 79, 192
Rydell, Mark 86

Sagan, Carl 131
Sandburg, Carl 126
Sarton, George 13
Satie, Erik 135
Scalapino, Leslie, 'bum series' 149, 151, 154–6, 162–3, 164–6
schizophrenia 198
Schwartz, Delmore 193
science-fiction 36, 40
*scientia* 94–5
Scottish Parliament 56
Scotus, Duns 76
Seidel, Frederick, 'The New Cosmology' 129
self 88–90
Self, Will 72, 73, 80
sensation 73, 85
Sexton, Anne 193, 201
Shakespeare, William 43–4
Shaw, Robert 162
Shelley, Mary, *Frankenstein* 45
Shelley, Percy Bysshe 5, 27, 36, 86, 105, 192
  *Prometheus Unbound* 29–30
Shepard, Paul 92, 102
Sinclair, Iain 173
Smith, Iain Crichton, 'The Space-Ship' 136
Snow, C. P. 3, 5, 10
  'two cultures' model 6, 55, 170, 177, 178
Snyder, Gary 105
sociology 13, 177
Sokol, John, 'Thoughts near the Close of the Millenium' 139
Space Shuttle 129, 136
space travel 128, 135–6
specialism 36, 81, 82–3, 85
Spender, Stephen, 'The Pylons' 59
spermatozoa 17–18
Spicer, Jack 163
spirituality 64–5, 66–8, 101
Stein, Gertrude 163, 179
Steiner, George 13–14
Stevens, Wallace 2, 172
  'Of Modern Poetry' 146–7
Stewart, Dugald 79, 84, 85, 86
suicide 193, 196–7, 203
Sun 8, 123–4, 133

supergravity 19–20
surrealism 22
Swift, Jonathan 52

Tanner, Joe 129
Tansey, Mark 157–8
Taylor, Mark C. 146, 157–8
Teasdale, Sarah 193
technology 56, 62–8, 94, 95, 121–2
telecommunications 39–40
telescopes 116–17, 128–33
Tennyson, Alfred Lord 5, 132, 147
themes 16, 165
Thom, Rene 158
Thoreau, Henry David 100
thought experiments 148, 151
Tiananmen Square protest (1989) 98, 159, 163
Tiffany, Daniel 7, 150–1, 153–4, 161
Tippett, Phil 43
Tolstoy, Leo 97
transformations 79–80, 155, 156, 181
translations 62, 66–7, 70
Troy 159, 163
Trueman, Fred 115
Truffaut, François 173
truth 76, 79–80
Tzara, Tristan 85

uncertainty principle 7, 148–9, 163, 186
unemployment 56
United States 137
universe:
  Big Bang theory 129, 139
  dark matter 136, 139–40
  size 136–7
Updike, John, 'Ode to entropy' 139
urban poetics 172–3
Ure, Dr Andrew 45

vaccines 94
Valery, Paul 1, 53
Valkeapaa, Aslak 100
Vaughan, Henry, 'I saw eternity the other night' 186
Vendler, Helen 160
Virgil 27, 55
virtual reality 42–7, 63, 66–7

walking 91, 97–8, 100–1, 105–6
Wall, Ian 4
Walter, Grey 37
Warren, S. Warren 5, 9–10, 202
Warwick, Kevin 209, 210
Wayne, John 43, 86
Whalen, Philip 163
Whitehead, Alfred North 179
Whitman, Walt 100, 118, 153
Whorf, Benjamin 152–3, 161
Wiener, Norbert 2, 3
Wilkins, John, Dean of Ripon 73
Wilkinson, John 184–6
Williams, Hugo 111
Williams, Raymond 204
Williams, William Carlos 24, 147, 172, 181
wit 20, 171–87
Wittgenstein, Ludwig 92, 153, 173, 174, 181, 182
word-association 199
Wordsworth, William 59–60, 73, 74, 79–80, 81, 85, 100
writing 179

Yeats, W. B. 1, 74–5, 79